DURHAM UNIVERSITY

Cha Thorp Warden

ARCHDEACON THORP, FIRST WARDEN, PHOTOGRAPHED BY EDIS
FROM THE PORTRAIT BY SWINTON IN THE CASTLE HALL

COLLEGE HISTORIES

DURHAM UNIVERSITY

EARLIER FOUNDATIONS AND PRESENT COLLEGES

BY

J. T. FOWLER, M.A., F.S.A.

HON. D.C.L. DUNELM, HON. CANON OF DURHAM, VICE-PRINCIPAL
OF BISHOP HATFIELD'S HALL, AND HEBREW LECTURER
IN THE UNIVERSITY

LONDON
F. E. ROBINSON & CO.
20 GREAT RUSSELL STREET, BLOOMSBURY
1904

PREFACE

WHEN I began the preparation of this book, I was afraid that a University not yet a century old would hardly afford enough material for a volume in the present series. And, indeed, the historical material is of necessity scanty as compared with that afforded by ancient Colleges and Universities. The want of it, however, leaves all the more room for architectural and biographical matter, and I hope that the descriptions of buildings and the notices of 'Durham Worthies' will be read with interest—at least by Durham men. The illustrations can hardly fail to be acceptable. The first and the last are from photographs by Mr. Edis of Durham, the rest from photographs kindly executed and contributed by Mrs. Powles, a lady whose early connexion with Durham gave her a special interest in the work.

The Appendices occupy a good deal of space, but they will not be found to be of the nature of padding. Number I. supplements Mr. Blakiston's collections. Numbers II. to V. contain matters connected with the

earliest days of the University not easily accessible elsewhere. Number VI. certainly deserves a more permanent
place than it has hitherto occupied. Numbers VII.
and VIII., will be useful for reference. In Number IX.
Mr. Leigh Smith has given us an admirable account of
athletics in the University. I have taken considerable
pains with Number X., but have not succeeded in
ascertaining all the dates as accurately as I could have
wished. In many cases the only authority is an old
calendar, and a man has commonly come into, or gone
out of, office for some little time before the issue of
the calendar of any particular year. The idea of
Appendix XI. is due to the publisher, Mr. Robinson,
who, when he saw the notice of the 'Verdant Green'
sketches (pp. 100-102), at once suggested a reproduction
of them as likely to prove an interesting and attractive
feature in the Durham volume. Appendix XII. is also
inserted at the suggestion of the publishers.

It will, perhaps, be thought by some that the index
is encumbered by many needless entries. My own idea
of an index is that, if it be worth making at all, it can
hardly be too full, and my practice is, if in doubt, to
insert an entry. It can do no harm, and the habit of
including 'needless' entries often prevents the neglect
of many which ought not to be omitted. But the more
experience I gain, the more thoroughly I am convinced
that finality in an index is unattainable. Whatever
pains you bestow upon it, you will find, sooner or later,

that there are things which ought to have been entered,
or to have been entered differently. And the more
condensed your index is, the more likely it is to be
subject to defects of this kind.

I have referred to our indebtedness to Mrs. Powles
and to Mr. Leigh Smith. I must also record here our
special thanks to Professor Lebour for his chapter on
the College of Science, to the late Principal Gurney for
his account of its buildings, to Sir George Hare Philipson and Professor Howden for materials connected with
the College of Medicine, to Professor Farrar for some
valuable initial suggestions, and for permission to print
his account of Dr. Jenkyns' lectures ; also to the Dean
of Durham (Warden of the University), for much kind
help in the revision of the proof-sheets.

J. T. F.

Winterton, Doncaster,
August 31, 1904

CONTENTS

APPENDICES

CONTENTS

LIST OF ILLUSTRATIONS

xi

CORRECTIONS

Page 23, note, line 2, *add* full-stop after ' 1831.'
Page 47, note, *add* ' pages 62, 65 '
Page 77, note, line 2, *read* ' lines 401, 402 '
Page 105, note, line 1, *read* ' az ', line 2, ' *vel cum.*'
Page 288, line 3, *erase* ' Rites of Durham.'

Page xi, line 6, *for* ' NORTH-EAST' *read* ' NORTH-WEST.'
Page 258, line 11, *read* ' worn with the gown.'

CHAPTER I

EARLIER FOUNDATIONS

§ 1. Durham College, Oxford.

No account of the University of Durham would be complete without some notice of earlier undertakings, the object of which was to connect the higher education with the Cathedral Church. Of these, the only one that came to any permanent result was the first in point of time—namely, the monastic College that was founded by Bishop Hatfield in the University of Oxford, and with which College the University of Durham may claim a sort of historic, though broken, continuity. The history of Durham College has, however, been so well worked out by the Rev. Herbert E. D. Blakiston[*] that there is little for anyone else to do in the matter but to avail one's self of his labours, and this I do with the fullest acknowledgment of my indebtedness to him in almost all that I now say on a subject that he has made so completely his own.

The monks of the Benedictine Order have always

[*] In his Introduction to 'Some Durham College Rolls,' in 'Collectanea,' Oxford Historical Society, vol. iii., and in his volume on 'Trinity College' (Oxford), in the present series, chap. i.

1

been pre-eminent among members of monastic foundations in the pursuit and promotion of learning.   And
in this respect the Benedictines of Durham were in no
way behind their brethren in the South of England.
Those of St. Peter's at Gloucester obtained a Hall in
Oxford for thirteen students in 1283, and in 1291 the
other great abbeys in the South combined for a general
monastic College, to consist of hostels to be united
with Gloucester Hall.   These were ultimately merged
in Worcester College, in the ancient part of which the
arms of some of the abbeys may still be seen.   But
previous to the Southern combination the great Northern
Abbey of Durham had made arrangements on its own
account.   We learn from a Bursar's roll of 1278 that
in that year Durham sent a clerk ' versus Exon.' (*sic*)
with 5 marks, and that a ' garcio ' was sent ' pro liberatura fratrum '—*i.e.*, for the purpose of conveying it.
In 1292 we find in ' liberatura facta studentibus Oxon.,
24*l*. 3*s*. 11*d*.,' which entry explains the former one.

We are told by the chronicler Geoffrey of Coldingham that Hugo de Derlington, Prior for the second
time from 1285-86 to 1289-90, sent monks to Oxford to
study, and made handsome provision for them.   There
is, however, so far, no mention of any building; but
the next Prior, Richard de Hoton (1289-90 to 1307-08),
is recorded by Robert de Graystanes to have prepared
a building in Oxford for the students from Durham,
and there is documentary evidence that five or six acres
or more had been acquired before 1291 for the site of
Durham Hall—namely, the area now occupied in great
part by Trinity College.   It was partly given by the
Benedictine nunnery of Godstow, and partly bought by

the Convent of Durham. To it were added some small holdings in the immediate neighbourhood. Soon after 1300 the Prior of Durham tried to have the great tithes of Brantingham in Yorkshire, then held by the abbey, appropriated to the new Hall to meet expenses, urging that the house consisted of ten, eight, or six monks at one time or other, and had already returned several learned men to Durham. The transfer, however, was not effected until about 1412. In 1315 the Convent of Durham sent church furniture and a number of books to the Oxford Hall. There is a list of these in the Durham Treasury, where also are similar lists and inventories up to 1456. There would, of course, be an oratory or chapel from the first, and the inventory of 1315 implies that there was one then. Among the books occur works on logic, physics, and metaphysics, as well as patristic and scholastic theology. The students (monks or novices) were supported in these early days by pensions, contributions, and presents from the Convent of Durham and its cells, notices of which constantly appear in the account rolls of the cells cited by Mr. Blakiston, and in those of the parent house, since published by the Surtees Society, and now again in our Appendix, No. 1. They would also receive from the Feretrar their shares of oblations at the shrine, and from the Chamberlain and Commoner allowances for clothes and commons. The Bursar appears to have sent £13 6s. 8d. (20 marks) regularly year by year—during the fourteenth century, at least— while all the obedientiaries made small contributions for the support of the house, providing the students with money for their journeys, and a man and horse to accompany them on their way to or from Oxford. They would themselves ride on horses belonging to the convent, and stabled at Durham or at Oxford, as the case might be. In *circa* 1330 and following years we find a pension of £10 from the church of North-allerton for half a year, or £20 yearly. The Oxford premises would include, besides the oratory or chapel, a sufficient number of living-rooms, with a small refec-tory or hall, dormitory, buttery, kitchen, stable, etc. Mr. Blakiston thinks that about 1380 there was a hall on the site of the present hall of Trinity College, with the still existing buttery and kitchen beyond it, that the upper chamber to the south of the hall was the oratory, and that the first chambers were those which appear in Loggan's view to the north-west of the old quadrangle. But the earliest existing buildings are too late in style to be the original ones.

It was to be expected that the famous literary Bishop Richard de Bury (1333-1345) would take a great interest in the Durham Hall, which had so far been maintained by the Prior and convent alone. Moreover, in 1334 Benedict XII. issued from Avignon the Bull 'Bene-dictina,' chapters v. and vi. of which enact that in every house a properly-paid teacher is to be appointed to instruct the monks in grammar, logic, and philosophy, and that one monk in twenty must be sent to the Universities for higher studies, and he is to have a fixed allowance. Accordingly, in 1338 the Bishop persuaded his former pupil, Edward III., to grant the Crown rectory of Simonburn in Northumberland to a house or cell, presumably the existing establishment, for a Prior and twelve monks of Durham studying in Oxford under statutes to be given by him. But neither this plan nor the Bishop's intention of bequeathing his great collection of books to the Durham Hall ever took effect. It appears that he died insolvent, without even a shirt of his own wherewith to cover his body,* and that his private goods were all seized by his creditors.

There was a design of establishing a Chair of Theology in the Durham house similar to one which had existed at Gloucester Hall from 1343, but that again fell through. During the long reign of Bishop Hatfield (1345-1381) we find about sixty references to the Durham house in the printed extracts from the account rolls, of more or less importance. In a Bursar's roll of 1348-49 occurs, among the expenses of brethren going to the cells: 'D'no Uthredo cum uno socio student. Oxon. 13*li*. 10*s*.'; and again: 'D'no Uthredo pro expensis suis versus Oxon. de præcepto Prioris, 40*s*.' In 1350-51 the entry runs, 'et socio suo studentibus Oxon.,' but in 1352-53, 'et sociis suis.' In 1358-59 comes the further payment of 13*li*. 6*s*. 8*d*., 'eidem d'no Uthredo incipienti in Theologia Oxon.,' and in 1359-60 an *extra* payment of 14*li*. for his inception charges. Dan Uthred at once came back to Durham loaded with his new honours, for we find, 'In expensis ij garcionum cum ij equis versus Oxon. pro d'no Uthredo et sociis suis reducendis, vij*s*. iiij*d*.' The latest entry of 13*li*. 6*s*. 8*d*. to Dan Uthred 'et sociis' is in 1366-1368, but there may have been entries of later dates in rolls now lost or perished. In 1367-68 the Hostillar gave 'd'no

---

* This statement has recently been remarkably confirmed (*Proceedings of Society of Antiquaries*, 1903-4, not yet issued).

Uthredo* versus Oxon. ex curialitate, 13s. 4d.' In
1373-74 John de Acley takes his place as head of the
' socii,' and in 1380-81 Robert de Blaclaw.   In 1381-82
the payment is only 10li., ' et non plus quia aliqui
eorum fuerunt domi causa pestilenciæ,' from which it
would seem that the recurrence of the Black Death in
1379 was still affecting Oxford.

Towards the end of his long reign, namely, in 1380,
Bishop Hatfield, in conjunction with Prior Robert
Berington of Walworth, took steps for the permanent
endowment of the Oxford Hall, the Prior undertaking
that the convent would continue to maintain four
monks if the Bishop would provide for four more and
eight secular scholars,† who were to be students in
grammar and philosophy.   The covenant was sealed in
1380, but the design was not carried out till some years
later.   The Bishop's executors handed over £3,000,
which was deposited in an iron chest in the custody of
William de Walworth, Mayor, and John Philipot, past
Mayor of London, Uthred de Boldon, and John de
Berington, a monk, and probably a brother of the Prior.

It was estimated that from the investment of the
£3,000 they would secure an annual income of 200 mark
(£133 6s. 8d.).   The money was partly invested in the
rectories of Frampton, Fishlake, Bossall, Ruddington, and
Laxton, and in lands near Durham and elsewhere   The
income so provided was made up to about £240 by the
pensions of £4 and £16 that had come for fifty years

---

* Uthred de Bolton, afterwards Prior of Finchale, and Subprior
of Durham, who was a famous Durham scholar, divine, and author.
See the Introduction to the Account Rolls, xxvi-xxviii.

† The Bull ' Benedictina,' referred to above, enacts that seculars
are not to be taught with monks

or more from the rectory and vicarage of Northallerton,* and by the customary contributions from Durham and its cells. Much of the capital was spent in stocking the estates and in providing necessaries for Oxford, including, probably, some of the buildings, also in expenses connected with the appropriation of the rectories. The pensions of the Rectors in possession had to be paid by the College during their lives, while the value of the benefices was declining. All the arrangements required the sanction of Bishops, Crown, and of successive Popes, thus entailing heavy fees and law expenses.

In the above-named agreement between Bishop Hatfield and the convent the latter bind themselves, under a penalty of £3,000, to maintain for ever the College which the Bishop had begun to build in Oxford on the ground belonging to the convent on Canditch, now Broad Street. The dedication is to be to the honour of the Holy Trinity, the Blessed Virgin, and St. Cuthbert, and there are to be special prayers for Bishop Hatfield and his family, Edward III., Queen Philippa, the Bishops of Durham, etc. The foundation is to consist of the eight monastic ' socii,' or student monks, chosen by the Chapter of Durham according to the Benedictine constitutions for general studies. One of these is to be selected by the Prior of Durham to be Warden or Prior of the new College or cell, which in Durham seems to have been commonly called ' the Oxford College.' They are to study especially philosophy and theology. The Warden is to hold a weekly Chapter, and the names of any offenders against order

* See Appendix, I., and ' Collectanea ' (Oxf Hist. Soc.) III, 14.

and discipline are to be sent to Durham. In conjunction with two Bursars, the Warden is also to
manage the estates, pay current expenses, make up the
accounts for the quarterly audit, and send a yearly
account to Durham; hence the number of compotus
rolls still preserved there. A 'socius,' or Fellow, is to
receive £10 a year, with allowances on taking the
degrees of B.D. and D.D. if there be a sufficient
balance.

The addition of eight secular scholars to the eight
monastic Fellows was a sort of anticipation of the
reaction against monastic Colleges that led Bishop Fox
to found Corpus Christi College at Oxford in 1517,
not, as he originally intended, for young monks of St.
Swithun's, Winchester, but, like most of the Colleges,
for secular students only. Hatfield's scholars were each
to receive annually 5 marks (£3 6s. 8d.), and were to
be selected by the four or five senior monks, four from
the bishopric, and two from each of the Bishop's lord-
ships of Allertonshire and Howdenshire. They were to
have a separate table together with the Warden's clerk
and the other principal servants, to have separate rooms,
to attend chapel and schools, to perform 'honesta minis-
teria' for the monks, and to have new tunics and hoods
twice a year. They might remain in the College for
seven years if they had good testimonials, but the Prior
of Durham alone could remove or expel them. They
were not required to take monastic vows, but they took
an oath to honour the monks and help the church of
Durham. They appear in the rolls as 'pueri.' The
Bishop of Durham was to be Visitor of the College,
but if he neglected his duty it was to pass first to the

Bishop of Lincoln, in whose diocese Oxford then was; and if he did not attend to it, then it was to pass on to the Archbishop of Canterbury. Thus, under Bishop Hatfield's scheme Durham Hall developed into a real College with a constitution, and eight 'students' or Fellows, one of whom was Warden, and eight scholars.

The College appears to have fulfilled its object in receiving the younger and more promising of the novices or monks of Durham to the benefits of the University, and in educating the secular scholars for various callings in the Church or in the world.

Mr. Blakiston has constructed an almost complete list of Wardens, all, as we have seen, alumni of the College. Some few dates that were unknown when he made his list may now be added from the Durham rolls. Six of the Wardens were afterwards Priors of Durham, and most of them held important offices. It will have been seen, from what has been said, that the College was not an independent foundation, as most Colleges were, but a cell of Durham Abbey, intended as a temporary home for Durham monks, and so the studentships were not like life Fellowships, but were only continued during residence in Oxford. In the fourteenth and fifteenth centuries persons not on the foundation rented rooms as modern undergraduates do, and there was a chamber for the monks of St. Mary's Abbey at York when they came to Oxford. It has been mentioned above that there are portions of the buildings yet remaining which may have belonged to the old Hall before it was a College. Bishop Hatfield's new foundation would naturally give an impetus to building operations, as well as render them necessary in order to provide accommodation for the increased number of inmates.

In the Bursar's roll of 1379-80 we find that the expenses of Dan John de Beryngton going to London and Northampton for £100 due from the King, 'ac eciam pro collegio Oxon. per Ep'm fundando, et aliis negociis ecclesiam tangentibus,' were £9 18s. 2d. for nine weeks. And in the same year we find: 'In solucione facta d'no Joh. de Acley, suppriori, in subsidium expensarum suarum circa reparacionem domorum et murorum loci in quo fratres nostri inhabitant Oxon. ex præcepto Prioris, viij*li*.'

Considerable sums were spent on a new chapel and other buildings shown in Loggan's view of Trinity College, and reproduced in Mr. Blakiston's two books. There we see the chapel, with its buttressed south wall and three good Perpendicular windows. The east and north sides of the quadrangle behind it appear to be of the same date, but the large dormer-windows were added by Dr. Kettell in the seventeenth century. The west side of the quadrangle was formed by the refectory, which collapsed when Dr. Kettell tried to make cellars under it in 1618; the present hall occupies the same space. The chapel was built in 1406-1408 at a cost of £135 18s., of which sum Durham contributed at least £35 18s. 4d. The principal altar and chapel were dedicated in 1409, and the two altars in the ante-chapel in 1414 and 1417. On the screen under the organ were these lines, dated 1418:

'Terras Cuthberti qui non spoliare verentur
  Esse queant certi quod morte mala morientur.'

Aubrey records that paintings of St. Katherine and of the taking of our Lord down from the cross were coloured over with green in the Commonwealth period, and that Dr. Kettell had said to the Parliamentary Visitor, 'Truly, my lord, we regard them no more than a dirty dish-clout.' They had doubtless formed the retables of the two altars in the antechapel. Aubrey further says that in the chapel windows were figures of St. Cuthbert, St. Leonard, St. Oswald, and others that he had forgotten, 'very good Gothique painting like those of New College, and I think better,' and in the east window 'northerne coates.'[*] There are still some fragments of original glass preserved in the windows of the library at Trinity College. There is no record, nor any reason to suppose that anything considerable in the way of building was done between 1408 and the dissolution, or that anything very remarkable occurred at the College during that period. There is such a delightful account in 'Rites of Durham' of the early education of the novices shortly before the dissolution that it must be quoted in this connexion. The unknown writer speaks here, as always, from personal recollection.

' Dane Richarde Crosbie m^r of ye novices.

'Ther was alwayes vj novices wch went daly to schoule w^thin the house for ye space of vij yere ['together,' Cosin MS.], and one of ye eldest mounckes that was lernede was appoynted to be there Tuter ; the sayd novices had no wages, but meite drinke and clothe for that space.

* Clark's Aubrey's 'Brief Lives,' ii. 23 ; Clark's Wood's 'Oxford,' ii 274 n.

The m^r or Tuteres office was' to se that they lacked
nothing, as, Cowles, frockes, stammyne, Beddinge, Bootes
and sockes, and whene they did lacke any of thes necessaries, the m^r had charge to caule of ye chamberlaynes for
such thinges, for they neuer Receyved wages nor handled
any money in that space but goynge daly to there bookes
w^thin the cloyster.   And yf the m^r dyd see that any of
theme weare apte to lernyng and dyd applie his·booke
and had a prignant wyt w^thall then the m^r dyd lett y^e
priour haue Intellygence, then streighte way after he was
sent to Oxforde to schoole and there dyd lerne to study
Devinity, and the resydewe of ye novices was keapt at
there bookes tyll they coulde vnderstand there service and
ye scriptures, then at the foresayde yeres end they dyd
syng there first messe.   The house was no longer charged
wth fyndinge them apparell, for then they entred to wages
to Finde them selves apparell wch wages was xx^s in ye yere
['and noe more,' Hunter MS. 45].   The eldest mouncke
in ye house had no more except he had an office ['y^t did
afford itt,' Hunter MS. 45].   his chamber where he dyd
ly was in the Dorter.'

This admirable system was doomed, however, to
speedy extinction.   The College came to an end when
Prior Whitehead surrendered all the possessions of the
abbey on December 31, 1540.   When the Chapter was
reconstituted as a secular foundation in May, 1541,
Prior Whitehead became the first Dean, and Edward
Hyndmer, the last Warden of Durham College on the
old foundation, was made first Prebendary of the first
stall.   The estates of the College reverted to the Dean
and Chapter, who are still the patrons of most of the
benefices, but the site and buildings passed to the

Crown in a second surrender in 1544, and were not regranted. Meanwhile the Chapter had attempted in 1541 to carry on the College with seven Fellows and four scholars, and George Clyff, who was Senior Fellow in 1540, was appointed Rector or Warden. But the old College was dead, and the new one was in a manner still - born ; it was given up within a year. Then followed an attempt to carry it on as a Hall for students at their own expense, but this also failed, as might have been expected. From the Crown the site and the derelict buildings passed to Dr. George Owen, of Godstow, and William Martyn, of Oxford, who sold them to Sir Thomas Pope, February 20, 1555, together with half of the grove of Durham College, then also in their possession. The other half had passed to Christ Church with Bernard College. Sir Thomas at once repaired the buildings for the use of Trinity College, which he founded, with new endowments, in 1555-56.

§ 2. The Proposed College of Henry VIII. in Durham.

In connexion with the scheme of Henry VIII. for the founding of new bishoprics out of the revenues of the monasteries, and for the remodelling of those already in existence, there was a plan for founding a College in Durham itself, which College was to form a part of his new Cathedral foundation. The following extracts are from the original drafts of the scheme of bishoprics, as printed by Henry Cole (London, 1838, p. 26), and again in 'Some Account of Durham College, Oxford,' by the Rev. Joseph Stevenson (printed at Durham in 1840, p. 14):

Duresme cum Cellis.

First a Provoste of the College ... ... cc*li.*
Item a Reader of humanytie in greke by
   the yere ... ... xx*li.*
Item a Reader of dyvynytie in hebrewe
   by the yere ... ... xx*li.*
Item a Reader bothe of dyvynytie and
   humanytie by the yere ... ... xx*li.*
Item a Reader in physyke ... ... xx*li.*
Item lx scollers to be taughte bothe gramer
   and logyke in hebrewe, greke, and
   lattyn, every of them by the yere
   iiij*li.* vjs. viij*d.* ... ... cc*li.*
Item xx studyents in dyvynytie to be
   founde x at Oxenford, and x at Cam-
   bryge, every of them by the yere x*li.* cc*li.*
Item a Scholemaster for the same scollers xx*li.*
Item an ussher ... ... x(*li.*)

This was a noble scheme, but it was not carried out. The principle of connecting education with the Cathedral Church was maintained on a much less extensive scale by the provision for a Grammar-school with a head-master and second master on the Cathedral foundation, and eighteen 'King's Scholars.' Thus, and by most liberal augmentation of the Grammar-school, as well as by the foundation of the University, has the Church of Durham for more than 625 years connected itself, or has been connected, with the education of youth.

§ 3. The Commonwealth College.

There was no great centre of learning in the Northern counties such as Oxford and Cambridge in the South, and when things had somewhat settled down after the great changes of the sixteenth century, men's thoughts turned in the direction of plans for a Northern University. In the first year of James I. the Corporation of Ripon petitioned for the foundation of a College there, 'after the manner of a University,' to be endowed from the alienated revenues of the collegiate and parochial church, which had been in the hands of the Crown since the days of Henry VIII., and the whole of that great parish was in a state of the utmost spiritual destitution. It does not seem to have occurred to the petitioners that the way to remedy this was to restore the Church organization, but they put forward the gross ignorance of the people as a chief argument in favour of their new scheme, one part of which was to provide for tutors who were to deliver discourses on market-days, and students, who were not only to acquire learning for themselves, but were to go about in the outlying villages to instruct the ignorant in the rudiments of religion. Accordingly, an order was issued for the establishing of a College, much distinguished patronage and substantial help were secured; but the project came to nothing, after all, and King James refounded the Collegiate Church, to the great benefit of the town and parish.

During the Commonwealth period there was a similar

movement for a College in Durham. Stress was laid on
the great distance of Oxford and Cambridge, and the
fact that those who went so far South seldom returned
to the North, whereas the proposed College would not
only keep Northerners in the North, but would attract
'foreigners,' and that so the general standard of learning
in the North would be raised. As in the former case of
Ripon, it was proposed that the new College should be
founded out of the plunder of the Church. On April 30,
1649, an Act was passed whereby all the Cathedral and
Collegiate Chapters in England were dissolved. The
Bishop, Dean, Prebendaries, and Minor Canons were
turned out of houses and homes, and thus the Castle,
the Cathedral, and the College were left empty and
desolate. The Puritans had no use for the Cathedral,
and both it and the residences connected with it soon
fell into decay. The lands were held by trustees, the
most prominent of whom was Sir Arthur Haselrigge,
whose rapacity led him to retain them in his own hands
as long as he could, and it was chiefly through his
obstruction that very little progress was made in the
disposal of them. The Cathedral and the Capitular
residences were standing empty, and the promoters of
the new College saw that they were ready to hand, and
that, if they could get hold of the endowments, they
could carry out their plan without any sacrifice on their
own part or the necessity of asking any one else to make
any. On April 24 and on August 20 petitions were
sent to Parliament through the High Sheriff similar
to the Ripon petition. The Parliament referred the
matter to the 'Committee of Obstructions for Sale of

Dean and Chapter Lands,' and instructed Sir H. Vane senior to write to the petitioners informing them that the House had taken their requests into consideration. In the spring of 1651 Oliver Cromwell was in Edinburgh, and a deputation from the petitioners rode over, and there waited on him in person. Their proposals met with his approval, and he wrote a letter to the Speaker Lenthall, praising the scheme as a pious and laudable work. Still nothing was done, and at the spring assizes of 1652 a third petition was sent, urging, in addition to other arguments, that the Parliament was indebted to the counties of Durham and Northumberland in the sum of £25,000 for buying off the Scots by maintaining their army after 1640. Nevertheless, the project disappears for four years. Weightier matters were occupying the attention of Oliver and his advisers. Yet the Protector was not unmindful of the proposed College, if there be any foundation for the tradition that he spent some days at the old manor-house still remaining at Houghal, and personally visited the Cathedral and other buildings, in order to judge of their suitability. If he did, it may have been on his way from Edinburgh, while the matter was fresh in his mind. However this may be, the project was seriously taken up in 1656, when Cromwell and his Privy Council issued an order for the founding of the College, and on May 15, 1657, letters patent were issued with provisions to the following effect.

1. The College is founded within the site of the old prebendal College, the Cathedral, and the Castle.

2. It is to consist of a Provost, two preachers or Senior Fellows, and twelve other Fellows, four of whom are to be professors, four tutors, and four schoolmasters. There are to be twenty-four scholars and twelve exhibitioners, beside eighteen scholars in the free school attached.

3. They are to be a body corporate, known by the name of the Master or Provost, Fellows, and Scholars, of the College of Durham.

4. The first Provost or Master is to be Philip Hunton, M.A.;* the Preachers, William Spinedge† and Joseph `Hill, M.A.;‡ the Professors, Thomas Vaughan, M.A.,§ John Kiffler, M.D., Robert Wood, M.A.,‖ John Peachill, M.A.;¶ the Tutors, Ezerel (Israel) Tonge, D.D,** Richard Russell, M.A., John Richell, John Doughty, M.A.; the Schoolmasters,

* Of Wadham College, Oxford; an eminent Puritan divine, of 'levelling' principles He achieved the distinction of writing a book which was burned at Oxford by decree of Convocation, namely, 'A Treatise of Monarchy,' 1643-44.

† Fellow of Exeter College, Oxford, Rector of Polshot, Wilts; ejected for nonconformity.

‡ Another learned Nonconformist, Fellow of Magdalene College, Cambridge, M A. 1649 His chief work was the augmentation of the Greek Lexicon of Schrevelius by 8,000 words.

§ Not to be confounded with Thomas Vaughan the alchemist, poet, and writer on magic, who was a Royalist.

‖ Of Eton and Merton College, Oxford; M.A 1649, Fellow of Lincoln College 1650 1660; a great supporter of the Commonwealth; ejected and went to Ireland in 1660, F.R.S 1681; died 1685

¶ Mentioned in Pepys' Diary, May 3, 1667, as having had a very red nose, though otherwise a good-natured man.

** A schoolmaster and alchemist in London; parson of St. Mary, Stayning; author of several anti-Papal works. After he left Durham he became a willing dupe and great ally of Titus Oates

Nathaniel Vincent, M.A.,* William Corker,† William Sprigg,‡ Leonard Wastell.§

5. The endowment is to be the Cathedral church and churchyard, the College, the free school, and all unsold properties attached to these.

6. The annual revenue is to be derived as follows: From the manors of Gateshead and Whickham, £117 15s. 8d., a second charge of £500 on the same manors, and a charge of £282 4s. 4d. from all rectories, etc., which had belonged to the Dean and Chapter. Also liberty to purchase lands to the extent of £6,000 a year.

7. All MSS., books, etc., belonging to the late Dean and Chapter are given to the College.

8. Ninety-one Visitors are appointed to hold office for two years only, and eleven gentlemen of the county are to be permanent Visitors. The Visitors are to redress abuses, remove refractory officials, and fill up vacancies. An appeal is granted to the Lord Chancellor, Lord Keeper, and Lords Commissioners for the custody of the Great Seal.

9. Right is granted to set up a College printing-press.

10. All members of the College are to be free from

---

* Chorister, afterwards chaplain, of Corpus Christi College, Oxford, under the Commonwealth. He was placed in the rectory of Langley Marish, Bucks, and ejected in 1662, after which he became an eminent Puritan preacher and prolific writer.

† Senior Fellow and afterwards Master of Trinity College, Cambridge; Proctor 1674. Friend of Dr. Seth Ward, Bishop of Salisbury, and of Dr. Isaac Barrow.

‡ Fellow of Lincoln College, Oxford, on the recommendation of Oliver Cromwell as Chancellor; ejected at the Restoration.

§ Rector of Hurworth-on-Tees 1651-1713.

serving in watching, warding, or mustering, hue and
cry, exempt from any public offices, their horses are not
to be required to ride post, and they are to be free
from all customs and taxes. They are to have a
common seal, and to do all things usual for a body
corporate.

The document is signed May 15, 1657.

It will be observed that here is no mention of University powers, no intention to rival Oxford and Cambridge, but only to found an independent College like
Eton or Winchester. We have no information as to
the number of students at any time,* but the Puritan
Provost and Fellows were established in the places of
the Dean and Chapter. It is a matter of the greatest
thankfulness that at this time the fabric of the
Cathedral appears to have remained without any
material damage. The old woodwork had been burnt
up in 1650, when the Scotch prisoners were quartered
in the church and had no coals allowed them. The
attitude of the Puritan divines towards the Cathedral
would probably be that of sheer indifference. They
were not thinking just then so much of sweeping
away the relics of popery and of prelacy as of improving
their own position and that of the College. Moreover,
it is not to be supposed that they were mere vulgar
iconoclasts of the Dowsing type, but men of some
culture. They were no sooner settled in their new
places than they petitioned for University powers; but
Oliver Cromwell died September 3, 1658, and nothing

---

* It is said that Dr. Ezerel Tonge 'had an excellent schoole
there (at Durham), and followed precisely the Jesuites' method of
teaching; and boyes did profit wonderfu.ly, as needes they must,
by that method.'—Aubrey, 'Brief Lives,' Oxford, 1898, ii. 261.

came of their attempt. In less than two months they sent a petition to Richard Cromwell, which seems to show that they felt themselves to be in somewhat evil case. The petition is worded in the most fulsome terms, but it does not show exactly what they wanted. Nothing is said about University powers.

But the new College does not appear to have attracted the numbers of students that were expected. The Quakers, led by George Fox, attacked it on the ground that it was to prepare candidates for the ministry, and to any kind of ministers they had 'conscientious objections'; the Churchmen of the North would have nothing to say to a Puritan and intrusive foundation. Oxford and Cambridge opposed it strongly when it aspired to be a University and to confer degrees. On April 18, 1659, petitions were sent from Oxford and Cambridge to Richard Cromwell, strongly deprecating the University idea, and on April 22 he directed that a grant which had been drawn up to make the College a University should not be sealed until further order. And while the members and supporters of the College were waiting, 'the blessed Restoration,' as Carlyle calls it in irony, and as some of us call it in deep thankfulness, put an end to the Durham College. With the Restoration came back not only the King, but the hierarchy, the Bishops, the Deans, the Canons, and all other Church officers who had been deprived during the Commonwealth. And the intruded Provost and Fellows of the new College had to vacate the places they were occupying in order to make room for those to whom they rightly belonged, and thus ended what is sometimes called 'Cromwell's College in Durham.'

CHAPTER II

THE PRESENT FOUNDATION: ITS CONSTITUTION AND ITS DEVELOPMENTS

THE University of Durham, like the Colleges in the ancient Universities, was in its origin essentially a religious and ecclesiastical foundation. Hence its motto, *Fundamenta ejus super montibus sanctis.* In point of date it is the earliest of all the modern Universities. It was in the year 1831 that the Bishop and the Dean and Chapter of Durham took the first recorded steps towards its formation. They were fully alive to the need for such an institution in the North of England. This need had long been felt, as is shown by what was done in the seventeenth century in order to provide great Colleges at Ripon and at Durham. And the great and increasing population of the Northern counties, together with their remoteness from the Universities of Oxford and Cambridge, the railway system being as yet in its infancy, brought the necessity into greater prominence than ever. There are signs also that the ecclesiastical body was influenced by a sort of panic at a time when all Church property was in danger, but in any case the founders proposed to supply the deficiency from their own resources. This, indeed, was in exact conformity with the principles on which they were themselves incorporated, the education of youth being enumerated among the objects of the Cathedral foundation, as set forth both in its charter and in its statutes.

The Chapter minutes are the great source of information with regard to the early history of the University, and this I shall now proceed to relate, so far as I have been able to gather it from them and from other authentic documents. The first of these is a letter from Dr. John Banks Jenkinson, Dean of Durham and Bishop of St. David's, dated August 31, 1831, addressed to the Revs. D. Durell, Archdeacon Prosser, and Charles Thorp, Prebendaries of Durham, drawing their attention to the critical situation in which the course of political events* seemed likely to place the Church of Durham, and giving notice that he would bring before the Chapter, at the September audit, a measure relating to an enlarged system of education to be connected with the Cathedral. The next step was that an 'Academical Institution or College or University' was projected by an Act of Chapter of September 21. No time was lost, for on September 28 the following plan was recommended by the Dean to the Chapter for 'Durham College.' It was to be in connexion with the Dean and Chapter, and supported by their funds; they, subject to the Bishop's visitatorial authority, were to be the governing body, with limitations to be specified. The Dean and a Master or Principal, who was to hold a

* The Reform Bill of 1832 was in progress during the greater part of 1831

prebendal stall, were to maintain the ordinary discipline, assisted by two Tutors with stipends, one of whom was to be Censor. There were to be three Professors, namely, (1) of Divinity, with a stall; (2) of Greek and Latin, with a stipend; (3) of Mathematics and Natural Philosophy, with a stipend. Also Readers in other branches, according to circumstances; also one teacher of German and one of French, each with a stipend. The nomination of the Master or Principal and of the Professor of Divinity, if provided for by stalls, was to rest with the Bishop, while the other Professors were to be named by the Dean with the approbation of the Chapter. In case the Master or the Professor of Divinity became infirm or incapable, a substitute was to be named by the Bishop, and paid out of the stall held by such Master or Professor. The students were to be: (1) Twenty scholars with chambers, and £30 a year or a table, to be named by the members of Chapter in rotation; (2) ordinary students providing for themselves, but subject to College rules; (3) occasional students, admissible to one or more courses of lectures. The admission of the two last classes was to rest with the Dean and Master (Principal). The funds were to arise from one fifth of the net proceeds of the deanery and stalls, to be charged as vacancies occurred; meanwhile the expenses were to be met by an annual vote not exceeding £2,000. The Chapter accepted the above plan with these changes, viz., for 'Dean and a Master or Principal' reading 'a Master or Principal,' and for 'Dean with the approbation of Chapter' reading 'Dean and Chapter,' and for 'Dean and Master (Principal') reading 'Dean and Chapter and Master (Principal).' After some minor details had been settled, it was agreed that the Dean, who was not present, should be requested by the Sub-dean to communicate with the two Archbishops and with the head of the Government, and that the Chapter were willing to receive any aid that might be offered for the benefit of the new academical institution.

The next day (September 29) the Bishop wrote to the Rev. C. Thorp, saying he had heard from Dr. Gaisford (then a Canon of Durham), who had counselled reserve in the publication of particulars, that he thought this was sound and wholesome advice, and he hoped the Chapter would profit by it.

On October 1 it was agreed that the Bishop should be consulted as to the obtaining of a charter for the 'College,' and that application should be made to the purchasers of the two archidiaconal houses on the Palace Green for the option of a repurchase on account of the proposed College.

On November 21 the Chapter thanked the Bishop for his handsome proposals contained in a letter of November 20, viz.: (1) The appropriation of three stalls; (2) a gift of £1,000 outfit, of £1,000 annually (eventually increased to £2,000), and the use of the house near the Castle during the Bishop's incumbency. And they undertook to enfranchise the leasehold property known as the 'South Shields Estate,' to the amount of £80,000, equivalent to £3,000 a year, in order to provide for the expenses of the 'University,' and to abandon the prospective tax upon the stalls.

On December 9, in a printed paper issued by Arch-deacon Thorp,* he states that he is appointed pro-

* Appendix II.

visionally to the office of Warden, and on the 10th the Dean informed the Chapter of this appointment.

On December 12 the Chapter took steps towards the enfranchisement of the Shields Estate.

We next come to a momentous point in the history of the University, namely, the passing of the Act 2 and 3 William IV., which received the royal assent July 4, 1832. This Act expressly calls the new institution a University; it legalizes the sale of lands, etc., with reservation of minerals to the Chapter; it provides for a sum not exceeding £2,000 to be spent on temporary buildings, and a sum not exceeding £20,000 on permanent buildings; and it sketches the first outline of a legal constitution for the University—such University to consist of such Warden or Principal, Professors, Readers, Tutors, students, and other officers and persons, as the Dean and Chapter, with the consent of the Bishop, shall from time to time under their seal prescribe. The Dean and Chapter are to be the Governors, and the Bishop the Visitor.*

A year elapses, and on July 20, 1833,† we find an announcement of the staff (with some important blanks), and of the terms, charges, etc.‡ It is announced that students will be admitted in Michaelmas term, 1833. On the same day the Chapter ordered that the founda-

---

* It was at one time proposed that the minor canonries should be appropriated to the University as Fellowships (*Gentleman's Magazine*, February, 1832, p. 156).

† It may be noted that 1833 was the year from which Newman always dated the Oxford Movement, in which Keble preached his famous Oxford Assize Sermon, and in which the originators of the movement, including Hugh James Rose, agreed on the main points which they thought that they ought to bring before the public.

‡ Appendix III.

tion students should be lodged in the Archdeacon's Inn on the Palace Green, under the Bursar. Some weeks later the professorships had all been filled up, and a little pamphlet or prospectus, sometimes called 'The First Calendar,' was issued in Michaelmas term. It does not include the calendar proper, but contains lists of officers, members, and students, with announcements of terms, charges, courses of lectures, etc.* Michaelmas term began, and the University was opened on Monday, October 28, and closed December 18.

The entrance examinations had been announced for October 28.† Nineteen scholars, or 'students of the foundation' were admitted, and eighteen 'students.'

On February 15, 1834, the Warden was to be requested to draw up a form of statutes for the University; a draft of these was presented and read on March 15.

On April 4, it was agreed that

'The Academical Institution or College or University established by an Act of Chapter of the 21st September, 1831, be constituted a University, to be called the University of Durham, in connexion with the Cathedral Church of Durham, and under the direction and control of the Dean and Chapter of Durham as Governors thereof, the Bishop of Durham being the Visitor thereof, and a consenting party to all Acts of the Dean and Chapter relating to the said University.'

Then the various officers are enumerated, and the modes of their nominations and appointments are set forth.

On June 14 Mr. Salvin was to be directed to make

* Appendix IV.   † In the paper issued July 20.

plans, etc., for a hall, common-rooms, etc., on the west
side of the Green ; for as yet the handing over of the
Castle formed no part of the scheme.

An August 9 ' the University Hall,' probably a room
on the ground-floor of ' the Archdeacon's Inn,' was to
be enlarged at once, at the expense of £20, by the
addition of the Bursar's room.

On October 4 the Chapter agreed to an application
to the Court of Chancery for the purchase of two houses
at the prices of £2,172 and £3,700 respectively.

On November 21 provisional statutes were approved,
' the Chapter having founded the University and partly
endowed a College within the same.' In the same
minutes the phrase occurs, ' The Warden of the College
as Vice-Chancellor of the University.' These statutes
relate to the year and its terms, to the final examinations, to the general regulation and government of ' the
College,' and to the work of the Professors of Divinity
and of Greek.

On May 9, 1835, a sketch of the above statutes was
to be submitted to Mr. Walters, and his attention to
be directed to the Act of Parliament,

' it being the intention of the Dean and Chapter to act
strictly in conformity with the Act, but without unneces-
sary interference in the concerns of the University, and
that Mr. Walters be requested to give his opinion whether
the University may proceed under such a constitution to
act and confer degrees.' '   -

On May 30 the Warden submitted to the Chapter
a scheme for the education of schoolmasters in the
University, and on November 20 they sanctioned the

principle of the proposition. The schoolmasters were, of course, to be Church teachers, and they were to be admitted in the faculty of theology. Nothing, however, came of this excellent project.

On June 13 the Chapter decided to make a fundamental statute constituting a Senate and a Convocation, and to apply for a royal charter, and on July 20 the statute was enacted, in accordance with what had been agreed upon April 4, 1834, setting forth the constitution of the University in further detail, thus:

' 1st. That under the Bishop, as Visitor, and the Dean and Chapter, as Governors, the affairs of the said University shall be managed by the Warden and a Senate and Convocation.

' 2nd. That the Warden shall have charge of the ordinary discipline of the University, and shall convoke and dissolve the Senate and Convocation, in both of which he shall preside, having an original and a casting voice in each, and a previous veto in Convocation, subject to an appeal from not less than one-fourth of the persons present to the Dean and Chapter, and further to the Bishop of Durham in case of the dissent of two members of the Chapter from their decision.

' 3rd. That the Senate shall transact the ordinary business of the University, and shall be competent to originate regulations and other measures relating to it, but which shall not be in force until confirmed by the Convocation.

' 4th. That the Convocation shall confirm or reject what is submitted to it by the Senate, but shall have no power to originate or amend.

' 5th. That all regulations passed by the Senate and

Convocation shall be forthwith communicated in writing by the Warden to the Dean and Chapter.

'6th. That the first or present Senate shall consist of the said Charles Thorp, Henry Jenkyns, Temple Chevalier, Charles Whitley, and Thomas Williamson Peile,* and of William Palmer, Master of Arts.

'7th. That the Senate in future shall consist of the Warden of the said University for the time being, of the Professor of Divinity and Ecclesiastical History for the time being, of the Professor of Greek and Classical Literature for the time being, of the Professor of Mathematics for the time being, and of the two Proctors for the time being, and of one member of Convocation, to be nominated annually by the Dean and Chapter, and of such other persons as may hereafter be determined by statute.

'8th. That the first or present Convocation shall consist of the said Charles Thorp, the Warden, and of such persons as shall have proceeded to the degree of Doctor in any of the three faculties, or of Master of Arts in any of the Universities of Oxford, Cambridge, and Dublin, and shall be members of the University of Durham.

'9th. That the Convocation shall in future consist, besides the original members, of all persons regularly admitted to the degrees of Doctor of Divinity, Doctor of Civil Law, Doctor of Medicine, and Master of Arts, in the University of Durham, and conforming to the regulations thereof.

'10th. That degrees in the several faculties shall be conferred by the Warden in Convocation, but the Grace for a degree shall be allowed by the Dean and Chapter before it shall be allowed in Convocation.

'11th. That no one shall be admitted to a degree in the said University of Durham without the assent of the

* Mentioned in the statute.

Dean and Chapter, and of the Senate and Convocation, nor without residence for the requisite number of terms within the University, nor without going through the requisite exercises and examinations, nor without subscribing the three Articles in the 36th Canon, which are as follows. [The three Articles here follow.]

'12th. That the number of terms, and the exercises and examinations necessary for each degree, shall, until settled by statute, be determined by the Senate and Convocation.'

In 1834-36 public lectures were delivered by the Professors of Divinity, Greek, and Mathematics, and by the Readers in History and Law. These lectures were printed, and references to some of them will be found below, in the notices of their authors.

All the Readers delivered lectures in their various subjects, mainly designed for occasional or extraordinary students—*i.e.*, persons not members of the University, who were invited by advertisements in the local papers. The fee was 1 guinea for each course.*

On March 12, 1836, it was agreed that the University should have the use of the Chapel of the Nine Altars for morning prayers, and that unfixed benches should be placed in it. This arrangement continued until March 6, 1847, when it was arranged that the morning prayers of the University should take place in the Galilee (Plate I.); and so they continued during the removal of the organ, after which they were in the

---

* As showing what interest the Chapter took at this time even in the smallest concerns of the University, I may refer to a minute of December 12, 1835, that Mr. Whitley's application for soup-ladle, sugar-tongs, and glasses, was to be granted.

'Nine Altars' again until that part of the cathedral was placed in the hands of the workmen in 1871. The University then went back to the Galilee again, and the morning prayers, now often ·called ' Galilee,' have been said there ever since, one of the Cathedral bells being tolled for the service on each morning during term.

On June 1, 1837, the royal charter of the University was granted by King William IV., constituting it a true and independent Body Politic and Corporate, under and by the name of THE WARDEN, MASTERS, AND SCHOLARS OF THE UNIVERSITY OF DURHAM, with a common seal, to ' have and enjoy all the property rights and privileges which are assured by the said Act* to the University therein contemplated and authorized, or are incident to a University established by Our Royal Charter.' This charter was received in Convocation, and the seal was adopted on June 8, 1837, on which day the first degrees were conferred, under the sanction of the charter.   The seal is circular, having in the centre a copy of the cross found on the body of St. Cuthbert, and in the margin the inscription

✠ SIGILLVM . VNIVERSITATIS . DVNELMENSIS .
A.D. MDCCCXXXVII.

By an Act of Parliament passed July 15, 1837, the provisions of former Acts relating to the admission and enrolment as attorneys of Bachelors of Arts or Law of Oxford, Cambridge, and Dublin, are extended to Bachelors of Arts or Law of the University of Durham.

But the year which gave the University its founda-

* 3 William IV.

THE GALILEE

tion charter was memorable in other ways. On July 19, 1837, an Order in Council appropriated Durham Castle and its precincts, to be held in trust by the Bishop of Durham for the time being, for the uses of the University, subject to (1) the right of access of the clergy of the diocese to Bishop Cosin's library, which they still enjoy, whether for the use of the books or for the holding of diocesan meetings ; (2) the enjoyment by all officers of the diocese or palatinate of their offices, which has lapsed by the University having provided them with offices elsewhere ; (3) the reservation of the almshouses for the bedesmen until they should be provided for elsewhere, which provision has been made ; and (4) the provision of accommodation of the Bishop, as Visitor, in the apartments within the Castle or palace, then known by the name of ' the Senior Judge's Apartments,' together with other rooms, coach-house, stables, etc., which has always been carried out, so that the apartments are now called ' the Bishop's Rooms.' Thus, the University was at last most nobly housed, as will more fully appear in a later chapter.

On March 17, 1841, it was agreed that each of the three Tutors should have, in lieu of guarantees and Fellowships, £100 a year each, and the Vice-Master £100 instead of £50. The Tutors' stipends were raised to £150 in the following year.

The recommendations of the Ecclesiastical Commissioners led to some modifications of Bishop Van Mildert's intentions with regard to endowment, and by an Order in Council of June 4, 1841, it was provided that the office of Warden should be annexed to the deanery ; that a canonry should be annexed to each

3

of the Professorships of Divinity and Greek; that. the
Professorship of Mathematics should include that of
Astronomy,* with an increased salary; that a Professorship of Hebrew and Oriental Languages† should
be founded; and that eighteen Fellowships‡ should be
added to the six already established by the Dean and
Chapter. In 1839-40 certain estates were assigned to
the University immediately, and power was reserved for
,making future endowments, by which an additional
grant in money was made, and certain landed estates
formerly belonging to the deanery or prebendal stalls
were assigned to the University. A draft of a scheme
for transferring this property to the Warden, Masters,
and Scholars was approved in Chapter, November 20,
1841, and was directed to be sent to the Ecclesiastical
Commissioners. Thus, the University property now
consists of (1) the Castle of Durham and its precincts,
with Bishop Hatfield's Hall and other houses standing
on the ground bounded by the river on the east and
west, and by the Cathedral churchyard on the south.
(2) The South Shields Estate mentioned above. (3) The
farms of Houghal, Hallgarth, Mountjoy, Ravensflat,
and other smaller farms, together with the Great and
Little High Wood and the Smiddy Haughs (formerly
the race-course, but now used by the University and
other athletic clubs), all adjacent to the city, or nearly
so. (4) The Bearpark Estate, including the farms of

* The Professorship of Astronomy was suspended in December,
1871.
† This professorship was not filled up until 1880.
‡ The total number of twenty-four has since been reduced to six
by the Durham University Act, 1864, an Order in Council, 1865,
and an Act of Chapter, 1871.

Witton Hall, Sleights House, Bearpark Lodge, Bearpark and Stotgate, Hill Top, Whitehouse, Auton Fields, Moorsley Banks, and Arbour House, with Hill Top Plantation and certain fields. (5) Certain outlying lands in different parts of the county, some of which have been sold and the money invested. (6) Some houses in Durham suitable for University purposes, acquired by purchase from time to time.

The constitution of the University was modelled on that of Christ Church, Oxford, of which one of its founders, Dr. Smith, had been head. The government of it was vested by the Act of Parliament of 1832, under which it was founded, in the Dean and Chapter of Durham as Governors, and the Bishop of Durham as Visitor; while by the same Act the Dean and Chapter were made trustees of the property assigned out of the capitular revenues for the maintenance of the University. Accordingly, in the first calendar or prospectus—that of 1833—the names of the Dean and of the then twelve Prebendaries are placed above those of the officers of the University.

The general management was entrusted by the Chapter as Governors to the Warden, Senate, and Convocation, and since that time the Governors have but seldom intervened in the affairs of the University. The appointment to some of the chief offices rests with them in theory, but in practice it has been left more and more in the hands of the Warden, the Chapter accepting his nominations as a matter of course, or, in rare cases, perhaps, with some little demur on the part of individual Canons. Again, the Chapter have the power of altering their own statute of 1835, or of enacting

new statutes, and this they have often done at the
request of the Senate. They have, in fact, invariably
endorsed the requests of Senate or the nominations to
offices made by the Wardens, except on four occasions.

The first of these was when the Chapter, led by Dean
Waddington, took independent action and passed the
Regulations of 1865, embodying some of the proposals
of the Parliamentary Commission, towards which the
Senate were maintaining a somewhat hostile and ob-
structive attitude. The second occasion was when they
refused to concede more than a portion of a request
made by the Senate. The Senate requested in 1880
that Convocation should be represented by four members
instead of one. Chapter consented only to the election
of two. The third was when Dean Lake, in 1882, persuaded the Chapter to assign *ex officio* seats in Senate
to the Professor of Hebrew, the Master of University
College, and the Principal of Bishop Hatfield's Hall,
all his own nominees. And the fourth was in 1892,
when the Senate demanded possession of the title deeds
of the Shields Estate, and the Chapter consented only
to provide exact copies, being legally advised that
the originals belonged to the Ecclesiastical Commissioners, and not to them.

From the above exceptions, extending over about
fifty years, it may be judged how harmonious upon the
whole have been the relations between the Chapter and
the University. These relations, although they have
subsisted now for sixty years, have, at any rate since
the Act of 1841, been of a provisional nature; for in
that Act occurs the following clause :

'And that it shall be lawful, by the like authority,* with the consent of the said University, and also of the said Bishop and of the said Dean and Chapter, to transfer to the said Warden, Masters, and Scholars the whole or any part of the powers relating to the government of the University and the order and discipline to be maintained therein, which are now vested by the last-mentioned Act † in the said Dean and Chapter.'

Since the abolition of religious tests, and the establishing of the Newcastle connexions, a University governed by an ecclesiastical body has been felt to be anomalous. As early as 1862 Dean Waddington wrote :

'I should advise the Dean and Chapter to cede that position. To be under the direct control of an ecclesiastical body would certainly be injurious to the prospects of a young and liberal institution, and the duties of the office would be better performed by the Senate.'‡

The Chapter has not, however, acted on that advice, and in 1895-96 there was a strong feeling among some members of Senate and others connected with the University that its relations to the Dean and Chapter were not satisfactory. It was thought by many that the government of a University by an external body, few in number, existing mainly for non-University purposes,

* The authority of an Order in Council to be issued for the purpose, according to the provisions in Act 3 and 4 Vict, cap. 113, lxxxiii-lxxxv.

† That of 1832, which vested the government in the Dean and Chapter for the time being

‡ The first time Dean Waddington, as Warden, nominated the Proctors, namely, on June 16, 1863, the words 'on behalf of the Dean and Chapter' were omitted, as has been the case ever since.

and regarded as representing a single interest, was an anomaly that must greatly injure the prestige and rank of the University in public esteem, even if it worked well in practice, which was disputed.

Bishop Westcott, as Visitor of both bodies, wrote to the Dean on November 16, 1895, suggesting that a conference should be held between the Dean and Chapter and the Senate to consider whether the time had not come for transferring to the Warden, Masters, and Scholars of the University, as contemplated by the Act 4 and 5 Vict. (June 21, 1841), and as recommended in the final report of the Durham University Commissioners in 1863, ' the whole or (some) part of the powers relating to the government of the University, and the order and discipline to be observed therein,' which were then vested by the Act 2 and 3 Will. IV. (July 4, 1832) in the Dean and Chapter. On November 21 the Dean, on behalf of the Bishop and himself, invited the members of Chapter and Senate to a conference to be held at the Deanery on January 24. On December 20 a memorandum was addressed to the Bishop by seven members of Senate resident in Durham, urging many considerations in favour of the proposed transfer of powers. Memoranda were sent to the Bishop from the President of the College of Medicine and from the two members of Senate appointed by the College of Science, strongly in favour of the change under consideration.

Early in January the Canons declined to attend the proposed conference for interchange of opinions, and accordingly it had to be abandoned. But on February 11, 1896, a committee, including the Dean as Warden and another member of Chapter, was appointed by Senate to consider what steps it was advisable to take in order to obtain the transference of powers. They recommended that the Dean and Chapter should join the Senate in obtaining the opinion of counsel on the legal bearings of the case; that the Dean and Chapter on the one part and the Senate on the other should independently state the case; and that the two statements should be submitted to the same (one or more) counsel for a legal opinion thereon. The Chapter were of opinion that the University should act independently, and nothing further was done.

The Senate consisted originally of the Warden, the Professors of Divinity, Greek, and Mathematics, the two Proctors, and one member of Convocation nominated by the Chapter as their representative, so that it might almost fairly have been described as a subcommittee of Chapter, four out of seven being members of that body. There was a provision for the addition of such other persons as might afterwards be determined by statute. And to the seven original members of Senate have been added at various times the Professors of Hebrew (1882) and Medicine (1887), the Master of University College (1882), the Principal of Bishop Hatfield's Hall (1882), the Principal of the College of Science (1892), one representative of the Fellows (1857), two of Convocation (one 1857, a second 1880), one of the College of Medicine (1871) and one of the College of Science (1874), the President of the College of Medicine (1903); (the Professor of Medicine as such is now no longer a member of Senate).

The Convocation consisted originally of the Warden

and of a certain number of Doctors and Masters in the Faculties of Divinity, Law, Medicine, and Arts, from the Universities of Oxford and Cambridge, and consists at present of all such persons as have been admitted to like degrees in Durham, and have complied with the conditions required by the University in the case of all who desire to be members of Convocation. The Senate transacts the ordinary business of the University, and is competent to originate regulations and other measures, but the regulations have no force until confirmed by Convocation. Convocation can confirm or reject what is submitted to it by Senate, but cannot originate or amend.

The two Proctors are annually nominated by the Warden. Under him they conduct the proceedings in Convocation, and have charge of University discipline. The Senior Proctor attends more especially to Convocation and public examinations, and reports to Convocation whether candidates for degrees have fulfilled all the conditions required by the University. The Junior Proctor attends more especially to discipline, and sees that terms have been duly kept; but in the absence of either Proctor the other can discharge his duties. There are also four Proproctors, nominated annually by the Proctors. The Proproctors assist the Proctors in their duties, and can act for them in their absence. Up to 1882 there were only two Proproctors, but in that year the number was doubled in order to make better provision for the superintendence of examinations.

As University College and Bishop Hatfield's Hall are not distinct foundations, and have no Fellows or other elective bodies, the Heads of those houses are appointed and licensed by the Warden. The Fellows in Durham are Fellows of the University, not of any particular collegiate house, and the scholars, in like manner, are University scholars, wheresoever they may happen to reside. So, again, the system of ' combined lectures,' of late years so largely adopted in the older Universities, has been the only system in Durham ever since 1846, when a second house for students was opened, and the men in both houses attended lectures together. The unattached students, including the women students, afterwards joined these same classes.

The founders of the University from the first provided for the reception of students in such buildings on the Palace Green and in the Bailey as were then available, and appointed Censors and Tutors to watch over their conduct and to direct their studies. These accommodations were much enlarged by the addition of the Castle and its precincts, now held in trust by the Bishop for the benefit of the University, under an Order in Council of August 8, 1837. These buildings and their occupants at first went under the colloquial designation of ' the University,' which name was gradually superseded by that of ' University College,' although there is no ' College ' in the sense of a foundation or corporation distinct from that of the University.

The mode of living in University College is similar to that which is followed in the Colleges in Oxford and Cambridge, except that luncheon is served in Hall at a fixed hour. From 1837 to 1839 the first Warden presided over the College without a Master. From 1840 to his death in 1862 he presided as Master, with a Vice-Master living in the Castle. The mastership appears to have been vacant in 1863 and 1864 ; then the Masters followed in the succession given in the Appendix, No. X. There is a minute-book of the Council of the College from 1834 to 1873, from which the following notes are taken. In 1835 no *ægrotat* was to be received without a medical certificate, and it was proposed ' that all *ægrotantes* should have mutton broth and bread pudding sent daily to their rooms, and nothing else, and that they should not be suffered to dine with one another or in Hall.' Further restrictions with regard to meals were placed on *ægers* in 1842. The Censors were to interfere either with the number or with the duration of convivial parties at their discretion. There was to be no Sunday lecture during the summer term ; dinner was to be at four on week-days and two on Sundays, but the hour of two was soon altered to 5.30. On May 26 it was ordered that the students should be required to attend cathedral service on Ascension Day, but not on May 29, only no lectures should be given during Divine service, this distinction to be observed between the feasts and fasts of the Church and State holidays. On January 19, 1836, it was ordered that the students be required to attend evening service in the Cathedral every Wednesday and Thursday. On March 21, 1838, ' much desultory conversation took place on the fire in the castle,' and on October 24 ' the undergraduates were warned of the inflammable materials which composed the castle ' On October 31 gas furnishings were to be purchased for £162 19s. 6d. On June 20 in the same year there was a consultation on the improvement of the Green. In 1839 it was ordered that there should be

no hot meat breakfasts on Sundays, and the order had
to be renewed in 1842.   Many years later a regulation
to the same effect was made at Hatfield Hall, where it
is still in force.   At various times students were repri-
manded for having suppers or dinners brought into the
College from the town.   This was against the rules,
and   was   managed   secretly,   the   provisions   being
smuggled in from a shop in Saddler Street kept by
one ' Mother Clarke.'   From time to time men were
severely dealt with for what is now called 'ragging.'
In some cases the outrages appear to have been per-
sistent, malicious, and brutal ; in others they assumed
the character of harmless, perhaps beneficial, practical
jokes.   The excuses made by men who were ' convened,'
as it was termed, for being the worse for wine, knocking
in late, and so on, are of the usual kind.   In November,
1841, a gentleman who had gone to Newcastle was
' too late for the Durham coach.'   Another gentleman,
charged with being drunk, ' urged that he was not used
to drinking wine, and the cold air produced the effect,'
and so forth.   In 1852 a representation was made of
excessive credit for tobacco having been given to an
undergraduate, and two gentlemen having been summoned for shooting with an air-gun from the keep, it was
directed that the air-gun should be removed from the
College.   Another gentleman was summoned for sleep-
ing out all night.   ' Defence that he was visiting a
friend at lodgings in a public-house, and taken too ill
to return.   Term lost.'   In 1841 there is a reference to
work at the ' new Castle garden.'   In 1842 the Warden
was authorized to apply for the lease of the well above
Little High Wood.   On May 10, 1843, Mr. Billings

applied for permission to make some drawings of the Castle. Leave granted. These drawings would be for the five beautiful plates in his ' County of Durham,' published in 1844. In March, 1851, it is recorded that Mr. Butler presented to the College a picture of ' Old Joe the .letter-carrier,' and his letter offering it is copied into the book. This picture is now in the Common-room. In the first Council of Easter term, 1842, a good deal of business appears to have been done, yet there occurs the record, ' Much talk, no work.'*

In 1843 the University received its grant of arms, which is printed in the Appendix, No. VII. The fees paid amounted to £87 7s. 6d.

In 1844 Mrs. Pemberton, of Sherburn Hall, near Durham, in compliance with the recommendation of her late husband, John Pemberton, M.A., one of the first members of the University, founded a Fellowship of the annual value of £100, and two scholarships of the annual value of £30, to be called the Pemberton Fellowship and Scholarships. The appointment to the Fellowship was restricted to B.A.'s of Durham and members of University College, with a preference to natives of the county of Durham. The scholarships were also confined to University College, then the only collegiate house in the University.

In the year 1876, the members in the University then being low, the Fellowship was temporarily suspended, and the scholarships were divided into a Senior

* Leaves 43 and 254 of this Minute Book have been torn out, and passages here and there have been erased with the pen so as to be illegible.

Scholarship of £40 and two Junior Scholarships of £15 per annum, and were handed over to Newcastle. The Council of the College of Physical Science now determine the conditions on which the scholarships are awarded. The Fellowship was also transferred from Durham to Newcastle in 1882, and regulations were passed by which graduates in science were made eligible for it.

Besides the above, there are several scholarships of University and of private foundation, an account of which may be seen in the calendar. Among the private founders were Bishops Van Mildert, Maltby, and Lightfoot.

On November 20, 1845, the Dean and Chapter approved of facilities for the students attending the 'State services,' but not of enforcing attendance. Thus the days became holidays, which continued after the abolition of three of the services in 1859, and were the origin of the present 'Open day' in the middle of each term.

In June, 1846, it was proposed that a Readership in Anglo-Saxon and in the Ancient Literature of England should be established, but the project was not carried out.

With the especial view of placing academical residence within the reach of men of comparatively limited means, another house for the reception of students was opened in 1846, and named Bishop Hatfield's Hall, after the great Bishop who had contributed so liberally to the foundation of Durham College in Oxford in the fourteenth century.* That College was suppressed at the dissolution .of the monasteries, together with

* See above, p. 6.

Durham Abbey, to which it was attached; and its
revenues were, with those of the Abbey, granted to the
newly established Dean and Chapter by Henry VIII.
The Chapter thus, in a sense, represents the ancient
College as well as the Abbey, and it seemed fitting that
the name of Bishop Hatfield should be connected with
the new institution in Durham, since it was in some
respects similar to the College which that prelate had
promoted in Oxford. A large house in the North Bailey
formed the nucleus of the Hall. This accommodation
was enlarged by the addition of a considerable building
in 1849, and of the chapel in 1853. In 1895 a large
house adjoining on the south was bought by the
University and added to the Hall.

The characteristic features in what is called the Hall
system are that the rooms are let furnished, and all
meals are taken in Hall, the students paying for their
commons at a certain fixed and reasonable rate. In
these meals in common they obtain much better value
for their money than would be the case with separate
meals. Not nearly so many servants are required, and
there are no opportunities for extravagance at meals in
rooms, which, indeed, are not allowed unless in cases of
sickness.*

This system was introduced by the late Rev. David
Melville, the first Principal of Hatfield, afterwards
Canon of Worcester. It was advocated by him in
pamphlets and otherwise; it excited great interest in
Oxford; it suggested the opening of Halls for poorer
students in that University; and it has been adopted

* Many of the men now have afternoon tea, which they provide
for themselves.

at Keble College as being by far the most economical and, on the whole, satisfactory arrangement.

In November, 1848, a flag was presented to the University by Mr. Telfair and other friends, and ever since that time the University flag has been displayed on the Castle keep during term time, showing to the many who pass by Durham on the railway that the Warden, masters, and scholars are at home and engaged in their several duties.

In Michaelmas term, 1851, another Hall was opened in the house on the Palace Green, now known as University House, and formerly as 'the Archdeacon's Inn.' It was named after Bishop Cosin, the first Bishop after the Restoration, and a munificent benefactor to the diocese. This Hall was closed in 1864, and has ceased to exist. The money spent on it would perhaps have been better employed in enlarging Bishop Hatfield's Hall.

In Michaelmas term, 1870, a regulation was passed providing for unattached students who should reside in some houses or lodgings licensed by the Warden and Proctors. Women students admitted under the supplementary charter of 1895 are unattached; there is at present a house on the Palace Green in which several of them reside in charge of a lady.*

The nature of the examinations for degrees in Arts will be understood from the following regulations:

'No Grace for the degree of Bachelor of Arts shall be granted unless the petitioner has passed two public examinations.

* See further below.

'The first of these examinations shall be conducted by three examiners, nominated annually by the Warden, and approved by Convocation. The subjects and books to which it shall be directed shall be fixed by the Senate eleven months at least before its commencement, the subjects and books fixed for candidates for Honours being distinguished from the subjects and books fixed for other students.

'Everyone admitted to this examination shall be required to prove his knowledge of Scripture History, of one Gospel in the Greek, of three Greek plays, and six books of Virgil, or of equivalent portions of Greek and Latin authors, *melioris ævi et notæ*, of Arithmetic, and either of the first three books of Euclid or of Logic, and shall be examined in English Composition. Candidates for Mathematical Honours shall be required to prove their knowledge of only one of the three Greek plays, or its equivalent.

'All those who satisfy the examiners shall receive certificates, and shall be classed according to their attainments. The number of classes shall be determined by the examiners, but the order of the names in each class shall be alphabetical.

'The second and final examination shall be conducted by three examiners at least, nominated annually by the Warden, and approved by Convocation. Everyone who is admitted to it shall be required to prove his knowledge of the Evidences of Religion (Natural and Revealed), of one Gospel, and of the Acts of the Apostles in the Greek, except that, in the case of conscientious objectors, alternative subjects may be provided by the Senate.

'Students who are not candidates for Honours shall, in addition to the Evidences, one Gospel, the Acts of the Apostles, and English Composition, be required to prove their knowledge of one Greek and one Latin book, *melioris*

ævi et notæ, approved by the Senate, and of two at least
of such subjects as Senate shall determine. Particulars
respecting these subjects shall be published by the Senate
eleven months at least before the examination.

' Candidates for Honours shall, in addition to the
Evidences, one Gospel, and the Acts of the Apostles, be
examined in such subjects and books in Classical and
General Literature, and Mathematical and Physical Science,
as shall have been fixed by the Senate eleven months at
least before the examination; they may be examined also
in other subjects and books selected by themselves, provided these subjects and books shall have been submitted
to the Senate and approved by it six months at least before
the examination.

' Candidates for Classical Honours only, need not be
examined in Mathematics, nor candidates for Mathematical
Honours only, in Classics. Every candidate for Classical
Honours may be examined both *vivâ voce* and on paper.

' The examination for Mathematical Honours shall be
divided into two parts, as follows—Part I. : Euclid, Geometrical Conics, Algebra, Trigonometry, Analytical Plane
Geometry, Elementary Mechanics and Hydrostatics, Geometrical Optics, and Plane Astronomy. [The use of the
differential and integral calculus is not permitted in this
part of the examination.] Part II. : Differential and Integral Calculus, Differential Equations, Analytical Geometry of three dimensions, Newton's " Principia," i.-iii.,
and any of the higher portions of the subjects of Part I.
The examiners shall have power to excuse from examination in the Classical portion of the subjects for the Pass
degree those candidates who, having failed to obtain
Honours, yet have shown sufficient knowledge of the
subjects of Part I.

' All who satisfy the examiners shall receive certificates

4

and shall be classed.   For those who are judged worthy of distinction there shall be two separate classifications, one for such as have distinguished themselves in Classical and General Literature, and the other for such as have distinguished themselves in Mathematical and Physical Science. In each of these classifications there shall be four classes, the examiners being at liberty to leave any one or more of these classes vacant.   For those who are not judged worthy of distinction there shall be no classification, but the examiners may, if they think fit, divide the candidates by a line into two parts.

‘ Students not candidates for Honours shall be allowed, with the consent of the Warden and Senate, to take up one or more Honour subjects, with a view to obtaining an honorary class.

‘ No grace for the degree of Master of Arts shall be granted unless the petitioner is a Bachelor of Arts of the standing of nine terms at least from his admission to that degree.

‘ Any Bachelor of Arts of the requisite standing who has obtained Honours at the final examination for the degree of Bachelor of Arts, or who, after passing the final examination for the degree of Bachelor of Arts, has passed either the examination for a Licence in Theology, or the examination for the degree of Bachelor of Civil Law, or for the degree of Bachelor of Letters, or the examination for a Licence in Medicine, shall be admissible to the degree of Master of Arts without further examinations or exercises. Other candidates for the degree of Master of Arts shall pass such examinations or perform such exercises as the Senate may require.’

From 1837 to 1857 the exercises for the M.A. degree consisted in the passing of a public examination either in classical and general literature or in mathematical and physical science. Classes were awarded in these examinations. Since 1857 the exercise required from such as have not qualified as above after taking the degree of B.A. has been an essay to be approved by the Senior Proctor.

It will now be seen that provision is made for a course of academical residence and instruction similar to that which exists in Oxford and Cambridge. But the degree of B.A. can at present be obtained at the end of the second year of residence; up to 1865 the Arts course was one of three years.

Besides the Arts course, arrangements were made from the first for a course of theological study. This course is open to those who have passed the examination for B.A. in Durham or an examination of a similar character in another University, also to non-graduates of the age of nineteen who have passed an examination in Greek, Latin, and the elements of theology.

The minimum length of the course has been, since 1871, for graduates of Durham, one term instead of three as previously; for non-graduates, since 1846, two academical years—that is, six terms. From 1841 to 1846 the course was one of three years, and the class fell off in numbers to a very serious extent. The fact was that very few theological students could afford either the time or the expense. On passing the final examination the candidates receive a certificate called a Licence in Theology, and the status of Licentiate in Theology (L.Th.).

The theological students have always attended

lectures by various Tutors and Lecturers in addition to those of the Professor of Divinity, those on Hebrew, for example, which have never been compulsory, and some, attended by all, on the Greek Testament or other subjects in the course. Instruction in the composition of sermons has always been given by the Professor, and the students' written exercises are sent in to him.*   Until about 1860 the Professor of Divinity delivered a lecture in the Old Divinity School, immediately following the afternoon service in the Cathedral, lasting from 5 to 6 p.m.   Attendance at these lectures, which were on the Prayer-Book or some such subject, was required from all the students, whether in Arts or in Theology. They were highly valued by a few, but were regarded by the majority as a vexatious infliction, and soon after 1877 attendance at the afternoon service was made optional. '

Soon after 1864, when Dr. Farrar succeeded Dr. Jenkyns as Professor of Divinity, it was decided that honours in theology should be awarded to candidates for the licence who took in extra subjects, and since that time a class-list of first, second, and third classes has been established.

* Among the ' Reminiscences ' of William Rogers, who in October, 1842, entered at Durham as a theological student, being B A. Oxon., 1840, is this   He says that ' one of the Canons, Dr Wellesley, brother of the Duke of Wellington, and his image in a surplice, was very partial to me. . . .   He would . . . at times express the desire to read over my sermon—we had to write one every week—and was most punctual in sending it back on Tuesday morning   I verily believe he carried it off with him to preach at Hartlepool, of which he was Rector, but I never hinted at such a thing ' (' Reminiscences,' 1888, p 39)   But Dr. Wellesley was Rector of Bishop Wearmouth, not of Hartlepool.

In the creation of a theological course Durham anticipated the older Universities of Oxford and Cambridge by many years. Dublin had provided systematic instruction in theology long before. In 1790 the Irish Bishops decided to admit to Holy Orders only such as had graduated in Arts 'and attended one year's theological lectures. In 1833 a two years' theological course and theological examinations, as they are at present, were first established in Dublin. The first Professor of Divinity in Durham was appointed and the theological course established in the same year, and the first examination for the licence was held in the following year.

Until 1887 the degrees of B.D. and D.D. were open to Masters of Arts of Durham of the requisite standing on the performance of exercises of the nature of essays approved as satisfactory by the Professor of Divinity. Since 1887 the degree of B.D. has been granted besides to Bachelors of Arts of any University in the British Empire or Licentiates in Theology of Durham of at least four years' standing from their final examination ; to clergymen who have kept three or more terms by residence at Durham, have passed the final examination for the Licence in Theology, and are of, at least, four years' standing from such examination; and to any clergymen of not less than fifteen years' standing from deacon's Orders. In all cases a searching and comprehensive examination must now be passed. No person who has been admitted to this degree can proceed to D.D. unless he has previously been admitted to the degree of M.A. in some University of the British Empire.

The exercise for the degree of D.D., until further notice, will be—*either*

(*a*) A *published* theological treatise approved by Senate, *or*

(*b*) An examination consisting of two papers :

(1) On the Text and Matter of the Books of the Old and New Testament.

(2) On the History, Doctrine and Liturgies of the Church.

In 1837 a course of civil engineering and mining was established.* This, however, did not attract many students, and its objects have since been better secured by the foundation of the College of Physical Science at Newcastle-upon-Tyne.

In 1852 the Newcastle College of Medicine,† the Medical School of King's College, London, and the Senior Medical Department of Queen's College, Birmingham, were received into connexion with the University, and in 1870 the Newcastle College was taken into closer connexion, the particulars of which may be seen in the calendar. The principal Professors in the College of Medicine are Professors in the University, and in 1887 the Professor of Medicine was made *ex officio* a member of Senate,‡ the College retaining

---

* The University of Durham was thus ' the first to establish a School of Engineering,' and not Dublin, for which University that distinction has been claimed (W M Dixon, ' Trinity College, Dublin,' 1902, p 195). The Dublin school was founded five years later.

† On the early history of this school, see Dr. Embleton's ' History,' published at Newcastle in 1890, a paper by G. G. Turner in the *Durham University Journal* of February 8, 1896, p 8, and below, in the chapter on ' The College of Medicine.'

‡ In 1903 the President of the College of Medicine was made an *ex officio* member instead of the Professor.

the right granted to it in 1870 to elect a representative.

In the Medical Act of 1858 the University of Durham occupies the same position as other English Universities. In 1876 special examinations were instituted to qualify practitioners of fifteen years' standing for the degree of M.D. Many have availed themselves of these, but the 'Practitioners' M.D.' is naturally regarded with some disfavour by those who have obtained the degree in the regular way. In 1891 the degrees of Bachelor and Doctor in Hygiene were instituted, in addition to the degrees of Bachelor and Doctor in Medicine and Bachelor and Master in Surgery that had been provided for before, and in 1894 arrangements were made for granting the Diploma in Public Health. The College of Medicine has well maintained its reputation as a very important and successful University institution.

In 1865, by an Act of the Dean and Chapter, students became admissible to the degree of B.A. after a course of two years instead of three years as before ; the period of residence was to be eight months in each year, but this was reduced in December, 1871, to six months, and thus the terms in Arts and in Theology became equal in length. In the same year twelve out of the twenty-four Fellowships were abolished by an Order in Council, the proceeds to be applied to the Schools of Theology and Arts, the latter including Physical Science. It was further provided that no student who was not a member of the Church of England should be obliged to attend its services, and that no religious test or subscription should be required from any member of the University, except before taking the Licence in Theology or any degree in that subject, or becoming a member of Senate or Convocation, in which cases each person was to declare himself in writing to be a *bonâ fide* member of the Church of England. By the same Act was founded, in the Faculty of Arts, a School of Physical Science, which did not succeed in Durham, but which, in 1871, developed into the College of Physical Science, founded on October 24, with a full staff of teachers, at Newcastle-upon-Tyne, by the co-operation of the University with the North of England Institute of Mining and Mechanical Engineers.

The University endowed the new College with more than £1,000 a year, provided by the suppression of some of the Durham Fellowships. In March, 1871, four more Fellowships were abolished, leaving eight.

In 1874 this College was formally incorporated with the University, and obtained the privilege of electing a representative in the Senate, and in 1892 the Principal was made an *ex officio* member, so that there are now two representatives, as in the College of Medicine. In 1878 and 1882 regulations were made for the degrees of Master and of Doctor in Science, obtainable, like those in Arts, after a two years' course of study, by such as have obtained the Degree of Bachelor in Science.

In 1870 a regulation was passed providing that persons should be admissible as unattached students, on condition that they resided in some house or lodging approved by the Warden and Proctors. These students were at first in charge of the Junior Proctor, but, when their numbers began to increase considerably, a Censor was provided specially for them.

In 1871, in consequence of the passing of the University Tests Bill in Parliament, the religious qualification for a vote in Convocation or a seat in Senate was abolished.

In 1873 the Union Society was founded. There had been for many years small debating clubs and libraries at University College and at Bishop Hatfield's Hall. These clubs agreed to combine, some members of the staff helped on the undertaking by becoming life-members, and the Senate provided convenient rooms. The 'unattached' system had been in operation for about three years, and provided members of the Union Society other than those from the College and Hall. In 1894 it was agreed that subscriptions should be paid from the 'Central Finance Fund,' and thus all who were in residence became members of the Union Society. This arrangement has proved very beneficial in bringing all classes of men together, promoting good feeling among them, practising in debate and in management, and providing a good supply of papers and periodicals. This society interchanges privileges with the Union Societies of Oxford and Cambridge and with the Historical Society of Dublin.

In 1875 Codrington College, Barbados, was affiliated to the University, under regulations which are given at length in the appendix to the calendar. This College is much the oldest part of the University, for it was founded by Christopher Codrington, Captain-General of the Leeward Islands, and Fellow of All Souls' College, Oxford, who died in 1710. His estates in Barbados were left in trust to the Society for the Propagation of the Gospel, then lately incorporated, to found a College, with Professors and scholars, who should study divinity,

physic, and chirurgery. There are scholarships of the
aggregate value of about £300, three-fourths of which
are for theological students. Residence in the College
counts as residence in Durham, and the examinations
are precisely the same, the questions being sent in
sealed packets and the papers forwarded to the examiners
in like manner, the conduct of the examination being
entrusted to the officers of the College.

Fourah Bay College, Sierra Leone, was affiliated to
the University in 1876, under regulations in the calendar
similar to those of Codrington College. The Fourah
Bay College was founded by the Church Missionary
Society in 1827 for the purpose of training Africans
as schoolmasters, catechists, and clergymen. A scholarship is maintained by voluntary contributions from
members of the University in Durham to enable a
student to obtain a University course in the College.
The residence and examinations are conducted in the
same way as at Codrington.

In 1876 regulations were passed by which students
who had completed their course of study and examinations at any of the theological colleges named in the
calendar should be allowed to proceed to the degree of
B.A. in Durham after residing for three terms and
passing the final examination. In the same year, on
July 1, appeared the first number of the *Durham University Journal*, which was projected by Willmore
Hooper, B.A. Hatfield, and Fellow of the University.
It was predicted that the *Journal* would die a natural
death after the issue of three or four numbers; but it
has been pursuing a useful career up to the present
time, and has been of great service to me in the pre-

paration of the present volume. For some years it was ably edited by Mr. Hooper, who judiciously admitted into its columns much that is of permanent value.

There has never been any full course of instruction in Law in the University. Until 1872 there was a Reader in Law who delivered occasional lectures, and the regulations referred to ' the examination in Civil Law appointed by the Senate,' and ' the exercises required by the Senate,' but no examinations appear to have been held until 1878. Since that year, in which an examination for the B.C.L. degree took place, fourteen examinations, similar in character to those at Oxford and Cambridge, have been held, and forty-two candidates have passed. Of these, about half have proceeded to the degree of D.C.L. after the performance of exercises satisfactory to the examiners.

In 1882, at the end of the summer term, the Jubilee of the University was celebrated by filling the north window of the Castle Hall with stained glass, by a University concert, by the conferring of a large number of honorary degrees, by services at the Cathedral—at one of which the Visitor, Bishop Lightfoot, preached—and by a great dinner in the Castle Hall.*

In 1884 the number of Fellowships was reduced to the present number of six.

In 1886 the Senate tried the experiment of ' evening lectures ' for young men engaged in offices, shops, etc., during the day. Those who had attended the classes for not less than two years, and passed an examination

---

* For a full account of the proceedings, including a verbatim report of the sermon, see the *Durham University Journal* of July 8, 1882.

in the subjects taken, were to be admitted to the final
year's course of study in the University, and after three
terms' residence were to be eligible for the final examination for the degree of B.A. or for the Licence in
Theology. A preliminary class designed to prepare
men for the lectures was started in Durham, and at the
same time a course of evening lectures by some of the
ablest men on the teaching staff, the subjects being
St. Luke's Gospel, the Alcestis, the Æneid, Euclid, and
Arithmetic. But it soon appeared that there was no
demand either for the lectures or for the preliminary
instruction, and the scheme speedily collapsed.

In 1888 Professorships of Surgery and of Physiology
were founded in the University.

In 1889 the degrees of Bachelor and Doctor in Music
were established under regulations to be found in the
calendar. The honorary degree of Doctor in Music
had occasionally been granted before this time, but
under the regulations the musical tests are similar to
those required in Oxford and Cambridge.

In 1891 the degrees of Bachelor and Doctor of
Hygiene were instituted, and in 1894 a diploma in
Public Health. The conditions on which these are
obtained are stated in the Calendar.

In 1892 a Board of Faculties and a Board of Studies
were formed. The former consists mainly of the Professors, Tutors, and Lecturers in the various faculties
in Durham and in Newcastle ; the latter is the executive committee of the former, and consists of two
members appointed by Senate and two by each
faculty. The Board of Studies makes recommendations
to Senate with regard to curriculum, examinations, and

educational work, and makes a report to the Board of
Faculties twice a year at the least.

In 1893 the Heath Professorship of Comparative
Pathology was formed in consequence of a liberal
bequest by Dr. George Yeoman Heath.

In 1895 a supplementary charter was granted,
enabling the University to grant degrees to women,
and to hold Convocations in Newcastle-upon-Tyne or
elsewhere as well as in Durham.

In the same year the degrees of Bachelor and Doctor
in Letters were established under regulations to be
found in the calendar, and lectures on the subjects
required were provided in Durham and in Newcastle.
This year, also, the University arranged to examine
grammar-schools and other secondary schools. Provision is also made for extension lectures, and under
certain conditions certificates are granted to students
who have attended courses of local lectures.

In 1896 the Durham University Philosophical Society
was founded, and it held six meetings in 1896-97; the
Proceedings for that session were published in 1898.
Meetings have been held and Proceedings issued from
that time to the present. The members of the society
mostly belong to the Newcastle Colleges, the meetings are usually held at Newcastle, and the matters
brought before them are chiefly such as are especially
connected with the studies pursued there. But the
term 'Philosophical' is interpreted in a wide sense, and
literary and historical subjects have been brought before
the society by both Newcastle and Durham members,
and some meetings have been held in Durham.

In 1897 provision was made for a Professor of Music,

who was to be a permanent examiner and to deliver public lectures. The first Professor is Dr. Philip Armes, the organist of the cathedral, in musical learning second to none, and one who may be said to have created for music in the University of Durham the important position that it now holds. His public lectures are at present open to persons not members of the University, and attract very large audiences.

In Easter term, 1899, a hostel was opened for the reception of women students in any faculty except that of theology. These students attend the same lectures, and are on the same footing with regard to academical costume, discipline, etc., as other students. A scholarship and two exhibitions are tenable by women students only. The women's hostel was originally situated in Claypath, but in Easter term, 1901, it was removed to more convenient premises on the Palace Green, now known as the Women's Hostel, or Abbey House.

In October, 1902, lectures on Education were instituted. It may be remembered that a scheme for the education of schoolmasters was planned by the first Warden in 1835.* Diplomas in the theory and practice of teaching are granted after a year's course of instruction and examinations.

Just as we are going to press a private Hall has been licenced by the Warden for the reception of students in Arts and Theology, who will be in charge of resident officers. A large house in the South Bailey has been taken for their accommodation.

* See above, p. 28.

CHAPTER III

THE Palace Green (formerly Place Green) is a large and open square which the founders of the University hoped to convert into a College quadrangle that was to rival the famous Tom Quad at Christ Church, Oxford. This they were never able even to attempt, and it was laid out as it is now in 1838-39. Any one now standing on it will find himself almost wholly surrounded by University buildings. On the south side is the Cathedral (Plate II.), which is not only a Cathedral church in the ordinary sense, but is, moreover, the University church. On the north side is the Castle, with the rebuilt keep conspicuous on a terraced mound (Plate IV.), formerly the residence of the Bishops, not only in their diocesan but in their palatinate capacity, now the home of the University and of University College. The oldest of the venerable lime-trees (Plate IV.) date from time immemorial, and are shown in old engravings. The four smaller ones were planted in and after 1890, to take the place of four that were poisoned by escape of gas into the soil. 'Many generations of Durham's citizens, and of the sons of *Alma Mater*, have welcomed their return-

ing verdure after our long winters, and enjoyed their
pleasant shade in summer.'* Two stately elms on the
east side of the Green were blown down on 'Windy
Monday,' January 7, 1839. They were said to have
been planted in the time of Queen Elizabeth. Sections
of their trunks, 3½ feet in diameter, are kept at the
Castle. The young elms now growing along the north
side of the Cathedral churchyard were planted March 16,
1894, being then about 6 feet high and seven years old,
and the sycamore in the middle of the Palace Green
was planted by the Rev. William Greenwell a year later.
The house near the north-east corner of the Green is
occupied by the Master of University College.

On the west side are the old Exchequer buildings
(Plate IV.), which comprised within their massive walls
the Palatine Court of Chancery, together with chambers
for the various offices of the Palatinate Courts and the
preservation of the records of the bishopric, now all
filled by the University Library. Adjoining the Exchequer buildings on the south is Bishop Cosin's
Library, which accommodates not only the Bishop's
collection, but a part of the University Library, and in
which were formerly held all Convocations, but now only
the smaller ones.

Still further to the south are the new University
lecture-rooms, dating from 1881, and the Bishop's
Registry, built upon the site of the old County Courts
in 1820; this last is not a University building. At
the south-west corner is the Old Grammar-school,
rebuilt in Cosin's time, and now used as a University
lecture-room; this and the private house adjoining,

* *Durham University Journal,* February 8, 1890.

formerly the Headmaster's house, are the property of the University. Behind the Bishop's Registry are rooms which have been occupied by the Union Society since its foundation in 1873. On the east side of the Green is the house that served for Bishop Cosin's Hall (see above, p. 47), and also a range of buildings, formerly almshouses, erected by Bishop Cosin on the ruins of Bishop Langley's Song-School. The arms of the two Bishops, and an inscription now weathered away, were placed over the principal entrance. Their occupants, still called the ' beadsmen,' were transferred to a new building at the head of Queen Street in the early years of the University, and the almshouses were converted into rooms for students. In 1876 they were thrown into one large apartment open to the roof, and the University Museum was removed hither from the old Abbey Mill that is still standing below the Galilee.

At the south-east corner is Abbey House, or the Women's Hostel. The octagonal raised grass-plat in the centre, one corner of which is shown in Plate IV., and more of it in Plate II., is not without a certain interest of its own. It preserves the fitness of the old names—Place Green, Palace Green, and Viretum Palatii. It was made of the debris from the old keep, and it has often been said to cover the same amount of ground as the keep, though in fact it covers much more. When it was first made, certain waggish undergraduates, one of whom still lives to tell the tale, sowed mustard seed after dark so as to represent on a colossal scale the well-known inscription, ''The Gift of Cha. Thorp, Warden.' When the seed came up, it excited the wrath of the Warden's faithful henchman, John Moor, but the Warden himself regarded the signature with an indulgent smile, and sent for a man with a rake to erase the inscription.

To the east of the Green, and at a much lower level, is the North Bailey. The descent to the Bailey may be made either by the ancient street at the - south-east corner, formerly called Lyegate, now Dun Cow Lane, or round by Queen Street, formerly Ouens-gate, at the north-east corner, or by a flight of twenty-six steps in a narrow passage at about the middle of the east side, probably ancient.* The houses on both sides of the street are, with one exception, the property of the University. On the east side is the house of the Principal of Bishop Hatfield's Hall, adjoining which are the University Treasury Office and the Office of Works. Next on the south is the Hall chapel, and lower down, towards the river, the Hall buildings are situated.

Among the buildings which have been named, the Cathedral (Plates II., III.) claims the first notice, although, as it is not primarily a University building, we cannot devote to it in the present work more than a few words in passing. It is well known to be in the foremost rank of buildings of its class, not only in England, but in Europe. 'Durham by the Wear, and Pisa by the Arno, rank side by side,' said Professor Freeman, 'as the noblest examples of the Northern and the Southern Romanesque.' But some who have seen both think it hardly fair to Durham that Pisa should be even named in connexion with it, fine as Pisa un-

* The author of the 'Metrical Life of St. Cuthbert' (l. 7221), writing in the fifteenth century about events in the seventh, speaks of a man and his wife going to the church ' by styes.' ' Stiȝe ' is a ladder, or ascent by steps—provincial English, ' stee.'

From a copyright photograph]

THE CATHEDRAL, FROM THE PALACE GREEN

[*by M. E. A. Powles*

doubtedly is. The key to the history of Durham Cathedral is contained in its traditional designation of the ' Abbey,' not yet obsolete in Durham. It is, in fact, the church of the great Benedictine abbey established by the Norman Bishop William after the Norman Conquest in place of an earlier foundation, the church of which was called the ' White Church,' and which was not more than half monastic. It differed, however, from most other great abbeys in having the Bishop at its head instead of an Abbot, the Prior performing most of the duties of an Abbot, and residing at what is now the Deanery, while the Bishop occupied the Castle. Hence it happens that to this day the Bishop has, in addition to his throne, the first or right-hand stall in the choir, and the Dean the second or left-hand stall. And so in Durham Cathedral the *Decani* and *Cantoris* sides are reversed. The monastic buildings were all on the south side of the church, and were to a great extent converted into prebendal houses, so that at the present time the Warden, as Dean, occupies the residence of the Prior. The house of the Professor of Divinity is on the site of the guest-hall, and that of the Professor of Greek on part of the infirmary site; the remainder of that site is occupied by the house in which the present Professor of Hebrew resides.

Viewing the Cathedral from the Palace Green (Pl. II.), we see the vast building in its main bulk, with an addition at either end—at the east the ' Nine Altars,' formerly used as the morning chapel of the University; at the west the Galilee, so used at present.* The Sunday morning service of the University is that of the

* See above, p. 31.

Cathedral, held in the quire, where seats are assigned to
the University officers and undergraduates, who attend
in academical costume; some of the latter, however, are
accommodated in the north transept.   One of the
Cathedral bells is tolled not only for the University
morning prayers, but for some time before each Convocation, proclaiming to the neighbourhood the close
connexion that exists between the University and the
Cathedral. The Cathedral is indeed a noble inheritance,
shared by the University in no ordinary degree.   Its
grandeur and solemnity, its perfect proportions, its
venerable associations, must, one would think, impress
even the dullest minds, and have an educational value
far beyond that of any single building in any other
University.

  Turning to the north side of the Palace Green we
come to the Castle (Plates IV., V., VI.). It is approached
by a road carried on arches over what was the moat. The
great gate-house, now serving as the porter's lodge, is
a Norman structure, partly rebuilt by Bishop Tunstall
circa 1535, and unfortunately faced, some time before
1826, with as poor a ' Gothic' design as could well be
imagined.   But it retains its iron-bound doors, made for
Bishop Tunstall (1530-1558), and called *portas ferreas*
by William de Chambre, the chronicler.   In one of the
gates is a small wicket, about which an excellent story
has been preserved by Spearman, the local antiquary :*

  ' He (Bishop Crew) pressed Dr. Grey, yᵉ great ornament
of yᵉ church of Durham, and Dr. Morton, to read King

* Quoted by Ornsby, in the *Archæological Association Journal*,
xxii 53, and by Boyle, in his ' Guide to the County of Durham,'
p. 184, but without a proper reference in either case.

THE CATHEDRAL

James's declaration for a Dispensing Power in their parish
churches, which they declining, and arguing against it, he
angrily told Dr. Grey his age made him doat; he had forgotten his learning. The good old Doctor briskly replied,
he had forgott more learning than his Lordship ever had.
" Well," said the Bishop, " I'll forgive and reverence you,
but cannot pardon that blockhead Morton, whom I raised
from nothing." They thereupon tooke their leave of the
Bishop, who with great civility waited upon them towards
the gate, and yᵉ porter opening yᵉ wickett or posterne
only, yᵉ Bishop said, " Sirrah, why don't you open yᵉ great
gates?" " No," says yᵉ Reverend Dr. Grey, "my Lord,
wee'le leave *yᵉ broad way* to your lordship; *yᵉ strait way* will
serve us." '

Dr. Morton and Dr. Grey were both Prebendaries of
Durham; the latter died July 9, 1704, aged ninety-
four. The story is often told as if the Bishop had
wanted the great gates opened for himself on entering.
It really was that he wished to show all possible
courtesy to the departing Prebendaries.

On passing through the gates we enter the irregularly
formed and most picturesque court. It cannot rightly
be termed a ' quad,' being, in fact, a very irregular
pentagon, with buildings projecting into it. The south
side is occupied by the gate-house and by a short wall,
through which is the entrance to what is called the
Fellows' Garden. On the left or west side stands the
Great Hall (Plates V., VI.), with a block of rooms at the
south end of it; the kitchen and offices, being behind it,
are not seen from the court. In the north-west corner
is the Black Staircase, and near it the old well, recently
opened out, On the two northward sides are, below

Tunstall's gallery and chapel, and above and behind these the 'Norman Gallery' (Pudsey's solar or upper hall), faced with eighteenth-century 'Gothic.' The right-hand or east side of the court is formed by a buttressed retaining wall at the base of the mound on which stands the keep.

Each of these buildings may now be noticed separately.* The gate-house (see p. 68) retains a Norman arch, and vaulting evidently later than the arch, with a pelican in her piety on the central boss (*circa* 1250); there are other features of interest still visible, dating from the former half of the twelfth century; others, again, now concealed, are shown in old drawings. It is a lofty structure, with chambers over the vaulting (Plate IV.).

The block of rooms at the south end of the hall is a composite structure. Parts of its south and east walls may be early Norman. It was partially rebuilt by Bishop Fox, and again by Bishop Cosin, whose arms, impaled with those of the see, appear on the front. On the south side of the doorway is a loop $17\frac{1}{2}$ inches high by $7\frac{3}{4}$ inches wide, $2\frac{1}{2}$ feet above the present floor, and now blocked within by a partition wall. It may have been intended for the same purpose as the circular opening in Tunstall's staircase described below.

The Great Hall was built in the time of Bishop Bek (1283-1310) over a Norman undercroft.† Its internal dimensions are 101 feet by 35 feet, and 45 feet high.

---

* Most of them are well shown in Billings' plates of the courtyard and of the keep in his ' County of Durham '

† One little window of this undercroft is shown in Plate V., just on the right of the steps.

THE CASTLE, FROM THE PALACE GREEN

But Bishop Hatfield (1345-1381) added 30 feet to it at the south end, and lighted that end by two lofty two-light windows, which remain almost entire, with fine bold reticulated tracery, which, however, is much built up and obscured. This later extension, however, was afterwards walled off by Bishop Fox (1494-1501). Bek's doorway, a pointed arch of two orders, still remains, partly hidden by a porch added by Bishop Cosin,* and now much decayed (Plate V.). The buttresses terminating in turrets (Plate V.) were made by Bishop Cosin, and are supposed to enclose earlier ones. The side-windows were most of them re-made and brought back to their original length about 1847; but the one nearest to the great fireplace, though blocked at the bottom, has not been 'restored,' and so affords most valuable evidence of the date of this portion of the hall. And the crooks for the shutter still remain. The other windows appear to be copies of earlier ones. Those on the west side are of two long lights, each having a plain transom, and they present two interesting features—namely, stone seats in the lower parts of the splays, and on each central mullion

* It was proposed in 1847 'to remove the Palladian porch which has been built over the Gothic doorway into the hall, and to restore that doorway' Fortunately, this destruction and 'restoration' were never accomplished. One good thing, however, was done at this time A portion of the hall had been cut off at the north end to form a room known as the 'Black Parlour,' so called no doubt from some dark panelling. Over this was a room, formerly the Bishops' drawing-room, but then used as a lecture-room. The Black Parlour was used as a waiting and reading room by the senior members of the University. Both these rooms were done away with, and thus the hall was restored to its original limit northward. The new north window was put in at the expense of the Warden, having been designed after the remains of the old one.

a projecting knob, pierced for an iron bar to secure the
shutters. The windows on the east side have stone
seats, and each has three lights and geometrical tracery
with a plain transom. All the windows appear to have
been shortened when panelling was carried round the
hall, as shown in an old drawing made before 1850.
These windows appear in their shortened form in
Billings' 'County of Durham,' plate dated 1841. The
four-light window at the north end, which was filled
with heraldic glass by Kempe at the jubilee of the
University (1882), is, as has just been shown, entirely
modern. It contains figures of Bishop Hatfield,
St. George, St. Cuthbert, and Bishop Fox. The arms
represented are those of Bishops, Wardens, and Masters
of University College. At the foot of the window is
this inscription : ' Universitatis hujusce jam L annos
fundatæ memorem hanc fenestram alumni posuerunt
MDCCCLXXXII '; in the background are entwined labels
bearing the motto of the University, 'Fundamenta
ejus super montibus sanctis.'* The new oak screen,
gallery, and sideboard at the south end (Plate VI.), and
the panelled dado running all round, were designed by
Mr. C. Hodgson Fowler, F.S.A., of Durham, and were
completed in 1888. On the walls are many pictures,
including a series of thirteen English Archbishops and
Bishops in rochets and scarlet chimeres, said to have
been painted for Bishop Cosin; ten pictures of Apostles,
brought from Spain and bought by the Dean and
Chapter in 1753; a portrait of Bishop Van Mildert,
copied by Evans, a pupil of Sir Thomas Lawrence, from

* There is a full account of the window in the *Durham University
Journal* of July 8, 1882, p. 44.

From a copyright photograph]

[by M. E. A. Powles

THE CASTLE HALL, ETC.

the original by Lawrence at Auckland Castle; a large carving in oak of Bishop Crew's arms, with supporters, baron's coronet and mitre, etc., from Father Smith's organ-case; twelve portraits of the Prebendaries who were joint founders of the University (there is no portrait of the then Dean in this series), and some portraits of recent University worthies—namely, Bishop Maltby (Phillips); George Maltby, Esq., father of the Bishop (Sir William Beechey, R.A.); Henry Jenkyns, M.A., Professor of Greek, afterwards of Divinity (Burlison); Temple Chevallier, B.D., Professor of Astronomy and Mathematics (Cope, R.A.); T. S. Evans, M.A., Professor of Greek (Burlison); Joseph Waite, D.D., Master of University College (Lowes Dickinson); John Cundill, D.D., the first student in the University (Burlison).

Above the screen are portraits of Charles I., Charles II., and Bishop Cosin, and over these some pieces of old armour, banners of troops formed in Durham to resist the first Napoleon, the royal arms, and the great mitres from the top of Father Smith's organ-case in the cathedral. On either side over the screen is a sort of stone pulpit. These 'pulpits' or seats (Plate VI.) were made by Bishop Fox when, by curtailing the length of the hall, he cut off the minstrels' gallery. The portion of the hall added by Bishop Hatfield is now cut up into passages and rooms, which perhaps date, in part at least, from the time of Bishop Fox.

The whole of the present low-pitched and open timber roof appears to be of Bishop Hatfield's time. Portions of it may be closely inspected in the staircases and rooms at the south end of the hall, as may also the stone stairs to Bishop Fox's seats for trumpeters, etc., just mentioned ('sedes pro buccinatoribus aut aliïs musicis').* In the room No. 11 are four stone corbels, which were external before Hatfield's extension, and belonged to some corbelled parapet of Bek's time, or earlier, and in No. 13 is the upper part of one of Hatfield's south windows.

The great and wide fireplace retains its original character, though an iron grate for burning coal has taken the place of the old arrangements for burning great logs of wood. The smaller fireplace appears to be modern.

Through passages behind the screens of the hall we come to the buttery, which was certainly built by Bishop Fox when he shortened the hall. Its inner walls are half-timbered, and on the south side is a hatch opening from the north side of the kitchen. The hatch is in two compartments, on the right or west of which is the doorway from the kitchen. The spandrels over the openings are carved with Fox's badge of the pelican in her piety, the motto, *Est Deo Gracia*, and the date in Arabic figures, 1499.

The kitchen was constructed by Bishop Fox, inside a great square tower of Pudsey's date. This tower has sometimes been called a square Norman keep, but it shows no signs of any staircase to the top, nor of passages or chambers in the walls. Still, it is impossible to say what Fox may not have removed in order to build his three great fireplaces, which are still available. There are not many places where, as in Durham, two medieval kitchens are in constant use. The other is

* 'Hist. Dunelm. Scriptores tres' (Surtees Society), p 150

THE CASTLE HALL

the Abbey kitchen, now attached to the Deanery, as it originally was, not only to the Abbey, but to the residence of the Lord Prior. The roof of the Castle kitchen is considered to be a part of Fox's work, but it may have been made after he went to Winchester, for we are expressly told that at the time of his translation (1501) his buildings at Durham were unfinished. Besides the buttery, the pantries and other rooms connected with the kitchen and hall, now modernized, were built by Bishop Fox.

The great range of buildings adjoining the north-east corner of the hall forms the two northward sides of the pentagonal court. This consists of a stretch of Norman buildings extending from the hall to the keep, with Tunstall's gallery, staircase, and chapel abutting on almost the whole of the south side of them, and rising to about half their height, and Cosin's 'Black Staircase,' rising to the whole height, in the north-west angle of the court (Plate V.). The Norman work, which forms the main portion of this block, is of two periods, the earlier being that of Walcher or of William of Carilef, the two first Norman Bishops (1071-1096). The 'Crypt Chapel,' as it is called, belongs to the earlier part of this period, and is seen at a glance to be much earlier in style than any of Carilef's work at the cathedral.* It is strikingly like a chapel in the Abbaye aux Dames at Caen, founded in 1066, and has features similar to those of other buildings of the same date. The arches and vaulting are very early in character. The columns are lofty; their capitals have square abaci, corner volutes, and rude sculptures representing natural and

* See the plate representing it in Billings' 'County of Durham.'

grotesque animals, and foliage, etc. The capitals are all different. The following account of the most remarkable of them is from a description of the Castle chapels communicated by me to the *Durham University Journal* of July 12, 1878 :

'Angular volutes . . . on the sides—north, a face with long hair and beard, which has been supposed to represent the sun ; east, a horse facing towards south, where we have a man, who may be supposed to have alighted from the horse, and to be " in at the death," standing behind two dogs ; under the south-west angle a conventional tree; then, west, a fine antlered deer, with two other dogs fastening on his nose in order to bring him down. The bodies of the horse and deer are scored (lozengewise) as if to indicate their dappled coats.'

On the other capitals are rude masks, floral devices, trees, fruit, serpent, dragon, monstrous human figures, mermaid, and a star pattern that is found in later Norman work. The bases of the columns have simple mouldings and square plinths.

The joints of the masonry vary from about $\frac{1}{8}$ inch to 2 inches in thickness, the upright ones being generally thicker than the flat ones. The pavement consists of rhomboidal stone pavers laid in a regular 'herringbone' pattern, with a single row of square pavers running up the middle. An altar-space at the east end is raised by two low steps. The top of this is now plastered all over ; there has probably been a pavement of some sort. The original entrance was through a quite plain round-headed doorway at the foot of a spiral staircase contained in a turret on the south side, and leading up to the top of the Castle, but the present access is through a modern passage cut through the solid masonry at the south-west corner, and another modern passage has been made at the south-east corner to give access to the keep. The chapel is in plan a simple parallelogram, 32 feet 10 inches by 20 feet 9 inches, and it is 14 feet 10 inches high. Prior Laurence, in describing it, says:

'Fulget et hic senis suffulta capella columnis,
Non spatiosa nimis, sed speciosa satis.'*

There were three round-headed windows at the east end, but one has been destroyed in making the modern passage; the others have long been blocked by the mound of the keep. On the north side are two widely splayed windows, the openings of which were, unfortunately, much widened in 1840. There is a large recess for a square aumbry in the north wall near the east end. The south side has had a doorway and windows made in it, probably in Tunstall's time, so that its original character, but for the Norman doorway above mentioned, is gone.

Belonging to the same period as this very interesting chapel are the Norman undercroft of the Great Hall mentioned above (p. 70), some lower courses in various walls, and perhaps a small vaulted place below the present level of the courtyard. This place is 20 feet long by 8 feet wide, is divided into four compartments by round arches, and runs in a south-easterly direction from where Tunstall's chapel now is. It is probably

* 'Dialogi Laurentii Dunelmensis monachi ac Prioris' (ob. 1153), Surtees Society, vol. lxx., book 1., lines 01, 402.

the pit of a garderobe tower, access to which from upper and lower floors could be gained from the spiral stairs mentioned above (p. 76), or from those that connected Pudsey's lower and upper halls, or from some earlier stairs, if the building was itself as early as has been supposed.

We now come to the main portion of the northern range of buildings, namely, Bishop Pudsey's hall, with the solar or upper chamber over it. It is not very evident why Pudsey built a second hall, if, as we may suppose, an earlier Norman hall was standing at the time—namely, that of which the substructure remains till now under the great hall of Bek and Hatfield. But it is quite possible that two if not three halls or rooms of state may have been required at that time. Pudsey's hall stands over a substructure with pointed arches, blocked up at an early period, on the south side, a good example of the use of the pointed arch in construction before it came into general use in design. All the original door and window openings that remain in the hall and solar are round-headed.

The lower hall is concealed outside by Tunstall's gallery, which encloses its magnificent doorway, almost the only characteristic feature now visible.* The bottom of this doorway is about 15 feet above the present level of the courtyard, and it would probably be reached by a staircase similar to that of the north hall at Canterbury (afterwards the grammar-school, rebuilt 1855). The Canterbury staircase is the only one of the sort now existing in this country; it is a little earlier than

* There is a round-headed window-opening on the north side, now blocked up.

Pudsey's work at Durham, and very like it. It is roofed overhead, and has an ascending row of open arches on either side. The Durham one was most likely destroyed when Tunstall built his gallery. The arch of the Durham doorway is of three greater and two lesser orders, covered with the richest possible ornamentation, the very unusual details of which are well shown in Billings' 'County of Durham' (plate before p. 31). This fine doorway, which had long been concealed and forgotten, was opened out in Bishop Barrington's time, and now leads to the rooms constructed within the lower hall, the principal of which are the common-room of the University, formerly the dining-room of the Castle, and the Senate-room. The common-room is lofty and well proportioned, and its walls are covered with pictures, none of which are very remarkable, though they have a handsome effect; and there are portraits of some famous Bishops, which are always interesting. There are also full-length portraits of George I., attributed to Kneller, and of Caroline of Anspach, consort of George II., attributed to Vanderbank.

The walls of the Senate-room are hung with seventeenth-century tapestry representing Scripture subjects, and the chimney-piece is of good Jacobean work, the carving and panelling being carried up to the ceiling, and richly decorated with armorial shields, including the royal arms of James I. and the arms of Bishop James (1606-1617). In the anteroom leading to the Senate-room are portraits of James II. and Mary of Modena—the one attributed to Kneller, and the other to Lely—a portrait of Judge Jeffreys, and other paintings. Opening out of the anteroom, on the left,

is a small octagonal apartment in which is a portrait of
Charles I., said to be by Rubens, and one of Bishop
Tunstall. Beyond the Senate-room is the state bedroom, and on either side of the short passage to the
latter is a small apartment, one of which would perhaps
be occupied by the valet of the distinguished guest.
The bedroom is hung with seventeenth-century tapestry.
On the same floor are the rooms formerly occupied
by the Bishop's chaplain, and the anteroom to the
common-room, both entered from the Black Staircase,
and over these the Bishop's sitting-room and bedroom,
entered from the same staircase higher up. The sitting-
room is hung with seventeenth-century tapestry, representing scenes from the Old Testament. Such are the
rooms into which Pudsey's lower hall has been divided.
In the south wall of this lower hall have recently been
discovered, concealed outside by eighteenth-century
facing, and within by the plastering of the common-
room, three remarkable windows, insertions of the fifth-
teenth or sixteenth century. They are single lights
with four-centred heads, each with four cusps forming
a cinquefoil, and with a segmental rear-arch. The
openings are 5 feet 6 inches high by 3 feet wide. Each
has had leading up to it, within, a flight of five stone
steps ; these steps are complete in the case of two of
the windows. The upper portion of a fourth window
in the same series may be seen in a small apartment
connected with the Bishop's rooms; outside it is hidden
by a little window inserted in the eighteenth-century
facing. Here and in the adjoining passage may also
be seen part of the fine oak ceiling of the lower
hall in its original state. The same ceiling is con-

tinued over the common-room, but there it has been modernized.

The upper hall is commonly called ' the Norman Gallery.' It is now entered from the Black Staircase by a doorway with a plain round arch and rear-arch of later date than Pudsey's work, perhaps Early English. Along the interior, on the south side and west end, are arcades constructed in triplets. The central arch of each triplet is higher and wider than the side-arches, and is pierced by a window. All these windows, with two exceptions, have been destroyed for modern insertions, made when the south side was refaced by Bishop Barrington. Of the two that open on the Black Staircase, one is in its original state, but much weathered; the other retains only its original jambs and outer arch. The internal arches are decorated with bold chevron mouldings, and supported on scolloped brackets, the front ends of which rest on cylindrical shafts; the shafts are detached on either side of a central opening, but are attached to the piers that divide the triplets one from another.* At the east end of the arcade on the south side is a doorway with chevron mouldings, in a sort of internal porch, leading to the head of a newel staircase, now destroyed, but which would connect the basement with the lower and the upper hall, and perhaps with a garderobe tower. Near the west end of the same arcade has recently been found the lower part of another newel staircase, probably intended for the servants; it is connected at the foot with a passage that may have led to an early kitchen that has long disappeared. In that case the eastern stairs

* See Billings' ' County of Durham,' plate facing p. 32.

6

would no doubt be used by officers, guests, etc. The
arcades appear to have run along the north side as well
as the south side and west end; but if so, those on the
north side have long been destroyed. At the north-
west corner is a small chamber in a turret with a
vaulted roof of stone, with pointed arched ribs having
plain chamfers. The roof has originally been a high-
pitched one; one of its corbels is still visible above the
east side of the upper doorway. In the west gable is a
three-light window with flowing tracery of Hatfield's
time. This having gone completely to decay, a new
one, designed after the remains of the old one, has
recently been inserted. Other new windows have been
substituted for some with wooden frames, perhaps
of Barrington's time or earlier, that had gone to
decay.

The whole of Pudsey's hall, from the floor to the
roof, has long been in a state calling for grave anxiety
and skilful treatment. It may, indeed, have shown signs
of giving way soon after it was built; for Norman
buttresses have been added on the south side, and the
pointed arches mentioned above (p. 78) were probably
walled up at the same time. Tunstall's staircase and
gallery and Cosin's staircase would all help to buttress
up this wall, but whether any such thought was
present to the minds of their builders we do not
know.

Dr. Gee has lately found an account of repairs in
1750-51 (B.M., Add. MS. 9,815), from which it appears
that in 1750 the north wall was overhanging 3 feet,
and was in many places bulged out. About ten years
previously, chain bars had been put from the said wall

to the south wall, and timbers added to prevent the thrusting out of the walls by the roof. The south wall is described as much perished on the surface, and too ruinous to be pointed up, letting the weather into the rubble core, and requiring to be refaced. Accordingly, the north wall was substantially repaired and partly rebuilt, and the south wall was refaced, as we now see them. It is remarkable that no bulging or overhanging of the south wall is mentioned in 1750, for it has lately been found that when the present facing was put on, the wall must have overhung about 13 inches, and that it was prepared for the facing by cutting it away to an increasing extent towards the top. The old Norman buttresses were cut down to about the roof of Tunstall's gallery, strong timbers thrown across their stumps, and the new facing built upon these timbers and run up plumb.

The whole of the south wall now shows a maximum movement in its total height from the ground-level of 2 feet 1 inch; the movement, including a pushing out of Tunstall's gallery, is at present going on. It is thought that there is no immediate danger, but that something must at once be done to arrest the movement before it goes too far. Unfortunately, the solid rock on which the Cathedral stands has failed at this point, and Pudsey's hall stands on a bed of brown earth or loam that goes down to a depth of 22 feet. The whole matter is being most carefully investigated and considered, and we trust that the architects will be able to deal with it in the best manner possible.

Bishop Tunstall (1530-1558) built the gallery that abuts on the south side of Pudsey's hall and the

6—2

staircase leading to it. In order to do this he would have to remove the Norman stairs,* and whatever was over the Norman vaulting described above,† if they were still there in his time. The gallery is entered at its western end from Cosin's Black Staircase,‡ and at its eastern end from Tunstall's staircase, which is not on the newel plan, but has convenient stone steps about 7 feet 10 inches in length from side to side. Above the spacious staircase is the clock-tower, from which the clock, being out of repair, was removed a few years ago. The masonry consists of remarkably fine blocks of ashlar work, some of them 2 feet 6 inches by 1 foot 2 inches in their outer faces, in accordance with Bishop Tunstall's known views with regard to his buildings. §

Tunstall's gallery ('porticus valde speciosus')‖ is in two stories (Plate V., and the Plate of the courtyard in Billings' 'County of Durham'), having under it a long ground-floor apartment and passages, so that the upper floor is 11 feet above the level of the courtyard. The lower story has three little doorways, which at first probably led into as many small rooms, now thrown into one, which is decorated with carved oak from the Cathedral, and once served as the Tutors' reading-room.

---

* P. 78.   † P. 77.

‡ The exterior of the Black Staircase and of the west end of Tunstall's gallery appear in Plate V., on the right. The whole of the gallery is shown in Billings' plate.

§ When he built the tolbooth in the market-place, and found that the workmen had built the first story thereof with 'rough work,' he angrily asked, 'Was not the Bishop of Durham able to build that place of esher worke ?' (Mickleton MS. No. 10, p. 70, quoted in Raine's 'Auckland,' p. 64)

‖ W de Chambre in 'Scriptores tres,' 155.

The westernmost of these doorways now leads to the foot of the Black Stairs. The upper windows are of three lights, and the lower of two, all having square heads with labels over them, the upper ones being also transomed. Next to the clock-tower the gallery is more lofty, and here it has a large window, similar in character to the last-named, but of five lights. The interior of the gallery is hung with landscape tapestry of the seventeenth century, called 'verdure' tapestry, and is decorated by a long row of busts on pedestals. Within the large window hangs a beautiful panel of enamel glass, representing the Judgment of Solomon, and probably of German or Flemish origin. On a shelf near the gallery is a bell that used to hang in the gatehouse, but which, being cracked, is no longer fit for use. It bears the inscription 'Sancte Vincenti ora pro nobis,' in sunk old English letters, with the date 1495 roughly incised in Arabic figures. The doorway under the large window is modern, and leads to the modern passage into the crypt chapel. The windows in the clock-tower are of two lights; the gallery and tower are embattled, and the former has buttresses with two set-offs. On the outside of both are Tunstall's arms (sa., three combs arg.) surmounted by hood-mouldings. And in the tower, 4 feet above the floor and 3 feet 3 inches above the step below it, is a round aperture 6 inches in diameter, and widely splayed within, which seems to have been for the purpose of peeping out, and perhaps for shooting into the courtyard in case of need. There is a good stone bench about 10 inches below the inner opening.

The chapel, like the gallery, is constructed over a

ground-floor apartment, which is connected with the crypt chapel by openings of Tunstall's time; in these the modern door and 'borrowed lights' have been placed. This room has a large square-headed window like those in the gallery, and a small modern one. It now serves as a Junior Common-room. It forms a part of Tunstall's work. The chapel, originally built by Bishop Tunstall, has been lengthened about 16 feet, by Bishop Cosin, as appears from the masons' marks, and it now serves as the chapel of University College. The difference in the masonry of the more recent portion is very evident within; but on the outside Tunstall's work is well matched. The original east window has been used again, and side-windows have been added to correspond with the others. At present the interior dimensions of the chapel are 57 feet by 19 feet 3 inches at the west end, and 18 feet 3 inches at the east, and the height 23 feet 6 inches. The original length was 41 feet. In the jambs of the east window are two shields, the one on the north bearing Tunstall's three combs, the other bearing a cock, which was a Tunstall badge. The west end of the chapel is approached either from Tunstall's gallery or from his staircase. A small doorway leads into the antechapel, or space under the west gallery, the front of which has been twice set back in order to give more room in the chapel. In a portion of the Norman stair-turret, which has been worked into the west end of the chapel, are two blocked openings and an inserted doorway from the Norman stairs into the gallery of the chapel. Higher up is the mark of an old high-pitched roof on the east side of the tower, below which are loopholes intended to light the stairs,

now concealed by Bishop Crew's arms. The turret
is supported on its south side by a half-arch of construction, filled up underneath by the west wall of the
chapel, in which is the west doorway.

In the south side of the chapel are six windows—
namely, a square-headed one of three lights intended
for the antechapel, but now thrown into the chapel,
and over this a smaller square-headed window of two
lights for the gallery, which was at first, as in other
private chapels, spacious enough to accommodate the
household. East of these are four uniform windows, each
having three lights and a transom. In this south wall,
towards the east end of the older part, is a piscina,
which may be seen by removing part of the panelling.
The east window is similar to the others in design, but
has five lights. On the north side is a small doorway
which may have led to a sacristy, and east of this are
two windows corresponding with those on the south
side. The tops of the principal windows and their
upper lights, particularly the more recent ones, are so
obtusely pointed as to be almost semi-elliptical. The
roof is a lean-to of low pitch, panelled within to represent an ordinary roof of very low pitch, almost flat.
The principals are supported by figures of angels
holding shields with the arms of the see and of Bishops
Cosin and Crew. The floor is comparatively modern.
The fittings of the chapel are of various dates. The
carved oak stalls, with misericordes, are of earlier date
than the chapel itself, and came in 1547-48 from the
now destroyed 'upper chapel' in Auckland Castle.
There are four very fine stall-ends that would doubtless
come at the same time. One of them bears a shield

with the arms of the see impaling those of Bishop
Ruthall (1509-1523)—viz., a cross between four martlets,
on a chief two roses slipped. Another bears the same,
but with the sides reversed by a mistake of the carver,
who had perhaps worked from a matrix of the seal
instead of from an impression. This shield has been
regarded as an evidence of the arrogancy of Cardinal
Wolsey, who was said to have placed his own arms on
the dexter side, the place of honour, and those of the
see on the sinister side. But as the private arms aie
those of Ruthall, and not of Wolsey, the latter must
not be blamed for the mistake of a carver committed in
the time of his predecessor. Among the carved misericordes are representations of a man on horseback attacking a winged dragon with a spear, a dragon and mermaid,
a pelican in her piety, a man wheeling a woman in a
barrow, a pig performing on the bagpipes to a young
pig and a calf, etc. The screen and canopies of the
stalls at the west end appear to be Cosin's work. The
panelling on the walls was of a very poor and almost
mean description; but in 1878 the chapel was fitted up
with new oak panelling and a handsome reredos with
the Crucifixion, etc., in carved oak, and with some
additional stalls and benches, all from designs by Mr.
C. Hodgson Fowler, F.S.A. The east end had been
panelled with figures of Apostles and Evangelists drawn
on wood with hot tools. These panels had previously
formed the sides of a pulpit in the Cathedral, as we see
from old engravings. The pulpit was given to the
University April 19, 1845; the panels are now preserved
at the Chapter Library. The altar of carved and inlaid
oak, with Greek inscriptions, but somewhat diminutive

in size, has also gone to the Chapter Library. The two large gilt candlesticks were presented by the first Warden in 1836. Two of the Prayer-Books are in black letter and in handsome red morocco bindings with the monogram of Charles II.—viz., two C's crowned. A large Bible bound uniformly with these is now in Bishop Cosin's Library. The organ, plate, and other furniture belonging to the chapel in Bishop Cosin's time have for the most part disappeared. The organ-case was in its place in 1841, but it was made into a cabinet about that time. The plate was lent to the Cathedral about 1686-1689,* and, possibly, never re-turned. When Father Smith's organ at the Cathedral was finally taken to pieces in 1873, the choir organ (properly chair organ) was set up, with some internal additions and repairs, in the Castle chapel gallery, where it now is.†

There are brass plates in memory of William Edward Gabbett, Tutor, who died in an Alpine accident on the Dent Blanche, August 12, 1882, and of James Sadgrove King, of University College, who died September 7, 1899.

The exterior of Cosin's Great or Black Staircase (Plate V.) is conspicuous in the north-west corner of the court, rising to the same height as the halls of Bek and of Pudsey, and crested by a battlement continuous with the battlements on their buildings. It is lighted by square-headed two-light windows, and the arms of

* 'Miscellanea,' Surtees Society, vol. xxxvii., p. 218.
† In what has been said about the Castle chapels here and at p. 75, I have made great use of the article in the *Durham University Journal* referred to above, p. 76, which is now out of print.

Bishop Cosin (az., a fret or) appear on the exterior. The stairs have panelled risers, and the railings are very handsome, but are only lime wood stained black, not oak. There are no balusters, the place of these being supplied by boldly-carved foliage filling up the space under the hand-rail. The wood, having shown signs of decay and of becoming worm-eaten, has been recently treated with chemicals in order to preserve it. From the skylight of this staircase is suspended a cannon-ball by a wire hung on swivels, the object being, by means of its oscillations, to demonstrate the rotation of the earth. It was put up under the direction of Professor Chevallier soon after the experiment had been devised. On the floor are some Norman capitals and other remains rescued from the destruction of the old Church of St. Nicholas in the Market Place. The walls are hung with old paintings, etc., the most interesting of which are three old views of Durham and a very scarce engraving of Shincliffe Bridge as ruined by a flood in 1753.

The wall by the mound of the keep, extending from the chapel to the gatehouse, was built in 1664, and in a recess in this wall is a drinking-fountain of the same date, still supplied with water.* In the same year there was a contract for a fountain in the court, 14 feet high and $10\frac{1}{2}$ feet broad. If this fountain was ever set up, it was taken down at some time unknown. Bishop Tunstall had made a water-conduit to wash at, but this also has wholly disappeared. It may have been then that the water was laid on from the Abbey. A lead pipe leading northward from the Abbey still exists, in great part buried in the earth. In earlier times the

* See Billings' plate.

Castle was supplied from a well in the court mentioned by Prior Laurence.* This well has recently been opened out to a depth of 105 feet without the bottom being reached, and is now closed again. Some temporary woodwork over it appears in Plate V. on the right.

The Fellows' Garden, the name of which dates from the time when all the then Fellowships were held by members of the staff, is small but very picturesque, surrounded by ancient buildings on every side, and having a central lawn available for garden-parties, tennis, etc. In the yard adjoining are two covered fives-courts. The boat-house is, of course, down by the river.†

Returning now to the Palace Green, we see in the north-west corner, and close to the south end of the bridge that leads to the Castle gate house, the old Exchequer buildings mentioned above,‡ with Bishop Cosin's Library built against them on their south side (Plate IV.). The walls are very massive, about 7 feet thick at the bottom and 4 feet at the top. The entrance is by a doorway probably of the time of Bishop Neville (1438-1457). His arms (gu. a saltire arg.) and badge (the bull's head) appear on the front or east side of the building higher up. The jambs of the doorway have been cut away and the mouldings destroyed, but the lower portions of the original jambs with the bases of side-shafts are to be seen where they were buried

---

* 'Dialogi,' as cited p. 77, lines 411, 412.

† I cannot leave the subject of the Castle without referring to the fine general view of it in Billings' 'County of Durham' at p. 30.

‡ P. 64.

when the chiselling was done. One or two original
two-light windows still remain. In the centre of the
building has been a newel staircase with ribbed vaulting over the top, but most of this has been destroyed
to make room for modern and more convenient stairs
leading to the upper rooms of the University Library.
Bishop Cosin's Library has a separate entrance of its
own ;* its windows are large and plain in character.
The building passed to the University, together with
the Castle, but the books did not. They form
an independent collection, which is still the diocesan
library. The first books acquired by the University
were placed in the oaken gallery erected in Bishop
Cosin's Library at the sole expense of Bishop Van
Mildert.†

In the earlier years of the University accommodation
was provided for the Vice-Chancellor's Court and other
offices in new buildings in Queen Street, and then the
Exchequer buildings became available for the growing
requirements of the University Library.

* Over this entrance are Cosin's arms impaled with those of the
bishopric, and ensigned by a mitre, with the inscription, 'Non
minima pars ervditionis est bonos nosse libros,' which, having become almost illegible, has been recut on a new stone This inscription appears to be based upon a saying of Joseph Scaliger, quoted
in Hutchinson's 'Durham,' i. 533, note.

† As there is sometimes confusion in the minds of people at a
distance about the Durham libraries, it may be well to mention
that, besides the University and Cosin's Library, there is the
library of the Dean and Chapter, which includes a great part of
the library of the Abbey; this part consists, of course, chiefly of
MSS There is also the Cock Library at St. Oswald's Vicarage,
which contains a Sarum Breviary of 1556 (Pars Hiemalis), but not
much else of interest.

The following account of the library is taken from the University calendar, with additions :

The University Library was founded on the opening of the University, Bishop Van Mildert contributing, with other costly works, a collection of the Benedictine Fathers.

The library is under the direction of a Board of Curators, and is continually being augmented by purchase and presents of books. Books may be taken out by members of the University, under regulations fixed by the Curators.

The following were the principal benefactors in the early days of the University: Bishop Van Mildert, Bishop Maltby, Archdeacon Thorp, Rev. Dr. Prosser, Rev. Dr. Townsend, Rev. G. S. Faber, Rev. H. J. Rose, R. Surtees, T. Carr, Rev. T. L. Strong, Rev. C. Simeon, Rev. J. Collinson, J. Leybourne, Rev. E. S. Thurlow, E. Shipperdson, and Rev. T. Baker.

In more recent times the library has received the considerable additions known as the Routh, Maltby, Winterbottom, and Lightfoot Collections.

Dr. Martin Joseph Routh, President of Magdalen College, Oxford, some time before his death, made over to the University of Durham, by deed of gift, his extensive library. This collection came to the University in 1855, and consists of about 16,143 volumes of works now classified as Biblical, Theological, Liturgical, Classical, Church History, Bibliography, Topography, Travels, Law, and Miscellaneous. There is also an important series of political and religious tracts, from 1582 to the middle of the last century. These are now bound in volumes and catalogued separately. The library possesses, besides engraved portraits, a life-sized oil-painting and a marble bust of Dr. Routh, also a cap and wig that once were his.

Bishop Maltby, on his resignation of the See of Durham in 1856, presented to the University about 2,416 volumes, classical and miscellaneous, collected by him at Auckland Castle, with an endowment of £1,000 3 per cent. Consols, vested in trust.

Thomas Masterman Winterbottom, M.D., of Westoe, South Shields, bequeathed to the University his library, consisting of works in philology, the classics, and general 'literature, including a large collection of dictionaries and many works in various European languages. This library came into the possession of the University in 1859, and consists of about 5,147 volumes. There is a small portrait in oils of Dr. Winterbottom.

Bishop Lightfoot bequeathed to the University about 1,700 volumes, including the magnificent work of Lepsius on Egyptian antiquities. The rest are chiefly classical, philological, general, and archæological. The Bishop's theological books were left to the Cambridge Divinity School.

The total number of volumes in the University Library is about 34,300. There are printed catalogues of the Maltby and Lightfoot Collections.

A complete set of Migne's 'Patrologia Græca,' 166 volumes, and 'Patrologia Latina,' 221 volumes, was obtained by purchase in 1894.

The recent facsimiles of Biblical and classical MSS. are also being procured for the library.

The library possesses no important MSS., and is not particularly rich in early printed or very rare books. The following, with the exception of the two last, are in the Routh Collection.

1. Missale ad vsū ac cōsuetudinē Sarū. Parisiis, Prevost, imp. Byrkman, 1527, 3 kal. Mart., fol. [xvi. A 11.]

2. The Primer, London, Grafton, 1546, 4to., English (perfected in MS. after one in the Bodleian Library). [xvii. E 30.] Also the same as reprinted without name, place, or date, *circa* 1700. [xvii. F 1.]

3. Breviarivm Romanum (Quignon) Lugduni, Baltazard Arnoullet, 1543-44, fol. [xvii. B 2.]

4. Inivnccions geuen by the Kynges Maiestie, London, Grafton, 1548. [xvii. E 19.]

5. A simple and Religious consultatiō of vs Herman . . . Archbishop of Colone. London, Daye and Seres, 1548. [x. D 29.]

6. The Ordre of the Commvnion, Grafton, 8 March, 1548 (1548-49). [xvii. E 19.]

7. The booke of the common prayer. London, Whitchurche, 1549, Mense Maii. [xvii. B 14.]

8. The Boke of common práier. London, Grafton, 1552. [xvii. B 15.]

9. The Psalter or Psalmes of Dauid. . . . London, Grafton, 1552, 4to. (With the Calendar, Order for reading the Psalter, Mattins and Evensong, Litany and Suffrages, and the Collects, but without the Communion or occasional Offices, being indeed a Companion to Mattins, Litany,

and Evensong. Very rare. It is fully described in ' The Clerk's Book of 1549,' H. Bradshaw Society, Intr., p. xiv.) [xvii. E 28.]

10. Manuale ad vsum insignis ecclesie Sarisburiensis, Rothomagi, Valentin, 1554. [xvii. D 21.]

11. Sarum Breviary, London, Kyngston and Sutton, 1555. One volume only, no title; described in the colophon as ' Pars estiualis tam de tempore quam de sanctis portifarii (*sic*) ad vsum insignis ecclesie Sarum. [xvii. C 22.]

12. A profitable and necessarye doctryne, with certayne homelyes adioyned thervnto. (By Bishop Bonner). London, Cawodde, 1555. A very imperfect copy, perfected in MS. [viii. E 6.]

13. The Primer in Latin and Englishe (after the vse of Sarum). London, J. Waylande, 1555. [xvii. F 29.]

14. Serenissimi et Potentissimi Principis Jacobi . . . Opera. London, Norton and Bill, 1619. In red morocco, stamped with the royal arms and supporters, with a diaper of fleurs-de-lis, thistles in the corners and lions on the back, and provided with blue silk strings for tying it up. At the beginning, the king's autograph, ' Jacobus R., D.D.,' and an inscription in a copper - plate hand commemorating the presentation of the book to the King's former tutor, Peter Junius, dated at Greenwich, 11 kal. Jun., 1620. On the end fly-leaf is a copy of a letter from King James introducing Peter Junius as Ambassador to Frederick, King of Denmark, not dated. [lxx. B 5.]

15. Missale Parvvm pro sacerdotibus in Anglia, Scotia, et Ibernia itinerantibus, no printer's name or place, 1626. (In the original wrapper of limp vellum, with the remains of leathern thongs for tying it up.) [xvii. E 6.]
16. The Booke of Common Prayer. Edinburgh, Robert Young, 1637, with the arms and initials of Charles I. stamped on the covers. [xvii. B 16.]
17. A collection of 149 copper-plate engravings of French monasteries, mostly bird's-eye views. The plates have been a little cut down in binding. They now measure $18\frac{1}{2}$ by 25 inches, are folded down the middle, and are mounted on guards. Some are not dated. The dates of those which are range from 1674 to 1702. One has the inscription, 'D. Franciscus Vrayet delineauit, 1676,' and most of the others seem to be the work of the same hand. A few of the plates have references to the pages of some work which they seem to have been meant to illustrate—*e.g.*, that of St. Ouen's, Rouen, exterior, 'p. 197,' interior, 'p. 196.' A written memorandum is pasted in stating that there are only two other copies known, one 'in Bibliotheca Rotomagensi,' another 'in Bibliotheca Parisiensi de Arsenal,' and that there is a description of the author of the work in 'Hist. litteraire de la Congregation de St. Maur, auctore D. Tassin, Lutet., *c.* 1766.' On the lining of one of the old covers, which has been preserved, is the following note in Dr. Routh's writing: 'It was

7

stated to me on the authority of Mr. Pugin the Architect that there were not more than three Copies known of this Book.'

It appears from the work of Dom Tassin, an imperfect copy of which is in the King's Library at the British Museum, at p. 154, that one Dom Michel Germain, who was born in 1645, professed 1663, and died 1694, projected, and, indeed, wrote, a history of monasteries of the Congregation of St. Maur that was to be in three volumes, and obtained permission to print it under the title of 'Monasticon Gallicanum.' Engravings were made of most of the monasteries, but the work remained in MS. at St. Germain des Prés, where, as well as elsewhere, were collections of the 'plans,' so-called, to the number of 152. The remainder had not been executed when Tassin wrote in 1770.

In 1870 the plates were reproduced and issued under the following title : 'Monasticon Gallicanum, Collection de 168 planches de vues topographiques [par Michel Germain, d. 1694] représentant les monastères de l'Ordre de Saint-Benoit. . . . Le tout reproduit par M. Peignè-Delacourt, avec une préface par M. Léopold Delisle.' Paris, 1870, 3 vols., 4to. There is practically no letter-press.

18, 19. Gregorii Nazianzeni orationes, Ven. 1536 (etc.) [i. G 42], and Io. Wiclefi dialogorum libri quatuor, 1525 (etc.) [xiii. G 12], each

with the autograph of Archbishop Cranmer
and MS. remarks thereon by Dr. Routh.

20. Ecclesiasticæ Historiæ Eusebii Pamphili libri
novem, ed. Cacciari. Romæ, 1740. Reported
in 1887 as not being in the Bodleian nor in
any College library in Oxford. [xxxii. C 8.]

21. The large collection of Civil War and other
pamphlets mentioned above, p. 93. Many
besides these came to the library in volumes,
and are entered in the general catalogue.

22. A Fragment of the history of John Bull, with
the birth, parentage, education, and humours
of Jack Radical, with incidental remarks upon
ancient and modern Radicalism. By Horace
Hombergh, Esq., of the Middle Temple.
Durham, printed by F. Humble and Co., 1820.
Very rare.

23. MS. notes of the lectures of Dr. Jenkyns, by
John Low Low, ç. 1844, Richard Glover, c.
1851, Henry Ellershaw senior, c. 1857, and
J. T. Fowler, 1858.

The great doors next to Cosin's Library lead into
the masons' yard, at the back of which are two covered
fives-courts. Next to these gates, and fronting the
Palace Green, are the new lecture - rooms, built in
1881, partly on the site of buildings that had long
been used for lectures, but which had become too small
for the accommodation of the more numerous students
and lecturers. The largest of these rooms is about
70 feet long by 30 feet wide, and is open to the roof.

7—2

A narrow passage leads into a yard adjoining on the south, in which are the rooms of the Union Society, old buildings granted by the University and adapted to serve as reading-room, billiard-room, etc., in 1873. In the reading-room the debates are held, and on its walls are the very interesting drawings that led to the writing and illustrating of 'The Adventures of Mr. Verdant Green, an Oxford Freshman, by Cuthbert Bede, B.A.,' 1853-1856. The author, Edward Bradley, of University College, took his B.A. degree at Durham in 1848, and while at the University made many drawings illustrating the more humorous aspects of life in the Northern University (Plates VIII., IX., at the end of the Appendix). After he had gone down he transferred his hero to Oxford, and brought him before the world as an Oxford Freshman, some of the old drawings, with new ones adapted to Oxford, supplying the illustrations. Mr. Bradley's own account of them is as follows :

'These sketches originated "Verdant Green." I showed them to Mark Lemon, editor of *Punch*, to which I was then a contributor with pen and pencil, and he asked me to adapt the sketches to Cambridge, and said that he would publish them in *Punch*, with letterpress by Professor Tom Taylor (of Trinity College, Cambridge, afterwards editor of *Punch*). I declined this offer; but said that I would adapt the sketches to Oxford, which I did, and Mark Lemon accepted them for publication in *Punch*. Some . . . were utilized for "Verdant Green." . . . Subsequently I wrote letterpress to the sketches, and they were published as a railway book.'*

* *Durham University Journal*, ix. 150

The best of the drawings that refer to Durham are the two sets, each in nine compartments, which are headed, 'Ye Freshmonne, his adventures at Univ. Coll., Durham.'

'The first drawing shows his arrival at the old railway-station in Gilesgate. The scene as the bus passes Claypath Chains with its freight of students and boxes is very amusingly depicted. The road here is considerably lower than the footpath on each side, and the surrounding houses are cleverly sketched. The roadway was not then so good as it is now, and a hat-box is seen flying off at one side of the vehicle, while a trunk labelled " Glass, with care," is dropping off at the other.* In the interview with the Warden it is not difficult to distinguish Archdeacon Thorp's genial features. The view of Palace Green, with Verdant in search of rooms, is very funny, and the bird's-eye sketch of the Castle and its surroundings is also very clever. Having matriculated, Verdant is next seen disporting himself on the banks, to the great amusement of young ladies and alarm of several babies, with their nurses. His movements on this occasion are given in three compart-ments. In the centre one is a bevy of young ladies, who cast side-glances at the Freshman as they coyly march across Prebends' Bridge. On his way to his rooms he meets Dean Waddington, whom he salutes in a character-istic fashion, and of whom there is a striking likeness. The series ends with the familiar " wine " scene.'

So far the *Durham University Journal*. In one of the series described above Mr. Verdant Green is ' dis-mayed at the number of steps leading to the keep.'

* The moon, with a human face, is looking on with a merry twinkle.

He is standing in the crypt chapel, and beholding ideal flights of steps that might reach almost to the clouds. There are two other drawings representing 'Reading for the June Examinations.' The 'students' are lying down on the grass in the Fellows' Garden, mostly in attitudes suggestive of anything rather than close attention to the few books that are lying about. The following names are written under the prostrate figures, evidently striking likenesses: John Bolland, Collins, Fynes Clinton, Garth, F. M. St. John, Hon. A. G. Douglas.

After Mr. Bradley's death in 1889 the drawings came to the Union Society through Mr. George Neasham, author of 'North Country Sketches,' etc., then assistant at the University Library. Those entitled ' Ye Fresh-monne,' etc., the germ of Verdant Green, were bought for £12.

The next building, which completes the west side of the Green, is the Bishop's Registry;* then comes an ancient path to the 'Broken Walls' and the Banks, now known as 'Windy Gate' or 'Windy Gap,' formerly as 'Wyndshole Yett,' and next to that the old Grammar-school, long the Divinity-school, and still a lecture-room. There is an old saying, dating from the early days of the University, that the two heads at the sides of the east window represent the man who has been 'plucked' and the man who is 'through.' On the east side of the Green is the University Museum. The building has been sufficiently referred to above.† The collection dates from early days. Soon after the University was founded, the Rev. Thomas Gisborne, Prebendary of Durham, presented a collection of objects

* P. 64.   † P. 65

of natural history, which has received additions by donations from members of the University and others. There is an almost complete collection of British birds, but some are still wanting to complete the 288 species named in Selby's catalogue. Other contents of the museum that may here be mentioned are—(1) A *hortus siccus*, made in the county of Durham by Miss Deborah Wharton, of Old Park, in 1760-1802. The specimens are for the most part still in fair condition. (2) A large collection of antiquities from the Roman station at Binchester. (3) A life-sized plaster figure and a suit of clothes, hat, hat-box, stick, under-garments, and violin, that belonged to the once famous Count Joseph Boruwlaski, the Polish dwarf. It is recorded in his monumental inscription in the Church of St. Mary the Less that he ' measured not more than 3 feet 3 inches in height, but his form was well proportioned, and he possessed a more than common share of understanding and knowledge.' After having lived for many years in Durham, an ever-welcome guest at the prebendal and other principal houses, he died, September 5, 1837, in the ninety-eighth year of his age, and was buried in the Cathedral, near the west end of the north aisle, where his grave is marked by the letters ' J. B.' (4) A gold five-guinea piece of William and Mary, 1691, in perfect condition, presented by the Rev. George Townsend Fox. This fine coin is at present kept in the Registrar's iron safe. The museum is under the direction of a Board of Curators.

In the early days there was also a biological museum in a room on the Palace Green. This museum was formed by the Reader in Medicine, and employed by him in his lectures.   It appears to have ceased to exist in 1840-41.

The other buildings on the east side of the Green do not call for any particular remark, but the house that was formerly Bishop Cosin's Hall and those which now form the Women's Hostel are old enough to be interesting, and the latter have particularly good oak staircases.   The ground-floor of the first-named house was long used as a common-room for the unattached students.

Passing now from the Palace Green to the North Bailey we come to Bishop Hatfield's Hall.   The history of the Hall has been given above,* and there is not much to be said about the buildings.   The original house was for some time a large inn, and under it are extensive cellars.   The great room now used as the hall for dinner and the other meals was an assembly-room where the county balls took place, and the first Warden told the writer that he had had many a good dance on its floor in his young days.   On the walls are two portraits: one, Bishop Van Mildert, a copy of Sir Thomas Lawrence's portrait, presented by Archdeacon Watkins; the other, David Melville, the first Principal, painted by Mr. S. P. Denning, father of Stephen Poyntz Denning, of Bishop Hatfield's Hall, B.A. 1848, and given to the hall by the artist in 1852; also a large picture of St. Sebastian (a copy of one by Guido), presented by Mrs. Powles in 1876.   The room which was the Principal's drawing-room until the University provided him with a separate house, and which is now

* P. 45.

From a copyright photograph]

BISHOP HATFIELD'S HALL, FROM NEW ELVET

[by M. E. A. Powles

occupied by the Vice-Principal, was that in which the
dowagers played whist while the damsels danced. The
east side of the Hall buildings (Plate VII.) stands on
or in the line of the old outer wall of the abbey and
castle precinct, and there is a good stretch of this
wall in the garden to the north, below the Principal's
garden. The grounds on this side extend down a
precipitous slope to the river. The 'new buildings'
were added in 1847-48. They are good and substantial, and include twenty-eight sets of rooms.* The
present chapel took the place of a temporary one
in 1853. It was designed by a member of the University, James Francis Turner (B.A. 1851), subsequently Bishop of Grafton and Armidale. He had
been educated as an architect under Philip Hardwick.
His work shows great originality without any particular
faults either in design or in construction. In the east
and west windows is an ingenious combination of
geometrical and flowing tracery, so devised that every
line shall be continuous with some other line. In order
to effect this, the designer has boldly made the tops of
lower lights unsymmetrical, but the general effect is
nevertheless not unsatisfactory. The side-lights are
long lancet windows with tracery in the heads, another
unusual arrangement, and two-light windows with
simple geometrical heads. The building stands on a
substructure that was required in order to adapt it to

* The arms of Bishop Hatfield (qz. a chevron or between three
lions rampant arg) and the motto of the Hall, *Vel primus velcum
primis*, were carved over the two entrances at the expense of two
newly-elected Fellows in 1875, instead of the wine-party then
usually given on these occasions.

the slope in the ground. It was at first intended to be longer, but the needful funds could not be raised ; consequently it is too short in proportion, and barely provides the accommodation now required. The building fund was provided partly by subscription and partly by grants of Senate that amounted to £520. Since 1883 some great improvements have been made in the chapel. An excellent new organ, built by Harrison of Durham, has been placed in a west gallery with carved and panelled front, and a handsome oak reredos similar in character has been set up as a beginning of panelling to be carried all round the chapel. The ornamental woodwork was designed by Mr. C. Hodgson Fowler, F.S.A. There are two brass plates, one in memory of John Pedder, Principal, 1854-1859, who died July 12, 1890, the other, in memory of Herbert Julius Hancock, who died October 17, 1900, and of Ernest Alfred Gee, who died on St. Barnabas' Day, 1902, both members of the Hall, and both engaged in the work of the Universities' Mission to Central Africa. The daily choral evensong took the place of a perfectly plain service while the Rev. James Barmby was Principal (1859-1876). It is much valued by most of the men, and is very well attended.

The Hall has its own boat-house, asphalted tennis-court, and covered fives-court.

The only outlying building in Durham belonging to the University and employed for educational purposes is the Observatory. This is a small but substantial structure, consisting of a ground-floor for the Observer's residence, with. rooms above for the instruments, and the usual dome for the equatorial telescope. Mr. Salvin furnished the design, and the building was completed early in 1841. In the calendars of 1840-1842 are sub-scription-lists that show how a sum of £1,361 16s. was collected for the Observatory; this sum was afterwards increased to about £1,440. At their first recorded meet-ing, held June 16, 1840, the Curators expressed 'their thanks to the Dean and Chapter for their ready com-pliance with the request of the University, in granting upon favourable terms a lease of the ground upon which the Observatory is erected.' In 1839 a collection of astronomical instruments, including a transit instru-ment, a telescope of above 8 feet focal length, by Fraunhofer, mounted equatorially, and a clock by Hardy, was purchased by the members and friends of the University, to furnish the Observatory. In 1843 a great many observations were made in different ways in order to determine the latitude of the Observatory. The results corresponded with remarkable precision, and the mean result of all the observations was N. 54° 46′ 6·423″. The Duke of Northumberland in 1846 made an addition to the instruments by presenting an excellent refracting telescope. In 1850 an obelisk was erected in connexion with the Observatory by William Lloyd Wharton, Esq., upon a rocky knoll on his own estate, partly in order to provide work for the unemployed in a time of distress. Its purpose is to afford a well-defined mark due north* of the Observa-tory, by means of which the transit circle may be directed truly in the meridian. The statement of its latitude on the obelisk makes it out to be 1,200 yards

* It would have answered the purpose equally well if it had been placed due south

distant from the Observatory. The obelisk bears the following inscriptions on its southern face :

W. L. W.

ASTRONOMIÆ

DICAVIT

MDCCCL.

N. LATITUDE 54° 46′ 54″.

W. LONGITUDE 1° 34′ 56″·25 (= 6 MIN. 19·75 SEC.).

MAGNETIC $\begin{cases} \text{DIP} \\ \text{VARIATION W.} \end{cases}$ JUNE 1854 $\begin{matrix} 70°\ 36′. \\ 23°\ 45′. \end{matrix}$

—— ABOVE SEA LEVEL (HALF TIDE) 292 FEET ——

On the top of a block of stone a little to the south of the obelisk,

100 FEET

BELOW THE SUMMIT.

The Senate voted their thanks to Mr. Wharton for this obelisk on December 3, 1850.

In 1891 the Fraunhofer equatorial was dismounted, and was replaced by one of equal aperture and modern construction by Sir Howard Grubb. An Almucantar of 6 inches aperture, constructed by Messrs. T. Cooke and Sons, was added to the equipment in 1900, and is placed in a new building to the south-east of the old Observatory. With the acquisition of this instrument, the activity of the Observatory as a place of astronomical research has greatly revived under the direction of Professor Sampson, F.R.S., and the results that have been obtained are well known to astronomers.

The Observer resides at the Observatory, and observations are regularly made. The Observatory is placed under the direction of a Board of Curators.

CHAPTER IV

THE FIRST FOUR WARDENS

THE first Warden, Archdeacon Thorp, held the office from 1831 to his death in 1862; the second, Dean Waddington, from 1862 to his death in 1869; the third, Dean Lake, from 1869 to his resignation in 1894; and the fourth, Dean Kitchin, has held it from 1894 to the present time. It was truly remarked at the time of the Jubilee of the University in 1882, that 'the first of these periods was one of alternate success and failure, the second a time of transition and revival, the third of change and progress.'* The same may now be said of the fourth or present period, as was said of the third in 1882.

CHARLES THORP, the first Warden, was born at Gateshead Rectory, October 13, 1783, and was the fifth son of Robert Thorp, Rector of Gateshead and afterwards of Ryton, also Archdeacon of Northumberland, who was the second son of Thomas Thorp, Vicar of Chillingham. Archdeacon Robert Thorp was a man of learning, and the author of important works on the higher mathematics. His son Charles was educated at the Newcastle

* Professor Farrar in the *Durham Advertiser* of June 23, 1882.

109

Grammar-School and at Durham School. He matriculated from University College, Oxford, December 10, 1799, becoming B.A. in 1803, M.A. in 1806, B.D. in 1822, and D.D. in 1835. In 1803 he was elected Fellow and Tutor of his College, and in 1807, on the resignation of his father, he was presented by Bishop Barrington to the rectory of Ryton. In 1829 he was presented by Bishop Van Mildert to the second prebendal stall in Durham Cathedral, and on December 6, 1831, he was by the same prelate appointed Archdeacon of Durham.

When about this time the Bishop and the Dean and Chapter began to form their plans for the foundation of the University, Archdeacon Thorp was, so far as we know, the only person thought of to fill the office of Warden, to which he was appointed provisionally before December 9, 1831, and permanently in 1834. In that position he showed a constant zeal and warm interest, and made considerable pecuniary sacrifices, in support of what he sometimes called 'my University.' It was strictly a Church institution at first, and as such lay very near to the warm heart of 'the Old Warden.' But it was always intended that it should include all the faculties and branches of learning that existed in the older Universities, and not be a Church seminary, but a place of general education and learning. It was intended from the first that the education should not be expensive, but the nobility and gentry of the North sent their sons, and so the standard of expense was soon raised.* Then Oxford and Cambridge became more

* Canon Greenwell remembers three sons of noblemen and eight sons of baronets being at University College in his time, about 1840.

accessible by reason of the throwing open of scholarships, etc., and the development of railway communication.

From these causes, rather than from any faults or defects of its own, the young University after a few years seemed to be in danger of extinction, and then the 'Hall system,' explained above (p. 46), was adopted with considerable success, while the old mode of living went on at University College, and thus men of more or of less limited means were provided for. In the early years of the University it suffered from the foundation scholarships being in the private gift of members of Chapter; if these had been thrown open to competition from the first, they would no doubt have attracted many good men. Some of the early Tutors very much wished to have this done, and it is said that they agreed to resign if it was not done. But the Warden and senior members of Senate would not hear of it, and the scholarships were not thrown open until 1859. An Order of Chapter dated November 21 in that year runs thus: 'Agreed, that the scholarships now in the gift of members of Chapter be thrown open for competition to students in Arts,' etc.* The Warden, however, showed his wisdom in doing what he could to bring in new spheres of work. In 1837 the engineering course was established (p. 54), and in 1852 the College of Medicine was connected (p. 54). The Warden was seconded by a most able and zealous set of coadjutors, but, in spite of all that they could do, the numbers of students began to decline rapidly after 1850. The theological class, however, as com-

* One scholarship had been set apart by the Dean and Chapter in 1840 as a University Classical Scholarship.

pared with the Arts course, and after the shortening of the course from three years to two in 1846, continued to flourish under Dr. Jenkyns, as it did for some time under his successor, Dr. Farrar.

In 1860 and 1861 the total numbers in the University were at a very low ebb, and some members of Senate were so dissatisfied that they asked for a Royal Commission to inquire into its condition. The old Warden was now nearly eighty years of age, and was little likely to welcome anything of this kind. Professor Chevallier, who had been on the staff of the University almost from the first, spoke of the petitioners as 'Catilines.' The unhappy termination of the Warden's lifework for the University, first in its want of success, then in the action taken by his colleagues, and finally in the work of the Commission, before which he never appeared, broke the old man's heart and spirit, and he died at Ryton Rectory, October 10, 1862. The Commissioners had been sitting from February 21 to March 7 in the same year. The writer remembers the old Warden very well as he was before these last troubles came upon him, namely, from October, 1858, to June, 1861, when he had passed his seventy-fifth year. He was then a bright, cheery, kindly, and dignified old gentleman, with more than a touch of the Northumbrian burr in his utterance. He often walked about on the Palace Green in his handsome silk gown and velvet cap, watching the men come out from lectures, and ready with a kind word or two with any undergraduate whom he happened to know, and many there were who not only experienced his splendid hospitality, but met with other kindnesses at his hands that never were made known.

One gentle rebuke to a student may be mentioned here, as showing what a change has come over us in the course of half a century, in the matter to which it refers. Meeting a student one day, he took him kindly by the hand, and said, with all the *r's* well burred, 'I am very sorry, Mr. N., to hear that you have contracted the vile habit of *smoking*. I do not like smoking in my University.' That last phrase, mentioned also above, gives the key to his whole attitude towards the University. He loved it as his own child, but was too much inclined to keep all power in his own hands, so that, as one of the hostile witnesses said before the Commission, ' the Dean and Chapter were simply managed, the Convocation was simply dictated to, and the Senate was simply checkmated.' This may be put in an exaggerated form, but it shows at any rate that the Warden had what he believed to be the interests of the University thoroughly at heart.

The Archdeacon was a High Churchman of that old school that existed before the Oxford Movement began. He was most careful to maintain the old traditions in the Cathedral, and desirous to establish good traditions in the University. Hence his care to have everything good and handsome at the Castle, as well as to have all the buildings in good repair and well cared for. But, unfortunately, he lived at a time when people were everywhere rushing recklessly into 'restoration,' so called. That meant the sweeping away of all that was considered ' inharmonious' or ' out of keeping,' and the conversion of ancient buildings into new ones, as far as might be. Hence the costly mistake of the new ' keep,' as it is called, although consisting wholly of sets

8

of rooms and staircases. Hence the sweeping away of all the old woodwork in the Great Hall, and the proposed destruction of Cosin's porch. But the Archdeacon valued old work for its own sake, and consequently much carved oak that had been turned out of the Cathedral was brought to the Castle, and has been thus preserved, while much more has been lost or destroyed. And a portion of the oak screen that long surrounded the 'feretory' in the 'Nine Altars' was brought to the University Library, where it serves to screen off the Maltby Collection. In these and in many ways the old Warden has left memorials of the warm interest that he always felt in everything connected with the University which he had so largely helped to found, and over which he so long presided. During the whole of his tenure of office as Warden, the Archdeacon was Master of University College, with a Vice-Master residing at the Castle.

GEORGE WADDINGTON was a son of George Waddington, Vicar of Tuxford, Notts. He was born there on September 7, 1793, was educated at the Charterhouse from 1808 to 1811, and was admitted scholar of Trinity College, Cambridge, in 1812. In 1815 he graduated B.A., being Senior Optime in the Mathematical Tripos and full of University distinctions. He was admitted Minor Fellow of Trinity in 1817 and Major Fellow in 1818, proceeded M.A. in 1818, and D.D. about 1840, and was an original member of the Athenæum Club at its foundation in 1824. About 1826 he was ordained, having published several books of travel. In 1833 appeared his 'History of the Church of England from the Earliest Ages to the Reformation,' in 2 vols.;

2nd ed., 1835, 3 vols.; and in 1841 his 'History of the Reformation on the Continent,' in 3 vols. In the same year he was presented by his College to the perpetual curacy of St. Mary the Great, Cambridge, and to the vicarage of Masham with Kirby Malzeard, in Yorkshire; he was, moreover, collated to the prebendal stall of Ferring in Chichester Cathedral. He was installed in the deanery of Durham September 25, 1840, and, according to the Order in Council of 1841, succeeded Archdeacon Thorp as Warden of the University in 1862, being then nearly seventy years old. A man of that age could hardly be expected to show much activity on succeeding to a post which he had never desired, but he showed liberality and wisdom in promoting the interests of the University. And, as a matter of fact, before his death the number of students had almost doubled, an increase partly due, probably, to recommendations of the Commission of 1862, but partly to his good management in carrying them into effect. He was a man of a stately presence, and his magnificent appearance as he stood in the Dean's stall was greatly enhanced by his singularly fine head of snow-white hair. He had a grand, sonorous voice, and his splendid delivery in reading and preaching still lives in vivid remembrance. He could never have been fairly charged with any tendency to asceticism, but rather the reverse. He was fond of old English sports, and used to visit the boxing-booths at Durham Races. It was said that he objected to a dinner 'without a bird,'* his cellar was superlative, and he considered that any pictures or other works of art—unless it were the culinary art—were

* 'Reminiscences of William Rogers,' 1888, p. 39.

8—2

quite out of place in a dining-room. He could use forcible language upon occasion, as once when the conversation turned on smoking, and he said, ' I abominate the stink of tobacco !' A mischievous lady asked Archdeacon Bland, ' What did the Dean say, Mr. Archdeacon ?' That gentle dignitary replied, 'The Dean says that he dislikes the scent of the cigar.' The Dean, overhearing, said aloud, ' What I *say* is, that I *abominate the stink of tobacco!* He was never married. He died July 20, 1869, ' revered for his kindness, generosity, and integrity,'* and was buried in the Cathedral yard amidst the universal regret of the citizens of Durham. There are full-length portraits of him in the new library at the Cathedral and at the County Hospital. The former was fitted up in his time, and to the latter he was a munificent benefactor.

WILLIAM CHARLES LAKE succeeded to the wardenship and to the deanery at the same time at the age of fifty-two, and in his full strength of mind and body. He was born in London on January 9, 1817, and was the eldest son of Captain Charles Lake of the Scots Guards, a Waterloo hero. Two or three years of his childhood were spent in France and Jersey, where French became almost a native tongue to him, and one which he could never entirely forget. At nine years of age he entered Rugby. About two years later— namely, in 1828—Dr. Arnold came to Rugby, so that the boy's mind was formed under the influence of that famous master, and he became the lifelong friend of his schoolfellows, A P. Stanley and C. J. Vaughan. In November, 1834, he went from Rugby to Oxford as

* Professor Farrar in the *Durham Advertiser* of June 23, 1882.

scholar of Balliol, and was there a pupil of Tait (afterwards Archbishop), together with Sir Benjamin Brodie,
E. M. Goulburn, B. Jowett, S. Waldegrave, and other
men of note.   In 1838 he was elected Fellow of Balliol,
and in 1842 became Tutor.   In 1852-53 he was Senior
Proctor.   He became very intimate with Tait, who
when Archbishop occasionally visited him in Durham,
and once, at his request, delivered a short address to
the men in Galilee.   He was ordained in 1842, and in
1858 became Rector of Huntspill, a benefice in the gift
of Balliol College.   Two years later he succeeded to a
prebendal stall in Wells Cathedral.   Having served on
three Royal Commissions upon education, and being a
Liberal in politics, he was nominated by Mr. Gladstone
for the deanery of Durham in 1869.   Thus he became
third Warden of the University, a position for which
he was in many respects exceedingly well adapted,
and which he filled with a great measure of credit.
Considerable changes took place under his management,
mostly arising out of the recommendations of the Commission of 1862.   The first important measure that he
promoted was the removal of the School of Physical
Science to Newcastle, and the founding and endowment
of the College of Science there.*   Another change was
the bringing of the College of Medicine into closer connexion.†   A third was the affiliation of Codrington
College and Fourah Bay College, and the association
with the University of many English theological Colleges.‡   Other changes under Dean Lake's wardenship
have been referred to above,§ and it was in his time
that the new lecture-rooms were built.   In 1894 he

* See above, p. 56.   † P. 54   ‡ Pp. 57, 58   § Pp 59-61,

resigned the deanery in consequence of failing health,
· and with it the office of Warden, at the age of seventy-
seven. He had remained a bachelor until 1881, when
he married Miss Katharine Gladstone, a niece of the
Premier. He died at Torquay December 8, 1897, at
the venerable age of eighty. Mrs. Lake is still living,
and she edited the volume of ' Memorials' of the Dean,
published in 1901, which includes his autobiography,
an account of his work in Durham as Warden and as
Dean, and much interesting correspondence. As Dean
of Durham he took great interest in the ' restoration' of
the Cathedral, which was completed in 1876, the necessary funds having been provided by the Ecclesiastical
Commissioners. As a theologian he was a moderate
High Churchman, becoming more decidedly such as
he grew older. The policy of persecution led him to
join the English Church Union, of which, after a short
time, he became a Vice-president. He also preached
for the E.C.U. on various occasions. In 1880 he joined
Dean Church and others in trying to procure some
modification of the Public Worship Regulation Act,
and it is supposed that at that time he had great
influence with his old friend, Archbishop Tait. Like
many other men with strong wills, tempers not always
under control, and great confidence in their own judgment, Dean Lake was sometimes at painful variance
with colleagues who would gladly have worked peace-
ably with him. But at the same time he was capable
of much kindness, and when at his best he was a most
genial host and delightful companion. Then his friends
forgot the friction in the past, and when he left Durham
there were those who felt that, after all, it was an old

friend who was going away, and they were sorry to think that they should see his face no more.

GEORGE WILLIAM KITCHIN, the present Warden, succeeded on the resignation of Dean Lake in 1894. He was fourth son of the late Rev. Isaac Kitchin, Rector of St. Stephen's, Ipswich, and was born at Naughton Rectory, Suffolk, December 7, 1827. He was educated first at Ipswich Grammar-School, then at King's College School and College, and lastly at Christ Church, Oxford. He became student of Christ Church in 1846; B.A. 1850; M.A. 1853; D.D. (by decree of Convocation) 1883; D.D. (by Diploma of the University of Durham) 1894; Tutor of Christ Church 1853-54; Censor and Tutor of Christ Church 1860-1863; Junior Proctor, also Tutor to H.R.H. the Crown Prince of Denmark, 1863; Honorary Student of Christ Church 1896. On September 9, 1863, he married Alice Maud, daughter of Bridges Taylor, Esq., of the Foreign Office, and Elsinore. From 1868 to 1883 he was Censor of non-collegiate students in Oxford, and from 1883 to 1894 Dean of Winchester. While at Winchester he took great interest in the fabric of the Cathedral and in the documents belonging to or connected therewith, and in 1889 he was elected a Fellow of the Society of Antiquaries. On his coming to Durham, he at once threw himself heartily into the work of the University. He has always shown a special interest in the higher education of women, and it was in 1895 that the supplementary charter was obtained to enable them to proceed to degrees. In the same year degrees in Letters were established and the examination of schools was provided for.*

* P. 61.

CHAPTER V

SOME OTHER DURHAM WORTHIES

I SHALL divide these into two classes, the first including those who have come from other Universities to work in Durham, the second including some of our own alumni who have become distinguished by their writings or otherwise. In both classes there are living men of whom much might be recorded, but there are difficulties in the way of selecting for special mention any of one's contemporaries, while omitting others. In the following notices, therefore, I propose to include those only whose connexion with the University, whether by office or by matriculation, is of earlier date than my own.

§ 1. OXFORD AND CAMBRIDGE MEN INCORPORATED AT DURHAM.

The founders of the University were most careful, in appointing the first Professors and Tutors, to secure the best men that they could find. The first who acted as Professor of Divinity was HUGH JAMES ROSE, sometime scholar of Trinity College, Cambridge, B.D., and Christian Advocate. But he never really held the

120

appointment. In March, 1834, he announced his deter-
mination not to accept the professorship, having only
come to Durham in the latter part of October, 1833.
During the few months of his residence he worked
extremely hard, but all the time he had to contend with
most distressing attacks of asthma, being, in fact, a confirmed invalid.   He lived in the vacant prebendal
house next adjoining the College gateway on the north,
now used for the Chapter offices.

He took for the subject of his inaugural address
' An Apology for the Study of Divinity,' and it was
delivered before the Bishop, the Dean and Chapter, and
the University, in 1834, probably at the beginning of
Epiphany term.   It is a very able and learned address,
and a second edition of it, revised, was published in
1835.   In Easter term, 1834, the ordinary lectures
were delivered by his brother, the Rev. Henry John
Rose, then Fellow of St. John's, Cambridge, but on
April 15 he himself delivered a second ' terminal '
lecture before the same auditory as before and in the
same place, entitled ' The Study of Church History
recommended.'   This lecture was highly commended
by John Henry Newman, and on the other hand it
was vehemently denounced by men of an opposite way
of thinking.   The lecturer had expressed an unfavour-
able opinion of Milner as a Church historian, and had
strongly condemned Jortin and Mosheim.   This was
said to be a manifesto on the part of the new University
against the whole school of which they were exponents,
but after a while the storm blew over.

In February, 1834, Rose was appointed Domestic
Chaplain to the Archbishop of Canterbury, Dr. Howley,

a result of friendly relations which had subsisted between them for more than sixteen years. When Bishop Van Mildert had earnestly begged him to come to Durham, the Archbishop made no secret of his distress that there should be any difficulty in the way. The only difficulty, indeed, was Rose's health. He long shrank from embarrassing himself and others by coming to Durham as an invalid, but at last he yielded, and with the result that we have seen. His work in Durham was, in fact, but an episode in his life, and it would hardly come within the plan of the present work to occupy over-much space by giving full particulars of his life before and after. This has been admirably done by Burgon in his 'Lives of Twelve Good Men,' and it may be sufficient here very briefly to enumerate the main facts of his short but eventful life, as gathered from Burgon's detailed account.

He was the elder son of the Rev. William Rose, and, was born at Little Horsted Parsonage, June 9, 1795. He was precocious as a child, and as a boy pursued his studies with rare diligence under his father's roof. He collected seals, and pursued as 'hobbies' heraldry, chemistry, drawing, poetry, and 'preaching.' At fourteen he was invited to read with Lord Sheffield's little son, and at eighteen he entered at Trinity College, Cambridge, where in 1814 he gained the first Bell's Scholarship, and in 1815 was elected scholar of Trinity. He made a great figure in the Union Society, and was joint-author of a mock examination paper that appeared in the *Annual Register* for 1816. He took his B.A. degree in 1817 as 14th Wrangler, his turn being classical rather than mathematical. He was ordained

deacon December, 1818, and priest December, 1819,
having married Miss Anna Cuyler Mair on June 24 in
the latter year. As a curate his labours were divided
between parish and pupils, and he wrote many pamphlets
and articles. He was presented by Archbishop Manners
Sutton to the vicarage of Horsham at the end of 1821,
and in 1828-29, strange to say, he had a controversy
with Dr. Pusey, in which the latter appeared as the
champion of German Protestantism. Soon, however,
Pusey's views underwent a complete change, and he
withdrew from circulation two learned volumes that he
had written in opposition to Rose.

About this time, as Christian Advocate and Select
Preacher, Rose published several important discourses,
and he is said to have exercised an influence in Cambridge deeper even than that of Charles Simeon. In
·1830 he left Horsham, being appointed by the Archbishop to Hadleigh in Suffolk. In the next year he
took an active part in launching the *British Magazine*,
and in originating the great Church movement of 1833.
It was he who really organized the little band of
Oxford men that began it. It was in June, 1833,
that he invited Froude, Perceval, Keble, Newman, and
William Palmer of Worcester College, and those who
thought with them, to a conference at Hadleigh.
Keble was not present, being a man who shrank from
'meetings,' nor was Newman, who relied more on individual and separate action than on combined efforts.
As he remarks in the 'Apologia,' 'Luther was an
individual.' All this time Rose was harassed by his
dreadful asthma, and in 1833 he resigned Hadleigh,
accepting in exchange the small livings of Fairstead in

Essex and St. Thomas's, Southwark; the latter he retained to his death, making due provision, no doubt, for his periods of non-residence. Then came the call to Durham and his six months' trial there, described above. From 1833 to 1836 he was heartily with the writers of the 'Tracts for the Times,' but when in the latter year a new spirit came over them, and they became, as he thought, disloyal to the English Church, he could no longer give them his entire sympathy—they had arrived at a parting-point: nevertheless, he continued to be on the most brotherly terms with them.

In October, 1836, notwithstanding the unfortunate result of the Durham venture, he was induced by Archbishop Howley and Bishop Blomfield to accept the office of Principal of King's College, London, where his teaching and his holy life made a great impression upon the students. He had a high sense of discipline, and deprecated the applause of the students, considering that, however well meant it might be, it was hardly consistent with the respect due to his office. But the inevitable breakdown in health came in about six months, as had been the case at Durham. From time to time he had to go away for change of air, once he was prostrated by influenza, and on October 13, 1838, he embarked in order to go to Rome for complete change. On this last journey he was accompanied by his wife and a faithful female servant. The party had only reached as far as Florence about the middle of November. There he became so much worse that he could go no further, and there he died, aged only forty-three and a half years, on December 22, 1838. He was buried in the English cemetery, where his grave is marked by a marble altar-tomb, with a Latin inscription much too long to be given here. But no tribute to his memory could be more affecting than that of the venerable Archbishop Howley, who wrote on the first leaf of a MS. presented by Mrs. Rose to the Lambeth Library:

> ‘ Multis ille bonis flebilis occidit,
> Nulli flebilior quam mihi.—W. Cantuar.’

The first Professor of Greek and Classical Literature was Henry Jenkyns, M.A., who was appointed in 1833.* He was scholar of Corpus Christi College, Oxford, 1813-1818, B.A. 1817, Fellow of Oriel 1818-1835, B.D. and D.D. 1841. As Greek Professor he read a public lecture on ‘ The Advantages of Classical Studies ’ on February 25, 1834. It was printed at the time.

After the resignation of Hugh James Rose in 1834, his brother, Henry John Rose, having lectured for a short time, Mr. Jenkyns, assisted by Mr. Chevallier in 1835, performed the duties of the Professor of Divinity until 1839, when the third stall, which was attached to that professorship, fell vacant, and then he resigned the Greek Professorship, which latter he had held from 1833, was inducted into the third stall October 26,

---

* It is said that this professorship was first offered to Edward Parr Greswell, author of ‘ Harmony of the Gospels,’ etc , and Fellow of Corpus Christi College, Oxford, but that he declined both this office and the presidency of Corpus in order to be more free for literary work. It appears that on August 16, 1833, John Henry Newman wrote to Hugh James Rose thus : ‘ I find Froude has mentioned to you the name of our friend Eden (Charles Page Eden, Tutor and Dean of Oriel College) as a man likely to suit for the Greek Professorship at Durham ’ (Burgon, ‘ Twelve Good Men,’ 1888, ii. 309).

became Professor of Divinity, and took his Doctor's degree in Oxford and Durham. As Professor he long continued to discharge his duties with great distinction, and many graduates of Oxford and Cambridge came to Durham for the benefit of his teaching. An admirable account of his lectures was written in the form of a leaflet by his successor, Dr. Farrar, on the occasion of the acquisition by the University Library of Mr. John Low Low's MS. notes of many of them. A reprint of this leaflet will be found in the appendix. The divinity students admired and respected him, but few indeed ever had the honour of a word with him, unless it were in connexion with the sermon exercises sent in. We felt that we were 'too young to be acquainted with so great a Doctor,'* that he belonged to a sphere altogether beyond our ken, and no one presumed to take the slightest liberty with him. It is said that his brother Canon Dr. Townsend, described him thus, ' Cold as ice, clear as ice, and hard as ice,' and those words exactly represent him as he appeared to his class. Yet he would now and then excite smiles and smile himself at some touch of his own caustic humour, whereby he would at rare intervals enliven the rigid decorum that always prevailed in his lecture-room, namely, the Old Divinity School, formerly the Grammar-School. Mr. Low Low writes as follows ·†

' None who had the privilege of attending the lectures of Dr. Jenkyns will ever forget them. He taught his scholars to take nothing for granted, but to make sure of everything from good authority. They had not only the

* See Aubrey's ' Brief Lives,' i. 300.
† ' Diocesan History of Durham,' 1881, p. 320.

opportunity of acquiring much knowledge, set before them in the clearest manner, but were inflamed by the desire of acquiring more. The text-book for early ecclesiastical history was Eusebius in the original Greek, construed daily by the students ; for liturgies, Cardinal Bona,* whom the Professor held in high and deserved esteem for his candour and exactness. Every student had to write a sermon every week, an excellent training† for those who were soon to be called upon to provide, perhaps, more than one weekly.'

In and after October, 1859, about half of his lectures were taken by the Rev. James Barmby, who then came to Durham as Principal of Bishop Hatfield's Hall. In 1864 Dr. Jenkyns resigned his professorship, but he continued to hold his stall up to the time of his death, April 2, 1878, at the age of seventy-three. There is a portrait of him in the Castle hall, also a brass plate to his memory in the south transept of the Cathedral.

Upon the resignation of the Divinity Professorship by Dr. Jenkyns in 1864, Dr. ADAM STOREY FARRAR, the present Professor, was appointed by Bishop Baring, but he did not succeed to the canonry connected with it until the death of Dr. Jenkyns. Dr. Farrar is not inferior to his predecessor in learning, and is as great a contrast as possible to him in some respects. His genial and sympathetic disposition, his extraordinary powers as a lecturer, and the kindly interest that he takes in individual men who are desirous to learn, all

* The great work of Cardinal Bona ought not to be described as a 'text-book'; we never saw it, but the Professor was constantly quoting it.

† See above, p. 52. Such training would hardly be possible now, with so much ' training ' of another kind, commonly regarded as more important

conduce to the great popularity which he has always enjoyed.

The first Professor of Mathematics was JOHN CARR, M.A., formerly Fellow of Trinity College, Cambridge. He had been Headmaster of Durham School for twenty-two years, and had been most successful in that capacity. He was appointed Professor June 20, 1833, but died October 30, and was buried on November 6 in the north transept of the Cathedral, where his resting-place is marked by an architectural monument designed by Rickman. The following letter, written by Robert Surtees, the poet and historian of Durham, shortly before his own death, will be read with interest here:

'To J. G. NICHOLS, ESQ.

'MAINSFORTH,
'November 15, 1833.

'DEAR SIR,

'I sent you a Durham paper with an account of the opening of the Northern University. I send you another which records the honoured end of my poor friend John Carr, whom I loved next to my heart. His scholars are subscribing to found a Carr scholarship, and to give an annual Carr golden medal.

'The new University is hailed by all parties as a rising star (a northern light, may I say?) of bright and unsullied lustre. Everything seems propitious, and the wealthy Cathedral Church of Durham has devoted a large portion of its revenues to the new institution; but the death of Carr has thrown a gloom on the general feeling. He died probably more deservedly and sincerely lamented than most persons recorded in your obituary. He was eminently distinguished as a mathematician, having taken a [second]

Wrangler's degree at Cambridge, and was, perhaps, not less distinguished as a classical scholar. He peculiarly excelled in pure Latin composition, but his private char- acter was to me his chief recommendation. Kind, un- obtrusive, gentle, but independent ; most pure, most blameless, wrapped up in domestic feeling, and neither meddling nor caring for the world, I firmly believe he had not an enemy. His death has cast a gloom over Durham. Raine will send you a better account ; if not, use this. There was a quiet, unobtrusive independence about him which I never, perhaps, saw equalled ; a purity and delicacy of mind and manners arising from the union of a complete education and the most perfect sense of honour, united to the most unaffected simplicity of manner. As to a schoolmaster, he never looked like one ; but he sent good scholars to Cambridge. No boy ever left Durham without loving him ; and between Raine and Carr there was an excellent master. Poor Carr could teach, but he could not govern, except by kindness. . . .

'Yours,

'R. S.'*

Dr. Raine adds in a note that Mr. Carr was of an ancient family seated at Stackhouse, near Giggleswick, and that he was educated at Giggleswick School. In 1811 he was appointed Headmaster of Durham School, and in 1817 was presented by the Dean and Chapter to the vicarage of Brantingham, which he held till his death.†

* 'Memoir of Robert Surtees,' Surtees Society, 1852, p. 439.
† See a notice in the *Gentleman's Magazine* of November, 1833, p. 471, based on the above letter   There is also an account of his funeral. It seems that members of the new University ' put on mourning for fourteen days.'

9

The first Senior Tutor, Thomas Williamson Peile, and the first Junior Tutor, William Palmer, were both distinguished men.

Peile was of Trinity College, Cambridge, B.A. 1828, 18th Wrangler, and bracketed second in the first class Classical Tripos, also second Chancellor's Medallist. He was elected Fellow of Trinity in 1829, and in the same year was appointed Headmaster of Liverpool Collegiate School. In 1833 he appears at Durham as a Senior Fellow and as Senior Tutor and Censor. In the calendars he occurs as Senior Censor and Tutor of 'the University College' in 1837, and as Vice-Master in 1841. From 1841 to 1854 he was Headmaster of Repton School; then he held parochial charges till 1873, when he retired; and he died November 29, 1882, aged seventy-six.

Palmer was a brother of Roundell Palmer, first Earl of Selborne, and is not to be confounded with his namesake, William Palmer of Worcester College, the liturgiologist. He was a demy of Magdalen College, Oxford, took a first class in the Classical School, was admitted B.A. in 1831, and obtained two Chancellor's prizes. In 1832 he was elected a Fellow of Magdalen, and in 1833 he was a Senior Fellow of the University of Durham, and also Junior Tutor and Censor. He appears as a Curator of the Library in 1837, and as a member of the Senate from 1838 to 1841. But, as he became Tutor of Magdalen in 1838, he must then have ceased from Tutor's work in Durham. From 1840 to 1853 he was making many efforts toward reunion with the Greek Church, to which communion he sought admission, but he was unwilling to be rebaptized, and a second baptism was made a necessary condition. On February 28, 1855, he was received into the Roman Church without rebaptism, and he resided in Rome until his death on April 4, 1879.

The Readers in the various subjects of Law, History, Medicine, Moral Philosophy, Natural Philosophy, Chemistry, and Modern Languages,* were for the most part men who either at the time of their appointment as Readers, or subsequently, were distinguished in the various branches of learning that they pursued. In 1835 the Readers in Law and in History delivered inaugural lectures that were printed. One of them, CHARLES THOMAS WHITLEY, Senior Wrangler 1830 and M.A. 1833, Fellow of St. John's College, Cambridge, long served the University in various ways. In the prospectus of 1833 he appears as a 'Junior Fellow,' and as Reader in Natural Philosophy, which readership he continued to hold until 1855. The first calendar was issued in 1837, and in that and the following calendars he appears as University Librarian 1837-1855, as Tutor of University College 1837-1849, Tutor in the University 1850-1855, Vice-Master of University College 1842-1855, Proctor 1837-1847, and in alternate years until 1853. He is first named as F.R.Ast.S. in 1843. In 1849 he was made Honorary Canon of Durham, and in 1854 appointed by the Dean and Chapter Vicar of Bedlington. The University of Durham conferred on him the honorary degree of D.D. in June, 1884. He died April 22, 1895. He translated Poinsot on 'Rotatory Motion,' published at Cambridge in 1834.

The following words, written by the elder Dr. Raine

* See the first calendar or prospectus, reprinted in Appendix IV.

in 1833, no doubt express what was a general feeling in Durham with regard to the University in these earliest times.   He writes:

'We have merely room to observe, and we do so with peculiar satisfaction, that whether we regard the munificent endowment, the talent and respectability engaged in the new establishment, or the spirit which manifestly pervades it, it promises to be productive of the most beneficial effects upon genuine science and sound literature.   May the blessing of God attend it !'*

We have seen that the infant University was unfortunate in almost immediately losing two of its Professors by death.   Their places were not filled with any precipitation, and during the vacancies the work was no doubt done as well as it could be in the circumstances. And when the places were filled first-rate men were again obtained.   For thirty-six years the name of TEMPLE CHEVALLIER was closely bound up in all that concerned the University.   Before he came to Durham he had been Second Wrangler and Second Smith's Prizeman, also Fellow and Tutor of St. Catherine's College, Cambridge, then 'Catherine Hall,' and was Hulsean Lecturer in 1826 and 1827.   His second volume of Hulsean Lectures is entitled, 'Of the Proofs of Divine Power and Wisdom derived from the Study of Astronomy, and on the Evidence, Doctrines, and Precepts of Revealed Religion ' (1835).   It is said that this volume suggested to Whewell the fundamental idea of his famous Bridgewater Treatise upon Astronomy and General Physics, in which, however, Chevallier's

* 'Brief Account of Durham Cathedral,' 144.

previous labours in the same field are not acknow-
ledged.

Chevallier was a mathematician and lecturer of great
ability, as well as an eminent theologian. He was
appointed Professor of Mathematics in 1835, and
continued to hold this professorship after a new Professorship of Astronomy was united to it in 1841.* He
lectured on Hebrew in 1834 and 1835, and was Reader
in Hebrew from 1835 to 1871. In Epiphany term,
1835, he was delivering divinity lectures. About 1835
he undertook, in addition to his University work, the
perpetual curacy of Esh, near Durham, having been
allowed by the Chapter to take clerical work, provided
that it did not interfere with his lectures, etc. On
March 11, 1836, he delivered a public lecture, which
was printed, on ' The Study of Mathematics as condu-
cive to the Development of the Intellectual Powers.'
From 1835 to 1864 he was Registrar to the University.
In 1846 he was made Honorary Canon, and in 1865
Residentiary Canon of Durham. He published many
papers on astronomy and physics ; an English translation of the Apostolic Fathers, etc., with a full introduction—first edition 1833, second edition 1851 ; and an
edition of Pearson on the Creed, 1849, second edition
1859. In the former edition of Pearson he acknowledges
help from Hugh James Rose, and in the second he has
inserted some notes written by Dr. Routh in a copy of the
eleventh edition of Pearson now in the Routh Library.

Mr. Chevallier was always an active member of
Senate, though not.what would now be called ' pro-
gressive.'† He was greatly interested in the first

* See p 34.   † See p. 112.

engineering school, begun November, 1837, and opened
January, 1838, in the second school (1865), and in the
College of Science (1871). I was his only Hebrew pupil
during the greater part of 1858-1861, the number
of theological students being then very small. He was
an excellent Hebrew scholar of an old-fashioned type,
was animated and interesting in his way of teaching,
and would do anything in his power to help one either
in or out of lecture. Sometimes he would go off into
some digression which might have little or nothing to
do with the matter in hand, but which was sure to be
inspiring and instructive. He very much objected to
steel pens, and said that whoever invented them ought
to be made to breakfast on them every morning.
Towards the latter end of my time he asked me over to
spend from Saturday to Monday with him in his then
lonely parsonage at Esh. Mrs. Chevallier had died
some time before, and none of his children were living
with him. On the Saturday evening he showed me the
transit instrument in the observatory in his garden, and
I then beheld for the first time the impressive spectacle
of the motion of the earth as it passed a fixed star. He
had just received the Surtees volume of ' Miscellanea '
(1861), containing Dean Granville's ' Remains and Correspondence,' which interested and amused him very much
at the time, and me also. That was my first introduction to the Surtees Society, for which he had edited the
' Sanctuarium Dunelmense ' in 1837. On the Sunday I
was much struck by the simple and impressive way
in which he preached to the villagers, not using any
manuscript. He resigned his parochial charge in
1869.

When I returned to Durham in January, 1871, he had failed very considerably, and I think that at first he hardly remembered me. He was, however, much interested in the Moabite Stone, which had recently been discovered, and showed me some casts of fragments, Dr. Ginsburg's book, etc. He also paid great attention to the building operations of the rooks, which he observed through a telescope from his windows as they were going on beyond the river in the spring of that same year. Not long after this he had a paralytic stroke, and at once resigned all his University appointments.

He died November 4, 1873, and was buried at Esh. In the 'Nine Altars' at Durham is a brass plate with this inscription :

DOMINUS ILLUMINATIO MEA.

TEMPLE CHEVALLIER, S.T.B. HUJUS
ECCLESIÆ E CANONICIS, UNIVERSITATE
DUNELMENSI SCIENTIÆ MATHEMATICÆ
PROFESSOR, ASTRORUM ACERRIMUS INDAGATOR,
SUPER ASTRA MIGRAVIT DIE IV MENS. NOVEM.
A.G. MDCCCLXXIII, ÆTAT. SUÆ LXXX.

IN TE DOMINE SPERAVI.

There is a fine portrait of him by Cope, R.A., in the Castle hall, but it is not very satisfactory as a likeness.

The next Professor was SAMUEL WAYMOUTH, whose early death left the professorship again vacant in about a year. It was then held for twenty-one years by, ROBERT JOHN PEARCE, late Senior Fellow of Gonville and Caius College, Cambridge, and Third Wrangler,

Subwarden at Durham 1880-1895, and now Vicar and
Rural Dean of Bedlington. The present Professor is
RALPH ALLEN SAMPSON, F.R.S., who was appointed in
1895, having previously been Professor of Mathematics
at the Durham College of Science at Newcastle-upon-
Tyne. His work in connexion with the Observatory is
referred to above, p. 108.

Upon the resignation of the Greek Professorship by
Dr. Jenkyns in 1840, the Rev. JOHN EDWARDS, M.A.,
was appointed by Bishop Maltby, but not until June,
1841, to the stall and chair thus vacated. Mr. Edwards
was the youngest son of the Rev. Edward Edwards,
Prebendary of Lincoln, previously Headmaster of the
grammar-school at Huntingdon, and Rector of All
Saints' in that town, and afterwards Rector of Offord
Cluny. He was born at Huntingdon in 1789, and was
educated at the grammar-school under his father. His
immediate preparation for the University was under
Dr. Maltby, afterwards Bishop. He entered at St.
John's College, Cambridge, and afterwards went to
Jesus College. He was ordained in 1811 to the curacy
of Brampton, Hunts, and in 1814 was presented by
Tomline, Bishop of Lincoln, to the small rectory of
South Ferriby in Lincolnshire, where he never resided.
He was second master at the Richmond Grammar-
School from 1814 to 1821, and in 1816 married Louisa,
daughter of Robert Cooch, Esq., of Huntingdon. In
1821 he moved to Warboys, Hunts, as curate-in-charge,
and took pupils. In 1826 he became an assistant-
master at Harrow under Dr. Butler. In 1828 he was
appointed Headmaster of the Bury St. Edmunds
Grammar-School, and held that appointment up to his

going to Durham in 1841. Bishop Maltby had a high
opinion of Mr. Edwards' classical attainments, based
upon full personal knowledge, and the appointment was
justified by the event. The Professor discharged his
duties in a conscientious and efficient manner ; he
enjoyed the affectionate respect of his pupils, and, if he
was not a brilliant teacher, at any rate he was conscientious, sound, and accurate. From his frequent
references in his lectures on Thucydides to Poppo,
the commentator on that historian, 'Poppo' was the
sobriquet by which he was generally known. Long
before he came to Durham he published a small volume
entitled, 'Epigrammata e purioribus Græcæ Antho-
logiæ fontibus,' with a dedication to his friend Edward
Maltby, D.D. He died April 1, 1862, aged seventy-
three, and was buried in the Cathedral churchyard.

THOMAS SAUNDERS EVANS, the next Greek Professor,
held office in Durham for nearly twenty-eight years.
He was born March 8, 1816, and was fourth son of
David Evans, Esq., of Belper. We are told that as a
child he showed quite a passion for architecture, and
that he made an accurate drawing of the west front of
Lichfield Cathedral from recollection. And all through
life he continued the habit of making sketches of architectural designs in the margins of books, or wherever
he could find a convenient space, when the fancy was
on him. At nine years old he was sent as a pupil to an
uncle, with whom he remained two years, during which
time he received a thorough drilling in the Eton Latin
and Greek Grammars, and was made to learn by heart
a portion of Vergil every day. At twelve he went to
Shrewsbury School under Dr. Butler, and was at once

placed in the lower fifth form.   Here he soon employed
his leisure time, of which school-boys then had more
than they have now, in writing Latin or Greek verses
on the passing incidents of school-life.   And in 1834
he wrote a prize poem in Latin hexameters, which
was pronounced by Dr. Butler to be 'worthy of Vergil.'
In April, 1835, he entered at St. John's College,
Cambridge.   While there he was fond of walking and
swimming, but did not take much part in organized
athletics.   He was famous for impromptu renderings
into Latin and Greek verse, took several College prizes,
and in 1838 won the Porson Scholarship.   He failed,
however, to gain a place in the Mathematical Tripos,
and so was debarred from Classical Honours.   Here-
upon he wrote a satirical Greek poem entitled
Μαθηματογονία, which was praised in the highest
terms by such scholars as Butler, Maltby, and afterwards Mayor.   He took his B.A. degree in 1839, and
then spent a year in Cambridge.   In 1840 he visited
his brother at Sedbergh, and wrote a very amusing
account of the Yorkshire rustics in the style of Tacitus,
but in English.   In 1841 he was appointed a classical
master at Shrewsbury under Dr. Kennedy, and there
he formed a life-long friendship with that great scholar.
He was ordained deacon in 1844, and priest in 1846,
and in addition to his school-work he undertook the
curacy of St. Mary's, Shrewsbury.   He appears at this
time to have devoted more attention than ever to
Hellenistic Greek, a study which he pursued with
unflagging ardour to the end of his life.   In 1847 he
went to Rugby as a master under Tait.   There he was
at the same time composition master to the sixth form

and master of the lowest form in the school. Dr. Goulburn afterwards promoted him to the mastership of 'the twenty,' a group of boys next in rank to the sixth form. This advancement of Mr. Evans is thought to have done much to help forward that reputation for polished classical scholarship which Rugby has always enjoyed. While at Rugby he married, in 1849, Rosamond, fourth daughter of John Broughton, Esq. In 1862 he was appointed by Bishop Baring to the canonry in the Cathedral to which the Professorship of Greek is attached. He was delighted with Durham; his fame as a scholar had preceded him, and he was cordially welcomed as a new and most genial element in the social and intellectual life of Durham at that time.

All seemed to promise well for him, but in the course of the year his wife's health, which had been delicate for some time, began to fail altogether, and she died in November, 1863. The bereavement was a terrible blow to him, and he was never the same man again. At first he tried to beguile his grief by carving out of a block of salt an elaborate model of an imaginary cathedral, which interesting production is now in the Chapter Library. He was a man of many resources. He led the life of a scholar, he discharged his duties as a Professor to the great profit and delight of successive generations of students, he brought up a young family, and he found solace in such recreations as were suited to his habits of mind and body. He frequently took long and solitary walks. It is said that he once walked as far as Darlington, eighteen miles, absorbed in thought, and on his arrival asked, 'Where am I?' But as time went on he seemed to be always glad to have a companion, and 'walks with Evans' still remain among the most cherished memories of such as had the privilege of joining him on those occasions. He spent a good deal of his leisure time in the game of bowls, or in dragging a heavy roller up and down the ' Prebends' Walk,' which latter form of exercise suited him both as leading to some tangible benefit and as affording opportunity for meditation. He was nominated as Subwarden January 27, 1872, but only held the office till the June following; he had, indeed, little taste for the ordinary business of Senate or of Chapter, and was not very regular in his attendance at either.   But when any question arose which he thought specially concerned him, he gave it his best consideration, studied it carefully, and then gave his judgment clearly and decisively.   Debates in Convocation are of rare occurrence, but when there was one he usually enlivened the proceedings by some characteristic remarks.   Thus, when it was proposed to admit graduates of the Scottish Universities to *ad eundem* degrees, he described their non-collegiate system as ' curriculum ridiculum.'   When there was a proposal to admit women students, he predicted that there would be ' ocular telegraphy.'   He was very fond of this kind of word-play, and once, when Mr. Greatorex temporarily undertook the duties of precentor, the Professor remarked, ' Greatorex, inter-rex !'   He once remarked that the bedrooms in his house were ' like the ten tribes, in a state of dispersion.'   And, again, criticising the Revised Version, ' " In your love of the brethren, love"; you might as well say, "In your plum-pudding, plums."'   But these were the witty flashes of his lighter

moments. Once, being asked, in the presence of a
young man who was professing to be an 'agnostic,'
what was the meaning of that word, he said: 'The
term explains itself; it means an ignoramus.' Then,
turning to the young man with kindly humour, 'I
knew your father, and I will not say anything about it
to any one,' treating him as a naughty boy. But all his
jokes were *sibi et amicis*. Once, referring to some one
whom he disliked, he said, 'I never joke with that
man.'

When the 'Speaker's Commentary' was undertaken,
the part offered to him was the First Epistle to the
Corinthians, the second being assigned to his son-in-
law, the Rev. Dr. Waite. Evans's work proved, as
might have been expected, to be eminently characteristic
of the man, both in language and in matter. Dr. Waite
truly remarks that it ' was not only a new departure
from the stereotyped form of commentary, but it excited
greater interest, and was considered more original than
that of any other contributor,' and that it is ' a
treasury of materials for preachers and future expositors.'
Soon after the appearance of this commentary the
University of Edinburgh conferred on its author the
degree of D.D. That he was not employed on the
Revised Version of the New Testament was in consequence of a formal request from Archbishop Thomson
that no one in his province should be asked to take
part in it, and Evans was not sorry to be thus excluded.
When the 'R.V.' came out, he strongly disapproved of
it, and he wrote trenchant criticisms in the *Expositor*
(vols. iii., v.). Archbishop Benson wrote : ' He would
controvert its principles and details by the hour, and I

never felt what absorption was until he went with me
to Lindisfarne, and, I am certain, never saw it.' That
is a most characteristic touch. As a preacher in the
Cathedral he was always original, striking, and interesting. From time to time he printed single sermons,
usually by request. The *Durham University Journal*
of November 9, 1889, pp. 219, 220, contains a list of his
sermons and other publications, twenty-two in number,
besides twenty-five contributions to 'Sabrinæ Corolla.'

For about three years before his death his health was
failing, and no change of air and scene, nor any medical
treatment, produced more than temporary benefit. He
died, May 15, 1889, aged seventy-three, at Weston-
super-Mare, where his two sisters resided, his unmarried
daughter and his two sons being with him at the time.
They brought him to be buried in the churchyard
of Durham Cathedral by the side of his wife, a son who
had died at the age of eight, and two children of his
elder daughter, the wife of the Rev. Joseph Waite, D.D.

There are many interesting reminiscences of Professor
Evans in a memoir, by Dr. Waite, prefixed to a post-
humous collection of the Professor's Latin and Greek
verses issued by the Cambridge University Press in
1893. Dr. Waite quotes or refers to Mr. A. Sidgwick,
Archbishop Benson, Rev. H. J. R. Marston, Dr. Sanday,
Dr. Hornby, and others who knew and admired his
gifted father-in-law.

Mr. Evans was succeeded in his canonry and professorship by the present Professor, Dr. HERBERT
KYNASTON, whose elegant scholarship, as was that of
his predecessor, is always at the service of the University
and of his friends.

JAMES BARMBY came to Durham in 1859 as Principal of Bishop Hatfield's Hall, Mathematical Tutor, and Assistant to the Professor of Divinity. He had passed through a distinguished career at Oxford : first as a scholar of University College, where his father had been a Fellow ; then he obtained a first class in Mathematics, and a second in Classics ; and finally he was elected to a Fellowship at Magdalen College, where he was Mathematical Lecturer from 1846 to 1859. On June 21, 1859, he married Katharine E. Wood, second daughter of Charles Wood, Esq., J.P., of Street House, Glastonbury, by whom he had four sons and two daughters. At Durham his lectures were highly valued, particularly those on the higher mathematics. As Principal of Hatfield he made a distinct mark, especially in connexion with the chapel, which he at once furnished in a seemly manner, and where he introduced the use of the surplice, and established that bright and hearty choral service which ever since has been associated with Hatfield Chapel in the minds of Hatfield men. In 1875 he left Durham in order to take the Chapter living of Pittington, and in 1894 he was promoted to that of Northallerton, where he died on May 9, 1897, after a painful illness of some weeks' duration, borne with Christian patience and fortitude. At Durham he produced a volume of ' Plays for Young People,' and wrote many Lives of the Popes in the ' Dictionary of Christian Biography.' At Pittington he wrote the ' Life of Gregory the Great ' (S.P.C.K.), exposition of the Epistles to the Hebrews and the Romans in the ' Pulpit Commentary,' ' Gregory the Great ' in the ' Post-Nicene Fathers,' the Hatfield Latin hymn ' Jam

noctis adsunt tenebræ,' Christmas carols, etc., and
edited for the Surtees Society 'Durham Parish Books'
and 'Memorials of St. Giles's.' His finding the Pittington Parish Book (1584-1697) and his preparation
of a paper on the church for the Durham Archæological Society directed his attention to parochial
history and antiquities, in which latterly he took
great interest. He was thinking of editing a volume
on Northallerton, when his fatal illness put an end to
all his work. The last thing he published was an
article in the *Expositor*—5th series, vol. iv. (1896, ii.),
pp. 124-139—on the Pauline expression δικαιοσύνη
Θεοῦ, which excited considerable interest and approval in Germany as well as in England. He had
previously expressed an original view on the same
difficult subject, which has been generally accepted, in
his commentary on the Epistle to the Romans. Though
a man of letters, he threw himself heartily into all the
details of pastoral work, and was greatly beloved and
respected in both his parishes. He was Rural Dean of
Easington 1890-1894, and of Northallerton 1894-1897.
In 1893 the University of Durham conferred on him
the honorary degree of D.D., and in presenting him
the Professor of Divinity said :

'The Rev. J. Barmby has proved his solid theological
learning by historical works and erudite contributions to
our great theological dictionaries. While here he was a
thoughtful, instructive, and accomplished lecturer. He
administered the affairs of the Hall, over which for many
years he presided, with notable wisdom and attention;
and since he has retired into parochial work he has translated abstract theology into pastoral action, and has exerted

himself to elevate and civilize the people entrusted to his care.'

I may refer also to an 'In Memoriam' notice in the *Guardian* of May 19, 1897, p. 807.

He was succeeded as Principal of Bishop Hatfield's Hall by WILLIAM SANDAY (1876-1883), now Lady Margaret Professor of Divinity and Canon of Christ Church, Oxford ; ARCHIBALD ROBERTSON (1883-1897), afterwards Principal of King's College, London, now Bishop of Exeter ; and FRANK BYRON JEVONS, the present Principal.

Before passing on to Durham alumni I must mention, besides those already named as having served the University with special distinction, Dr. WILLIAM GEORGE HENDERSON, the venerable Dean of Carlisle, who has edited many liturgical works for the Surtees Society ; EDWARD MASSIE, of Wadham College, Oxford, of whom Dr. Waite writes : 'He was a most elegant scholar. I attended some of his lectures on Æschylus. It was a perfect treat to hear him translate the choruses in the " Agamemnon." They seemed to inspire him. He was in other respects a most charming man'; JAMES GYLBY LONSDALE, described by Dr. Waite as 'a most accomplished scholar and a man of very subtle intellect'; and, of late, Dr. ALFRED PLUMMER, Master of University College and Tutor 1874-1902, and Subwarden 1895-1902. His contributions to literature are, like those of Drs. Sanday, Robertson, and Jevons, so well known that they need not be further referred to here.

10

§ 2. Original Durham Men.

George Hills (University College), a son of Rear-Admiral George Hills, was born in 1816, and was educated at King William's College in the Isle of Man. He matriculated at Durham in October, 1833, took his B.A. degree (4th class) in 1836, and his M.A. in 1838. He was ordained deacon and priest in 1840, and served under Dr. Hook as senior curate and lecturer at St. Peter's, Leeds, till 1848. Dr. Pusey offered him the first incumbency of St. Saviour's, but this he declined. From 1848 to 1859 he was Vicar of Great Yarmouth, where three future Bishops were curates under him. In 1850 he became Honorary Canon of Norwich. In 1858, on his nomination to a bishopric, he received from his University the degree of D.D. by diploma, and on St. Matthias' Day, 1859, he was consecrated first Bishop of British Columbia, the arms of which diocese preserve the memory of his connexion with the University in their most prominent characteristics— viz., arg., a cross patée quadrate gu. Bishop Hills was a pioneer and a confessor whose work was remarkably successful. In 1879 the mainland of British Columbia was formed into the two dioceses of New Westminster and Caledonia, and in 1900 Kootenay was formed out of New Westminster, to be at first under the Bishop of that diocese. In 1892 the senior Bishop resigned and came to England. In 1894 he accepted the charge of the small parish of Parham in Norfolk, where he died on December 10, 1895.

'A man of iron will, but as gentle as a lamb in his intercourse with those he loved, and very courtly to all.

He was a High Churchman after the school of Dr. Hook, and no one seems to have realized what a fight he fought for the faith against the schism led by his own Dean (Mr. Cridge). During this both his house and his cathedral were fired by the mob, and he was frequently pelted with mud and stones. His memorial are the dioceses he built up in the great West.'*

He joined one clergyman when he arrived in 1859; he left twenty-five in 1892. He found no church; he left Vancouver's Island overspread with churches. He found a few thousand colonists settled in the vast colony of British Columbia; he left 100,000 prosperous people -presided over by three Bishops and upwards of fifty clergy.

JAMES SKINNER (University College) was born June 23, 1818, the youngest son of John Skinner, Dean of Dunkeld and Dunblane, grandson of one Bishop of Aberdeen and nephew of another, and great-grandson of John Skinner, an Episcopal clergyman who in the eighteenth century endured much persecution on account of his religion, and is still known for his 'Verses in the Scottish Dialect,' among which is 'Tullochgorum,' mentioned by Burns as 'the masterpiece of my old friend Skinner.' James Skinner's mother died of consumption two years after his birth, and he is described as 'a delicate, fragile child.' At ten years old he went to school in Aberdeen, in 1832 to Marischal College in that city, and in October, 1833, he entered at Durham, being only fifteen years of age. He is described as then having the appearance of a youth of twenty, bright and cheerful, a general favourite, and the reverse of

* Correspondent of the *Church Times*, December 20, 1895.

10—2

studious, except towards the close of every term, and in preparation for the Debating Society, in which his powers as a speaker soon became well known. The fact was that his great popularity and his enjoyment of social pleasures interfered very much with anything like close study. Yet he appears to have passed all his examinations at the right times, for he became B.A. in 1836, Licentiate in Theology in 1839, and M.A. in 1840, having passed the examination for M.A. in 1838, with second class honours in Classics.

He was ordained deacon in 1841, and priest in 1842, having previously been third master in King William's College in the Isle of Man. He would have gone as curate to Dr. Hook at Leeds, but there was no vacancy, and he went to Archdeacon Wilberforce as curate at Burton Agnes. There he met many eminent Churchmen, and was as one of the family at the rectory; but he suffered so terribly from quinsy that he could not face another winter in the East Riding, and in the autumn of 1843 and in 1844 he took work at Windsor, where he came in contact with the soldiers, and where he soon made a great impression as a preacher. In July, 1845, he undertook the chaplaincy of the military prison at Southsea, and laboured among the men for about a year, after which he went to St. Mary's, Reading, and there lived and worked among the poor. In 1846 his health broke down, but in August of that year he was able to go as chaplain to Corfu. There he remained until May, 1850, when he was to have become Incumbent of St. Mary's, Glasgow, but his health broke down again for a time. From 1851 to 1857, with some absences occasioned by delicate health, he was senior

curate of St. Barnabas', Pimlico, and that at a very
trying time. There his striking appearance and earnest
preaching held crowded congregations, as it were, spell-
bound, and the religious convictions of many were
greatly strengthened. While at St. Barnabas' he pub-
blished a 'Guide to Advent' (1851), an admirable
devotional manual, a second edition of which was soon
required. At last he was compelled by ill health to
resign his charge and to rest from active work for four
years.

During this period he devoted himself to the study
of moral and mystical theology and spiritual works.
He published 'Warnings and Consolations,' being notes
of sermons at St. Barnabas, and a Guide to Lent. He
also performed his share in a joint work to be entitled
'A Synopsis of Moral Theology.' This portion of the
work was privately printed after his death (1882). After
a journey to Egypt in search of health, he was invited by
Lord Beauchamp to go to Newland as Vicar, and to be
the first Warden of the Beauchamp Charity. Here he
remained until 1877, when his health again failed and he
retired. While at Newland he originated and founded the
Clergy House of Rest at West Malvern. He attempted
to minister to a sisterhood at Ascot, but was unable to
continue in that work. Yet whenever his health permitted it he was always doing something, and in his
last years, which were spent at Bath, he translated the
'Manuale' of St. Augustine into English odes, under
the title of 'Cœlestia' (1881). He died at Bath December 29, 1881, aged sixty-three, and was buried at
Newland. Besides the works already mentioned, he published, in pamphlet form, 'On the Observance of Lent,'

1840; ' Guidance into Truth, what hinders ?' three discourses, 1856; 'The Revelation of the Antichrist,' 1861 ; 'Twenty-one Heads of Christian Duty,' 1864 ; ' A Plea for the Threatened Ritual of the Church of England,' 1865; 'The Bishops are Responsible,' 1877, and many others.

WILLIAM GREENWELL (University College) is so remarkably distinguished among Durham men, that in his case I make an exception, and include a memoir of a living person in these pages.

He was born at Greenwell Ford, Lanchester, March 23, 1820, the eldest son of William Thomas Greenwell, Esq., J.P. and D.L., and a brother of Dora Greenwell, whose prose and poetical writings are well known to many. He received his earliest education at a preparatory school taught by the Rev. George Newby, Vicar of Witton-le-Wear. He next went to the Durham Grammar-School, where his masters were Mr. Buckle and Mr. Luke Ripley, and where one of his schoolfellows was Henry Baker Tristram, now Canon of Durham. He entered at University College, and was matriculated in October, 1836. According to his own account, he did not do much work while an undergraduate, but he took his B.A. degree in June, 1839. Soon after that he entered at the Middle Temple, intending to go to the Bar; but as he was never well in London, he returned to Durham, and entered on the theological course in 1841. He took the licence in 1842, and the M.A. degree in 1843.

Born and brought up on the banks of the Browney, he was a keen and successful angler from early boyhood, and as he grew up he also developed a taste for shooting;

indeed, he began to shoot with a flint-lock long before he left school.* The Roman camp at Lanchester was on his father's estate, and when he and his brother Frank were boys they cleared out a considerable portion of a covered drain in the camp, dragging out the soil in an old fish-kettle. This was his first essay in archæological research. While at the University he belonged to an architectural society that existed for a few years, and he was an active member of the University College Choral Society.

He was ordained deacon by Bishop Maltby June 30, 1844, and priest June 28, 1846, and when he was examined for the diaconate he highly gratified the Bishop by reproducing his lordship's published discourse on the text 'Canst thou speak Greek?' and accordingly he was appointed to read the Gospel. He appears to have been ordained to the Pemberton Fellowship, which he held from 1844 to 1854. He was Bursar of University College from 1844 to 1847, and Chaplain in 1846 and 1847. In 1846 he became an original member of the Tyneside Naturalists' Field Club, and in the same year he made a tour in Southern Germany and Northern Italy. From 1847 to 1850 he was Perpetual Curate of Ovingham with Mickley, and then he went to live with Archdeacon Wilberforce, who was then writing his work on the Holy Eucharist, at Burton Agnes, as James Skinner had done before. While there he received an invitation from W. G. Henderson, then Principal of Bishop Hatfield's Hall, to help him, and he came, but only remained in the Hall for a very short time, for in 1852 he was appointed

* Percussion caps came into use between 1820 and 1830.

Principal of Neville Hall, Newcastle-upon-Tyne, in which office he was succeeded by James Raine the younger, afterwards Canon and Chancellor of York, in 1854. While at Neville Hall he edited, for the Surtees Society, the ' Boldon Book' and Egbert's Pontifical, having had his attention directed to this sort of work by his friend James Raine the elder.

The Newcastle meeting of the Archæological Institute took place in August, 1852, and at one of their gatherings (on August 31) he read a paper on those curious concentric circles carved on rocks in Northumberland and elsewhere, which have since been the subject of much discussion ; his paper first called attention to these interesting stones. The paper and the drawings that illustrated it were, unfortunately, lost, and were never published. At this time he belonged to the Newcastle Society of Antiquaries, and to the Literary and Philosophical Society. He also worked hard with the medical students among the patients during a great epidemic of cholera in Newcastle. In 1854 he was selected out of a great number of candidates, and appointed Minor Canon of Durham, an office which he has now held for more than fifty years. He was also Chaplain and Censor of Bishop Cosin's Hall from 1854 to 1864. During these years he worked at Durham documents, and employed much of his leisure time in shooting and fishing. In 1856 he began to form a collection of Greek coins, which afterwards assumed such dimensions and value that he sold it for £11,000 to Mr. Warren, of Lewes House, Sussex. In 1857, for 1856, was issued by the Surtees Society Bishop Hatfield's ' Survey,' under his editorship.

In 1858 a circumstance occurred which led to great and unexpected results. Some one happened to show him a bronze dagger that had been found in Ford West Field in Northumberland. He was also shown some flint scrapers and urns, with burnt bones, that had been found in levelling a cairn. In June and July of this year he opened two barrows near Ford, and shortly afterwards wrote an account of them which is in the Transactions of the Berwickshire Field Club, vol. iv., p. 390. This first essay in the exploration of barrows led to his opening a great number, first in Northumberland and then on the Yorkshire Wolds and in other parts of England, and he wrote an account of barrows that he had examined in the *Archæological Journal*, vol. xxii. (1865), pp. 97-117 and 241-264. This and the earlier paper just mentioned were the precursors of his famous work on British Barrows, which was published in 1878.

Some time about the middle of the last century his natural acuteness, together with his long experience in ' the gentle art,' helped him to a little invention that has made his name famous among anglers in distant New Zealand, and, indeed, all over the world. While fishing one day in the Tweed, he noticed that the trout were not taking the ' March brown,' as they were accustomed to do, but were rising freely at some other fly which he had not observed before. He caught some of these flies, and came to the conclusion that the best imitation would be a fly made with wings from the inside of a blackbird's wing, and the body formed of a ' cock-a-bundy ' hackle, tied with yellow silk. In the evening he ordered twelve flies to be so made by Mr. James

Wright, the fly-dresser at Sprouston.　Next day he had fine sport with the new fly, and again on the following day.　On the second evening all the anglers in the place met to name the new trout-fly, and the school-master proposed as a toast, 'Success to Greenwell's Glory.'　And 'Greenwell's Glory' has been well known ever since as one of the most killing of artificial flies.　Its name is enshrined in the 'English Dialect Dictionary,' vol. ii., p. 720, and in all modern works on angling.　There is also a salmon-fly named, after its inventor, 'the Greenwell.'

In 1860 the Surtees Society issued the second volume of the 'Durham Wills and Inventories,' edited by Greenwell, in continuation of the former volume, which was edited by Dr. Raine.　On July 25, 1861, Green-well joined the Berwickshire Naturalists' Field Club, and in or about 1862 he became a member of the Council of the Durham Archæological Society, then recently established.　On April 10, 1862, he was elected President of the Tyneside Naturalists' Field Club for 1862-63, and his presidential address appears in the Transactions, vol. vi., p. 1.　Notes by him on a tumulus and its contents at Grundstone Law are in the same volume, p. 34.

Some time about 1862 he was appointed Librarian to the Dean and Chapter, an office which he has held ever since, to the great advantage of the library.　He has been the means of the acquisition of large numbers of Government and other publications, and he has formed the fine collection of Anglian sculptured stones. He found the enormous mass of charters dating from the earliest times of the abbey in a confused heap at the library, and he induced the Chapter to fit up the large room over the College gateway for their reception. He then put them all into their present perfect order, and made a complete catalogue of the seals (*circa* 1875-1880).

On March 23, 1865, he was elected President of the Durham Archæological Society, to which office he has been unanimously re-elected every year since at the annual meeting. His addresses delivered on these occasions are reported in the Transactions. In the same year he was appointed Rector of the small parish of St. Mary in the South Bailey in Durham, which cure he still serves. There is an account by him of an ancient British burial at Ilderton, Northumberland, in Transactions of the Natural History Society of Durham and Northumberland, vol. i., N.S. (1865-1867), p. 143.

Some time in 1868 he happened to be at a meeting of the Society of Antiquaries in London, where, on being invited to take part in some discussion, he acquitted himself with such ability that the President expressed his regret that the rules of the society did not admit of his being elected a Fellow there and then. However, he was elected in due course before the close of that same year.

For two or three years, off and on, towards 1869, he was exploring those remarkable excavations in the chalk near Brandon in Suffolk, known as 'Grime's Graves.' He wrote an account of these in the *Journal of the Ethnological Society*, N.S. vol. ii., p. 419. On February 5, 1870, he took the oaths as a magistrate for the county of Durham. His next literary undertaking was the editing of the ' Feodarium Prioratus Dunelm-

ensis' for the Surtees Society, a work that occupied
a great part of two or three years. The volume was
issued in 1872 for 1871. In 1873 he gave an account
of some Lascells deeds in the *Yorkshire Archæological
Journal*, vol. ii., pp. 87-96. His work on British Barrows
was published in 1878, and in the same year he was
elected a Fellow of the Royal Society. In 1879 he was
made honorary F.S.A.Scot., and contributed a paper
on 'Chambered Cairns in Argyllshire' to the Proceedings
of that Society. On September 24, 1879, he delivered
a lecture on Durham Cathedral, which is reported in
the Transactions of the Durham Archæological Society,
vol. ii., pp. 163-234. This was reissued as a guide-
book in 1881, and a fifth edition of it appeared in 1897.
In 1882 he received from his University the honorary
degree of D.C.L. In 1887 he wrote a treatise on the
Electrum Coinage of Cyzicus, which appeared first in
the *Numismatic Chronicle*, and afterwards in a separate
form. To *Archæologia* he has made three contributions,
namely: 'Recent Researches in Barrows,' read 1899
and 1900, vol. lii., pp. 1-72; 'Antiquities found in
Heathery Burn Cave,' read 1892, vol. liv., pp. 87-114;
and 'Some Rare Forms of Bronze Weapons,' read 1901,
vol. lviii., pp. 1-16. He presented his collection of
objects from barrows and other places of interment to
the British Museum, where they now have a place of
honour as 'the Greenwell Collection,' and his collection
of skulls he gave to the New Museum at Oxford. He
has retained his great collection of bronze and gold
objects.

Since 1893 he has been taking an active part in the
preparation of 'The History of Northumberland,' six

volumes of which have now been issued. In 1895 he
slipped and fell in walking down Queen Street; the
neck of one thigh-bone was broken, and it was feared
that he might never walk again. Nevertheless, although
he was seventy-five years of age, he made an excellent
recovery under the skilful management of Dr. Selby
Plummer, and now walks with a stick, and with scarcely
any lameness. In that year he sold his collection of
stone implements to Dr. Sturge, of Nice, for £1,200.
In 1897 it was proposed at the annual meeting of the
Durham Archæological Society that his portrait should
be painted by subscription, and Mr. Cope, afterwards
A.R.A., was selected as the artist. The likeness is
striking, and the picture an admirable work of art.
The Canon is represented as seated, with a bronze spear-
head in his hand, and with gold and bronze antiquities,
' the Greenwell ' and ' Greenwell's Glory ' on a table by
his side. A beautiful autogravure of this portrait has
been done by the Autotype Company, London, and the
original hangs in the Chapter Library.

Besides the literary works already mentioned, he has
contributed many papers to the *Numismatic Chronicle*,
and others to the Transactions of the Durham Archæological Society. He also wrote the account of Anglian
Stones in the ' Catalogue of Sculptured Stones in the
Cathedral Library, Durham,' published in 1899. After
the death of the Rev. Arthur Duncombe Shafto
(February 28, 1900), he was appointed Chairman of the
Petty Sessional Division of Durham Ward, of the
magistracy of the county. All the time that he has
been a magistrate he has been a Poor Law Guardian;
also Chairman of the Assessment Committee since 1888,

and a member of the Durham School Board since its
foundation in 1871. He has long been a member of
the Standing Joint Committee of the County Council,
and was elected an Alderman in March, 1904. He is
an honorary member of the Cumberland and Westmoreland, the Derbyshire, and the Suffolk Archæological Societies. He is now (June, 1904), in his eighty-
fifth year, and, although he has long been liable to
severe attacks of gout, he is hale and hearty, and con-
tinues to discharge his duties at the Cathedral, at his
little Church, on the Bench, and at various Boards.
Last year he resumed his old recreation of angling, and
went in all weathers to the fish-pond at his old home,
where his nephew, His Honour Judge Greenwell,
now resides. His spirited efforts were rewarded by
the capture of over 100 trout, after which he re-
stocked the pond to be ready for another season.
During the present year he has returned to his favourite
sport, and on May 20 he stood for six hours in the
water or by the side of the Browney, and landed
forty-two trout. He has continued to make frequent
expeditions to the river, and to retain all his other
and varied interests, up to the time of our going to
press.

In this account of my old friend, who has always
shown the greatest readiness to hand on the lamp of
Durham archæology to any of us who would receive it,
I have confined myself entirely to main facts. A volume
might be written about his life, but this is not the
time or place for anything more than some such notice
as is here contributed to the series of 'Brief Lives' in
which it appears.

JOSEPH STEVENSON (University College) was the eldest
son of Mr. Robert Stevenson, surgeon, of Berwick-upon-
Tweed, and was born there November 27, 1806.   He
was educated first at Witton-le-Wear, and then at
Durham School, under Dr. Raine.   He next studied at
Glasgow, became a licentiate of the Presbyterian body,
and preached a trial sermon.   After that he followed
his bent in the direction of documentary research, and
found employment in London, first in arranging the
public records, then kept in St. John's Chapel in the
Tower, and subsequently in the MS. department in the
British Museum.   In 1831 he married a Glasgow lady,
and in 1834 was appointed a Subcommissioner of the
Public Records.   In London he had his children bap-
tized in the Church of England, to which he had become
himself attached.   He matriculated as a theological
student at Durham April 23, 1839, obtained the licence
in June, 1841, was ordained deacon and licensed to the
curacy of St. Margaret's, Durham in July, and was
ordained priest in December of the same year.   He does
not appear to have acted as curate at St. Margaret's for
more than about a year.   In 1841-1848 he was engaged
in arranging the charters and rolls preserved in the
treasury of the Dean and Chapter, and in making a
catalogue of the charters.   In 1846 he was made
honorary M.A.   In 1847-1849 he was curate at
St. Giles's, Durham, and in January, 1849, he was
instituted to the vicarage of Leighton Buzzard in Bed-
fordshire, which benefice he resigned in 1862.   He then
undertook the work of calendaring at the Public Record
Office.   On June 24, 1863, he was received into the
Roman Catholic Church.   About that time he resigned

his post as calendarer, but he continued to edit books in the Rolls Series. He also assisted Canon Estcourt in his work on Anglican Orders, and he reported on no less than twenty-four collections of MSS. for the Historical MSS. Commission. His wife, who had all along been accustomed to help him in his work, died July 11, 1869, and he entered St. Mary's College, Oscott. In 1872 he was admitted to the Roman priesthood, received a pension from Mr. Gladstone's Government, and was employed to examine the Vatican archives. In about four years he made thirteen folio volumes of transcripts, which are now in the Public Record Office. In November, 1877, he became a novice in the Jesuit Order, and then lived, first in Oxford, and then at the 'House of Writers,' 31, Farm Street, Berkeley Square, where he died February 8, 1895, in his eighty-ninth year. When eighty-six years old he received the honorary degree of LL.D. from St. Andrews. He was a man who did an immense amount of work, mainly in editing, and there are lists of his editions and other works in the 'Dictionary of National Biography,' and in the *Durham University Journal*, vol. xi., p. 170, so copious that we can here give only a brief abstract.

For the Maitland Club he edited eight works, for the Bannatyne Club two, for the English Historical Society four, for the Roxburghe Club four, for the Surtees Society seven, for the Church Historians of England collection seven, for the Rolls Series four— thirty-six in all. Besides these, he wrote nine other works, and he assisted Mr. James Paton in editing the Scottish National Memorials in 1890. His principal subject latterly was the history of Mary Stuart,* on which he wrote two important works. It is to be regretted that, in consequence of limited means, he was obliged to write and edit with a view to remuneration, and he did not always allow himself time for sufficient revision; hence it happened that some of his work was not so accurate as it might otherwise have been.

GEORGE ORNSBY (University College) was born March 9, 1809, and was the eldest son of George Ornsby, Esq., J.P. and D.L., of The Lodge, Lanchester. He was educated at Durham School, and for some time he practised as a solicitor in Durham. His antiquarian and historical proclivities brought him into close association with the elder Dr. Raine, the historian of North Durham, author of 'St. Cuthbert,' and of 'A Brief Account of Durham Cathedral.' On October 19, 1839, he matriculated, and entered the University as a theological student. Having obtained the Licence in Theology in 1841, he was ordained, and held in succession the curacies of Newburn, Sedgefield, and Whickham. In 1846 appeared his 'Sketches of Durham,' a book of more solid value than might be supposed from the title. In July, 1850, he was inducted to the vicarage of Fishlake, in South Yorkshire, on the nomination of the Dean and Chapter of Durham. While there he edited for the Surtees Society Dean Granville's 'Remains,' in vols. xxxvii. and xlvii., issued 1861 and 1865, the former of these being a volume of 'Miscellanea'; Bishop Cosin's 'Correspondence,' etc., in vols. lii., lv., issued 1869, 1872; the Household Books of Lord William Howard

* It has been noted as a coincidence that he died on the anniversary of her execution.

11

of Naworth Castle, vol. lxviii., issued 1878. The care and
skill with which these works are edited, and the value of
the introductions and notes, are well known. He undertook the editing of Dean Comber's 'Correspondence,'
but never got it done.   In 1872 his University conferred
on him the honorary degree of M.A., and in 1873 he
was elected F.S.A.   In 1877 he supplied the historical
introduction to a volume of sermons preached at the
reopening of the Cathedral.   In 1879 he was preferred
to the prebendal stall of Ampleforth in York Minster,
and in 1882 his excellent 'Diocesan History of York'
was published by the S.P.C.K.   Having relations and
old friends in Durham, and retaining a warm interest
in his early associations, he often came over, and those
of us who enjoyed the privilege of his friendship felt
that he never ceased to belong to the old place.   There
are still a few who well remember how his face would
light up with appreciative humour as he quoted quaint
passages from the writings of his favourite seventeenth-
century worthies.   He died after a very short illness,
April 17, 1886, aged seventy-seven, and, next to Fishlake, where he had lived for thirty-six years as an ideal
parish priest, there was no place where his loss was so
much felt as it was in Durham.

   JAMES SIMPSON (University College) came of a good
old stock of sturdy Westmoreland yeomen, and began
life as the teacher of a day-school at Shap.   On October 23, 1841, he entered at Durham as a theological
student, and in 1843 obtained his licence, having gained
prizes for Hebrew and Hellenistic Greek.   He was
curate, first at Chester-le-Street, and then at Morland,
near Penrith.   In 1857 he became Vicar of Shap, and

in 1863 Vicar of Kirkby Stephen.   True to his early
associations, he entered heartily into educational work,
and he was frequently consulted by Mr. Forster in connexion with his great measure dealing with elementary
education.   He took a keen interest in diocesan education, and in 1872 received the Lambeth degree of LL.D.
in special recognition of his services in the cause of
education.   In 1874 he was made Honorary Canon of
Carlisle.   Although in Holy Orders, he was several
times Mayor of Appleby, and he took an active part in
county business in various capacities.   He was long
connected with the Freemasons, and was Grand
Chaplain of England.   He was one of the founders of
the Cumberland and Westmoreland Antiquarian Society,
and its President from the time of its formation to his
death, which took place on March 9, 1886, in his sixty-
seventh year.   He was a business man rather than
literary, but many valuable papers by him are contained
in the Transactions of the above-named society.

The RIGHT HON. JOHN ROBERT DAVISON, M.P. (University College), was the second son of Edward Davison,
Perpetual Curate of St. Nicholas, Durham, and was
born in Old Elvet, April 12, 1825.   He was educated,
first at the Kepier School, Houghton-le-Spring, and
then at Durham Grammar-School.   He matriculated at
Durham April 24, 1841; passed the examination for the
B.A. degree in June, 1844 (4th class); and was admitted
B.A. January, 1845, M.A. November, 1847.   He studied
under the late Sir William Atherton, and was called
to the Bar by the Benchers of the Middle Temple
November 2, 1849.   He joined the Northern Circuit,
soon came to the front, and it was not long before he

11—2

was recognised as leading counsel.   In 1860 he married
Jane Anna, eldest daughter of the late Nicholas Wood,
of Hetton Hall.   In course of time he became so much
engaged in Parliamentary practice that he ceased to
travel on circuit.   He was constantly employed in the
railway contests of 1857-1863.   In 1866 he became Q.C.,
and in April, 1867, was made a magistrate for the county
of Durham.   He became Chairman of Quarter Sessions
June 29, 1868.   In the General Election of 1868 he
stood for the city of Durham in the Liberal interest,
and was returned, together with Mr. John Henderson,
the other Liberal candidate, Mr. J. L. Wharton, the
Conservative, being defeated.   He soon became a well-
known member of the House, and was a prominent
supporter of Mr. Gladstone.   At the close of December,
1870, he was appointed Judge Advocate-General, which
involved another election at Durham, in which Davison
was returned without opposition.   Near his residence
at Under-river House, Sevenoaks, he built and endowed
a church, dedicated in honour of St. Margaret.   He
had long suffered from some disease of the heart, but
went to bed in his usual health on Friday night,
April 14, 1871.   On the next morning he was found
dead.   He was buried, April 21, at the parish church
of Seal, near Sevenoaks.   His death made a profound
impression in his native city, where he was greatly
respected and admired by all classes of persons, including
those who were most opposed to him in politics.   In
1875 the 'Window of the Four Doctors' at the end of
the north transept of the Cathedral was reglazed,
partly by public subscription and partly by members
of his family, as a memorial of him.

JOHN Low Low (University College) was, I think, a
native of Dundee, and he received his early education in
the grammar-school of that town. As he grew up he
became warmly attached to the Episcopal Church, and,
with a view to Holy Orders, matriculated at Durham
October 22, 1842, as a theological student. In due
course he became a Licentiate in Theology in 1844,
B.A. 1846, and M.A. 1849, having been Gisborne
Scholar and Hebrew and Divinity Prizeman. After
serving as curate of St. Margaret's, Durham, from 1844
to 1847, he was curate-in-charge of Forest and Harwood
in Teesdale until 1873. Here he spent the best years
of his life as an excellent village pastor, at the same
time devoting himself to the study of theology, Hebrew
and Syriac, medieval archæology, Church history, and
liturgiology. In 1872 he went to Whittonstall on
the presentation of the Dean and Chapter of Durham.
About that time he became a member of a clerical
society for the study of the Hebrew Scriptures, founded
and long presided over by the Rev. S. A. Herbert,
Vicar of Felling. Very few members brought with them
so much knowledge as did 'Low Low,' as he was usually
called. The completeness of his preparation of the
portion to be read, his familiarity with the text of the
Hebrew Bible, and the lively interest he took in the dis-
cussions on particular passages, were remarkable. He
used to say that he dated his interest in Hebrew from
some little Hebrew grammar that he had at Dundee
when a boy. His mind during his waking hours was
never at rest. In him the *perfervidum ingenium
Scotorum* manifested itself in active thought and em-
phatic conversation, of which he had no lack, and he

could combine a keen sense of humour with deep reverence for holy things. He wrote the 'Diocesan History of Durham,' published by the S.P.C.K. in 1881, and 'Historical Scenes in Durham Cathedral,' Durham, 1887, besides a number of magazine articles and the like. In the latter end of 1887 he was made an Honorary Canon of Newcastle, but he did not long live to enjoy the distinction, for he died rather suddenly on February 9, 1888, aged seventy-one. 'Hospitable, genial, and humorous,' as he has been described, his well-known personality was greatly missed, not only in his own parish, but in the University and in Durham generally, where he was a frequent and a welcome guest. He was twice married.

CHARLES THOMAS ERSKINE (University College) was the sixth son of the Hon. Henry David Erskine, and was born at Alnmouth, January 6, 1821. In 1823 his parents came to reside in Durham, so that his earliest recollections were connected with the Cathedral, antiquities, and scenery of the old city. Here he became a distinguished and a loving son of the new University. A few years later the family removed to Edinburgh, where they were intimately associated with Scott, Jeffrey, Chalmers, and other literary and conversational notabilities. Charles was educated in Edinburgh and at Broomrigge, near Dollar, and in 1838 was admitted at the University of Edinburgh, where he remained only six months. On October 19, 1842, he matriculated at Durham as a theological student, but his tutors, perceiving his ability and attainments, soon urged him to enter the Arts course, which he did. In 1845 he obtained a double second class in the examination for the B.A. degree, and in 1846 a first class in Classics, and again became a Divinity student with the Van Mildert Scholarship.   He is described by a contemporary as a person of deep religious feeling, though he was not inclined to make a display of it.   At the same time he was conscientious and regular in the public duties of religion, and never missed the weekly Communion while resident in Durham.   He was a great lover of Nature, and ever on the look out for the earliest wild flowers in his walks about Durham.   He had a great fund of Scottish humour, and his quaint remarks were long remembered by his friends.   On June 28, 1846, he was ordained deacon and licensed to Tynemouth, and in the November following was elected to a Fellowship in the University.   In July, 1847, he was ordained priest, and instituted to the charge of St. James's Chapel, Stone-haven, where he laboured for eight years and did much for the advancement of the Church there.   He found some singular customs still surviving after the perse-cution of the Church of Scotland had ceased, as, for instance, the reading of the Burial Service in the house before the body was taken to the grave, followed by a silent interment in the Presbyterian manner.   These customs he broke through, and he soon began to have daily services and more frequent celebrations of Holy Communion, a 9 a.m. celebration being one of his 'innovations.'   However, he carried his people with him, and the fisher-folk were devoted to him.   In 1855 his Fellowship was about to run out, and he was obliged to leave Stonehaven for want of means to carry on his work.   In June of that year he settled at Hingham in Norfolk as senior curate, his now widowed mother, his

sister, and an aunt, accompanying him. In a few months'
time he took charge of Thelbridge, in North Devon,
where he remained for about a year and a half. Then
a new incumbent came into residence, and Mr. Erskine
removed to Exeter, where he assisted occasionally at
St. Olave's and other churches till the beginning of
1858, when he was appointed to the charge of the new
district of St. Michael's, Wakefield. He threw himself
very heartily into the work of the new parish; the
building of the church was completed within the year,
and in 1861 it was consecrated. On All Saints' Day of
that year he was at church as usual for the early
celebration, and on November 5 he died, having been ill
only four or five days. He was buried at Alverthorpe
on the 9th. His work was pastoral, not literary, but
after his death a volume of remarkable sermons by him
was published (London: Saunders, Otley and Co., 1864),
to which is prefixed an interesting memoir by the late
Bishop A. P. Forbes, from which these notes have been
extracted.

WILLIAM WALSHAM How (University College) was
born December 13, 1823, at Shrewsbury, and was the
elder son of Mr. William Wybergh How, solicitor, of
that town. He received his education at Shrewsbury
School under Dr. Butler and Dr. Kennedy, and went to
Wadham College, Oxford, in 1841, with the intention
of being a lawyer, and at first he read for double
honours. Soon, however, he discarded mathematics;
then he appears to have found a difficulty in applying
his mind to some of the subjects required for classical
honours, and in May, 1845, his name appeared in the
third class. From a child he had been interested in

botany, which was his favourite recreation all through life, and while in Oxford he obtained a Goodridge's Botanical Exhibition. On October 25, 1845, he matriculated at Durham as a theological student, and in the June following he obtained the Licence in Theology. On December 20, 1846, he was ordained deacon, and licensed to the curacy of St. George's, Kidderminster, under Mr. Claughton. From 1848 to 1851 he was curate at the Abbey Church in Shrewsbury, . and in 1849 married the eldest daughter of Canon Douglas of Durham, and also wrote the first volume of 'Plain Words,' of which nearly fifty editions have been issued. From 1851 to 1879 he was Rector of Whittington, Salop, and from 1879 to 1888 Rector of St. Andrew Undershaft and Bishop Suffragan of Bedford, his episcopal work being in East London. He was Bishop of Wakefield from 1888 to 1897, and on August 10, 1897, he died, after a short illness, in the West of Ireland. On August 12 he was buried at Whittington. It was for the Queen's Jubilee on June 20 in the same year that he wrote, at the request of H.R.H. the Prince of Wales, our present King, his noble hymn 'O King of kings,' to be set to music by Sir Arthur Sullivan. It must here be mentioned that in February, 1890, upon the death of Bishop Lightfoot, he was offered the bishopric of Durham by Lord Salisbury. There was much that might have attracted him in this preferment. He had resided in the University for the theological course, and had taken an *ad eundem* degree there. Durham was the old home of his wife and of her father, Canon Douglas. The position of Bishop of Durham was one of great dignity and influence, and the income more than double that of Wakefield. He would have escaped from many of the difficulties that were connected with his early residence in Wakefield. But he could not, as he said, see any argument in favour of ' deserting the half-finished work ' of organizing the young diocese to which he had been called, and so he declined the offer, assigning as one among other reasons that he had no academical distinction to qualify him specially for a diocese in which there was a University. The Diocese of Wakefield, generally, received the news of the Bishop's decision with delight and gratitude, though some of the Yorkshiremen were puzzled. Thinking mainly of the income, they said, 'It's not business.' Most of the Bishop's works were written at Whittington. There are altogether four series of ' Plain Words.' His most useful 'Commentary on the Four Gospels' (S.P.C.K.) was finished in June, 1868, and its sale has reached a total of over 223,000. It was followed by a volume on the Acts and Epistles by various authors. His next important work was ' Pastor in Parochia,' which has also had an enormous sale, and of his ' Manual for the Holy Communion' more than 657,000 copies have been sold. There were numerous volumes of sermons and addresses issued by him at various dates. Perhaps his most remarkable sermon was one preached before the British Association in Manchester Cathedral on September 4, 1887. Mr. Gladstone and Professor Huxley were greatly struck by it, and the latter mentions it with much respect in his book on ' Science and the Christian Tradition.' The Bishop greatly excelled as a hymn-writer, and besides hymns he wrote many poetical compositions of great

merit, both serious and humorous—indeed, he wrote
creditable hymns when quite a boy. And he may
be regarded as a very good example of the kind of men
that used to come from the other Universities for the
Durham theological course.

JAMES FRANCIS TURNER (University College) was a
son of Lord Justice Sir George James Turner. He
matriculated at Durham in 1848, took his B.A. degree
and a fourth class in Classics in 1851, obtained the
Licence in Theology in 1852, M.A. 1854, and was
Chaplain and Censor of Bishop Cosin's Hall 1852-1854.
On his previous architectural training and his designing
of the chapel of Bishop Hatfield's Hall, see above,
p. 105. He was Rector of North Tidworth, Wilts, and
Rural Dean until shortly before 1869, when he was
consecrated Bishop of Grafton and Armidale, having
received the degree of D.D. by diploma, December 15,
1868. In the latter part of 1892 he was compelled by
failing health to resign his see, and on April 27, 1893,
he died in Rome, on his way to England. He was
buried in the English cemetery there, and a handsome
monument, made in Rome from a design by Mr. C. C.
Hodges of Hexham, stands over his grave. He was a
vice-president of the English Church Union, and under
the auspices of the New South Wales branch delivered
a lecture at Sydney entitled 'Is the Church of England
going Romewards? A Reply to Dr. Vaughan.'

SAMUEL KETTLEWELL (University College) was a son
of the Rev. W. Kettlewell, who was curate-in-charge of
Kirkheaton in Yorkshire, 1826-1839, and kept a school
for boys in the rectory there. Here, no doubt, the
future author received his early education. He matricu-

lated at Durham, October 24, 1846, obtained the
Licence in Theology in June, 1848, and was soon after
ordained to a curacy at Leeds Parish Church with
Dr. Hook, Vicar of Leeds.   In 1851 he was appointed
Vicar of St. Mark's, Woodhouse, near Leeds, and here
he remained for twenty years, and then retired from
parochial work and devoted himself to study and
literary occupations.   He wrote works on the Rights
and Liberties of the Church, and on the Reformation in
Ireland, also a somewhat jocular little book on Church
Politics, and a Catechism on Gospel History.   Afterwards he made a special study of Thomas à Kempis and
the 'Imitatio,' and it was by his works on these subjects
that he made his reputation as an author.   In 1877 he
published a work on the authorship of the 'Imitatio,'
establishing the claim of à Kempis against all other
supposed authors, and in 1882 a kindred work on
'Thomas à Kempis and the Brothers of the Common
Life.' In 1888 he published a work on Christian Unity,
and, although his health was failing, he became associated with Archdeacon Wright in a translation of
'Meditations on the Life of Christ' by Thomas à
Kempis, and he wrote the valuable preface.   In 1860
he received the Lambeth degree of M.A., and in 1892
that of D.D.   He died November 3, 1893, aged seventy-
one.   He was one of the old race of literary licentiates,
but spent most of his life out of touch with the University.   He left £100 to the parish of Kirkheaton for
the poor.

JAMES RAINE (University College) was born July 11,
1830, in the North Bailey, Durham, a son of Dr. James
Raine the elder, who was the friend of Robert Surtees

the historian of Durham and of his friends, historian of
North Durham, author of ' St. Cuthbert,' and editor of
numerous books and papers, and who married Margaret,
sister of Dr. George Peacock, F.R.S., Dean of Ely.
Their son James was educated at the Durham Grammar-
School, and matriculated at the University, March 22,
1848. He took his B.A. degree in June, 1851, having
obtained a second class in Classics, and was. elected
Fellow in 1852. In June of the same year he passed
the examination for the M.A. degree with a first class
in Classics, and he took the degree, as also the Licence
in Theology, in 1853. He was ordained deacon in
September, 1853, and priest in December, 1854. From
1854 to 1856 he was Principal of Neville Hall at Newcastle, and from 1855 to 1895 Secretary to the Surtees
Society, for which society he edited ' Richmond Wills '
(1853) and ' Testamenta Eboracensia,' vol. ii. (1855).
Soon after his arrival in Newcastle, namely, on October 4,
1854, he was elected a member of the Newcastle Society
of Antiquaries, and soon became a contributor to the
Archæologia Æliana, as well as a member of the
council, and one of a committee appointed to superintend the printing of the society's publications.

In 1858 he removed to York, where he was curate of
All Saints' in the Pavement with St. Peter the Little.
He appears to have at once addressed himself to the
study of York documents, for he edited for the Surtees
Society the first volume of ' York Fabric Rolls' (1859)
and ' Depositions from York Castle ' (1861). In 1863
appeared the first volume of 'Fasti Eboracenses,' or,
'Lives of the Archbishops of York,' by Canon Dixon,
edited and enlarged by Raine; in 1864 'Hexham,' vol. i.,

in 1865 'Testamenta Eboracensia,' vol. iii.; and in 1866
' Hexham,' vol. ii., all for the Surtees Society. In 1866
he issued a pamphlet on ' Vestments in the Northern
Province.'   In 1867 he married a daughter of Dr. Key-
worth of York, by whom he had a large family of sons
and daughters.   He was Vicar of St. Lawrence, York,
1867-68 ; Rector of All Saints', Pavement, 1868-1896,
and also of St. Michael's, Spurriergate, 1868-1885 ;
Prebendary of Langtoft in York Minster, 1866 ;
Residentiary Canon, 1888 ; Prebendary of Laughton,
and Chancellor, 1891.   He was also chaplain to
the merchant guilds of the city. He did not allow
his devotion to documentary and other antiquities
to interfere unduly with his pastoral engagements,
and he was greatly respected and beloved as a parish
priest.

During the whole of his life he continued to edit
volumes for the Surtees Society—viz., in addition to
those mentioned above, 'Testamenta Eboracensia,' vol.
iv. (1869), 'Gray's Register' (1872), 'Memorials of
Fountains,' vol. ii. (1878), 'Prior Lawrence' (1880),
'Testamenta Eboracensia,' vol. v. (1884), and ' English
Miscellanies ' (1890).   In 1882 he was made Hon.
D.C.L. Dunelm.   In 1888 he edited and enlarged
Burton's work on Hemingbrough for the Yorkshire
Archæological Society, and in 1893 he brought out
·the York volume in ' Historic Towns.' For the Rolls
Series he edited ' Letters from Northern Registers ' and
' Historians of the Church of York,' 2 vols.   He also
made three contributions to the Associated Archi-
tectural Societies' papers, six to the *Yorkshire Archæo-
logical Journal*, and wrote several articles in Smith's

Dictionaries of Christian Antiquities and Biography, besides the account of antiquities in the handbook to the York Museum and the introduction to the second volume of ' Old Yorkshire,' 1881.

During his eight-and-thirty years of residence in York he became one of the best-known characters in that city. As a vice-president of the Yorkshire Philosophical Society he took great interest in the museum in their grounds, in which stand the ruins of St. Mary's Abbey. No excavation can be made in York without some objects of interest being found. All the navvies, sure of a reward, brought their finds to Canon Raine, and most of these found their way to the museum. The present railway-station is on the site of a Roman cemetery, and in the excavations for the lines of rail and for the subways a vast number of interments were disturbed, while innumerable objects of interest were found. Out of the many thousands of persons that pace the platforms in the course of a year, how few there are who are aware that they are walking over any number of buried Romans resting undisturbed beneath the pavement!

Raine never could get past an excavation. I remember once walking with him in York, and we stood by a deep hole, with two or three men at the bottom, who had just found something. It was a hoard of Saxon stycas. Of course they all went up to the Crescent, where Raine then lived, and we washed and examined them in the evening. This kind of thing was going on constantly. Canon Greenwell remembers that Raine was an eager collector of birds' eggs when a boy, and the love of collecting continued with him through life, to the great advantage, not only of the museum, but of the Minster Library, in which he took great interest. It was mainly through him that the Hailstone collection of Yorkshire books was secured for the library. He inherited his father's books, and besides them he formed a valuable collection of artistic pottery, coins, plate, pictures, old glass, etc., the sale of which occupied two days.

Early in 1896 his health, which had been somewhat declining for some time, began to fail rapidly, and on May 20 he died at the Old Residence in York. He was buried on Whitsun Tuesday in the York Cemetery, the Archbishop officiating at the Minster, and the Dean at the grave. A monumental tablet to his memory was shortly afterwards placed in the north choir-aisle of the Minster.

It was in 1872 or 1873 that I first became acquainted with him. I had copied the will of Margaret Piggott from the MS. book of Acts of the Chapter of Ripon, and had recently joined the Surtees Society. I think he recognised in me one who might, if encouraged, work for the society, and to the encouragement I received at that time from Raine, William Greenwell, and W. H. D. Longstaffe, is due the fact that I have since edited ten volumes for that learned body. Raine and I became life-long friends. Whether as a clergyman, as a man of letters, as a man of taste, or in his domestic relations, he was always to be admired, and I shall never cease to be truly sorry that we have lost him. He was, says one who knew him well, ' essentially an amiable man—bland, placid, and cheerful—ever ready to assist the inquirer, and to guide the student through the toil and weariness which are inseparable from antiquarian research.'*

JOHN HENRY BLUNT (University College) was born at Chelsea, August 25, 1823, and was educated at a private school. For some years he was in business as a manufacturing chemist, after which he matriculated at Durham, October 21, 1850, as a theological student. In 1852 he obtained the Barry Theological Prize and the Licence in Theology, and was soon after ordained to the curacy at Tynemouth. While there he was accused of teaching Transubstantiation, and in 1853 he published a sermon on the Real Presence, for the purpose of refuting that charge. He did not meet with any sympathy from Bishop Maltby, and soon after left the North for a curacy in the Diocese of Exeter; then he was appointed Travelling Secretary for the National Society, and curate of Over in Cambridgeshire. Next he was at Cowley and at St. Thomas's, Oxford, and was one of the first of the Anglican clergy in the nineteenth century to wear the Eucharistic vestments. To the *Oxford Magazine* (1861) he contributed a serial story, entitled 'The Curate of Northborough,' a thinly-veiled autobiography, with much local and personal colouring, and sketched in a somewhat humorous way. In 1861 he returned to the North, and was curate of Newbottle and Herrington in the parish of Houghton-le-Spring. While at Newbottle he organized a temporary polytechnic exhibition in some new sheds at Philadelphia, a pit village; this was very successful, and attracted

* Mr. Welford in *Archæologia Æliana*, xix. 130, where will be found an admirable obituary notice, illustrated by a characteristic portrait of Raine, with a facsimile of his autograph.

12

thousands of visitors. He also competed for a prize essay or treatise on Pastoral Work; his essay did not gain the prize, but it was published by Messrs. Rivington under the title of 'Directorium Pastorale.'

This was the beginning of an unbroken continuity of literary production rarely equalled in amount in the life of any one man. While engaged on the 'Directorium' he also edited the *North of England Magazine*, to the pages of which he was himself a principal contributor, but it lasted only from April to December, 1862. Dora Greenwell contributed to the first number 'A Country Rhyme,' in eighteen stanzas. From Newbottle he went to Tudhoe, in the parish of Brancepeth, then to Breamore, Hants, and then to live in Oxford without any curacy, to be free for literary work and near the Bodleian Library. By All Souls' College he was appointed Vicar of the small parish of Kennington, near Oxford, in 1868, and in 1873 he was recommended by Mr. Gladstone for the Crown living of Beverston, which he held until his death; this took place in London on Good Friday, 1884, somewhat suddenly, in his sixty-first year. He was a man of amazing vitality and energy, and often worked, not only through the whole of the day, but during a great part of the night; and an excellent memory, a rapid grasp of what he read, and an extraordinary facility in composition, all combined to make him one of the most prolific writers of the last century. He received from his University the distinctions of honorary M.A. in 1855, and honorary D.D. at the Jubilee in 1882. He was also a Fellow of the Society of Antiquaries.

The following is the list of his works as supplied,

presumably by himself, with the publishers' names, etc.,
to,' Crockford's Directory ' for 1884. A few additions
are here given in brackets. ['The Real Presence,' a
sermon, 1853]; 'Lectures on the Atonement and the
At-One-Maker,' 1855; ['The Position of the Priest at
the Altar,' 1858]; 'Three Essays on the Reformation,'
1860; ['Miscellaneous Sermons,' 1860]; ['The Curate
of Northborough ' (p. 177), 1861; edited the *North of
England Magazine*' (p. 178), 1862]; 'Directorium Pastorale,' 1864; 'Household Theology,' 1865; 'Ecclesiastical Year-Book,' 1866; edited *' Annotated Book of
Common Prayer,' 1866; ninth edition, 1883 [revised
and enlarged, 1884]; 'Christian View of Christian
History,' 1866; 'The Sacraments and Sacramental
Ordinances,' 1867; 'Key to the Knowledge and Use of
the Book of Common Prayer,' 1867; 'Key to the
Knowledge and Use of the Holy Bible,' 1868 [first
edition, 1865]; 'The Doctrine of the Church of England
as set forth by Authority of Church and State in
the Reformation Period,' 1868; *'Reformation of the
Church of England, its History, Principles, and Results,'
1868-1882, 2 vols.; edited 'Key to the Knowledge of
Church History,' 1869; edited *' A Dictionary of Doc-
trinal and Historical Theology,' by various writers,
1869-70; 'Parties and Principles in the Church of
England,' 1870; 'Union and Disunion,' 1870; 'Plain
Account of the English Bible,' 1870; 'Condition and
Prospects of the Church of England,' 1871; 'Key to
Christian Doctrine and Practice,' 1871 [and 1882];
'Companion to the Old Testament,' 1872; *'A Dic-
tionary of Sects, Heresies, Schools of Thought, and
Church Parties,' 1873 [new edition, 1886]; ['The

Beginning of Miracles,' 1873 ; 'The Poverty that makes Rich,' 1873] ; edited *' The Myrroure of Oure Lady ' for the Early English Text Society, 1873; 'Tewkesbury Abbey and its Associations,' 1874; 'Chapters of Parochial History' (Dursley, Beverston, etc.), 1877; 'Compendious Edition of the Annotated Book of Common Prayer,' 1876 ; 'The Annotated Bible,' 3 vols., 1878-1880; 'Companion to the New Testament,' 1881 ; *'The Book of Church Law,' third edition, 1881 [first edition, 1872]. At the time of his death he was engaged upon a 'Cyclopædia of Religion.'

Of the above works those marked with an * are the most important.

Other Durham alumni there are, happily still living, of whom much might be said. Among these I may mention Dr. THOMAS WILKINSON (University College), titular Bishop 'of Hexham and Newcastle,' and President of Ushaw College, who promotes the higher education of Ushaw students by sending them to the University, where they always reflect credit on their early training; Dr. JOSEPH WAITE (University College), many years Fellow and Tutor, and Master of University College, one of the best of teachers and kindest of friends; JAMES FRANCIS HODGSON, M.A. (Bishop Hatfield's Hall), strenuous in the elucidation of Church architecture; JOHN BULMER, B.D. (University College), late Fellow, and a very clever writer of Latin and Greek prose and verse ; and WALTER CONSITT BOULTER, M.A., most accurate of men, who is at the present time contributing ' Fasti ' and 'Athenæ Dunelmenses' to the *Durham University Journal*, where may be found many biographical notices that cannot be included here. There

are three Durham men at present on the teaching staff
of the University in Durham, six at the College of
Medicine, and two at the College of Science. That
there are not more Durham men on the staff may be
a matter of surprise. There are not wanting those
who are quite capable of doing the work of Professors
and Tutors, and doing it well, but who have not
received the higher appointments. The lists in the
Appendix, however, will show that the minor appointments have often been held by Durham men.

CHAPTER VI

A RETROSPECT

Durham, like other places, has much changed since I
came up in October, 1858, now nearly half a century
ago. But even then the new order of things had set in:
it had become a changed place. The old hierarchy of
twelve wealthy Prebendaries had been abolished, with
reservation of life interests, and of the last twelve Prebendaries of the foundation of Philip and Mary there
survived only four, namely: Dr. Henry Philpotts,
Bishop of Exeter; Dr. Charles Thorp, Archdeacon of
Durham and Warden of the University; Dr. Henry
Jenkyns, Professor of Divinity; and Mr. Henry
Douglas. Besides these four, there were, under the
new Cathedral Act, Mr. John Edwards, Professor of
Greek, Archdeacon Bland, Archdeacon Coxe, and Mr.
H. J. Maltby, son of Bishop Maltby, who were on the
same footing as are the present Canons.

Much had been done to the fabric of the Cathedral
not long before, including a great deal of well-meant
but unfortunate, 'restoration' and wholesale destruction of good seventeenth-century woodwork, but the
services were maintained much as they had been for a

long time previously.* I shall never forget the effect
that the weekday afternoon service had on me the first
time that I attended it.   The quire was dimly lighted
by wax candles on the darkening October afternoon,
and the anthem was that masterpiece of Dr. Blow, ' I
beheld, and lo ! a great multitude.' Those who know
that anthem and Durham Cathedral will understand
what I mean.   I soon became greatly interested in the
Cathedral services, took lessons in singing from Mr.
Matthew Brown, one of the gentlemen of the choir,
and usually attended the daily afternoon service, occupying a stall to which Matthew Brown handed me the
music whenever he could.   At that time there was no
early celebration of the Holy Communion in Durham ;
it was before the appointment of Dykes as Vicar of
St. Oswald's.   Those of us who valued the privilege
regularly remained for the weekly mid-day celebration
in the Cathedral, which once a month was choral, with
Dykes' music.

The Bishop, who had not for a long time resided
much in Durham, had entirely ceased to do so about
twenty-five years before this time, when the Castle
was made over to the University. · The University was a comparatively recent element in Durham
society, and as undergraduates we did not become
acquainted with many of the Durham people ; but I
at once found kind friends in Alan Greenwell, then
chaplain of the gaol, and J. B. Dykes, then Minor

---

* It may here be noted that the traditional custom of bowing
towards the altar on leaving the quire, so much objected to by
Peter Smart but upheld by John Cosin in the seventeenth century,
was observed by the Dean and by all the Major Canons, as well
as by most, if not all, of the Minor Canons, at this time.

Canon and Precentor, to whom I brought introductions.
Then, as time went on, I met with much kindness and
hospitality in the houses of the Warden, of Mr. Chevallier, of Dr. Holden the Headmaster of the Grammar-
School, and of Mr. Barmby the Principal of Hatfield
Hall. Quite at the end of my time I became acquainted
with that gifted lady, Dora Greenwell, and one of my
earliest literary efforts was a review of her poems in one
of the Church papers.

It is often said that our undergraduate days are the
happiest in our lives; certainly, if they were not the
happiest in my life, they were among the happiest, and
they have left in my mind a crowd of pleasant and
refreshing memories, whether of the interest one had in
one's work, the admirable teaching that the University
afforded, the kindness of one's seniors, the intimate
friendships among one's contemporaries, or that *religio
loci* which then came upon me as a sort of revelation.

At that time 'manners' were more attended to than
they are now. For example, I think that the Dons
always capped the Warden, and the undergraduates the
Dons.

Athletics, which now occupy so much of an undergraduate's time and thoughts, can hardly be said to
have existed in the sense in which they now do. They
were, I think, limited to the boating and a little cricket
in the summer. Boating has always been taken up
with great spirit from the very first days of the University; but only four-oared boats can be rowed on the
Wear, because an eight-oar can hardly be got through
Elvet Bridge, and there is not a long enough course
for an eight-oar race on either side of the bridge.

And one of the two available arches is easier to get through than the other, so that before every race there is a toss-up for the 'easy arch.' The Durham Regatta was begun by the University, and remained entirely in its hands for many years. For some years past the management has been shared with the school and the city, and it no longer always takes place, as it did formerly, on the last days of the summer term, but may be either then or at any time during term or in the vacation. There was for many years a pack of beagles, followed on afternoons during the hunting season by Hornby, the Principal of Cosin's, James, a chaplain of University College, and a few Castle men.*

Such as did not care for boating, cricket, or the beagles, were not forced into them in any way, so far as I remember. We walked a good deal on summer afternoons, two or three or more together, and it was commonly remarked then, as now, that about Durham you never need return by the same road that you start. A very common three-mile walk was up the South Road to Farewell Hall, and back by the lane to Potters' Bank and the Prebends' Bridge, or *vice versâ*, and, from its being much frequented by the tutors, this round acquired the name of 'the Tutors' Grind,'† by which it is still known. The men of the present time will be both surprised and amused to be told that we usually wore tall hats to walk in, and, indeed, whenever we were not in cap and gown or in our rooms. A straw hat might now and then be seen in the summer, but

* A note on athletics in recent times will be found in Appendix IX.

† This became in after-years a favourite walk of Professor Evans. See above, p. 139.

never a cap, except a 'square.' There are many representations of cricket-matches and also of boat-races in
which the players, as well as the spectators, are wearing
tall hats, and it is quite possible that in the earliest days
of the University cricket may have been played in tall
hats here. I remember that during my first week, after
the entrance examinations were over, a man who had
been up for a term or two proposed a morning walk to
Finchale Abbey, and set the example of going in cap
and gown. Two or three of us who were quite 'fresh'
supposed he ought to know, and did the same. When
we returned I think someone made a remark, but it did
not seem to be thought anything very extraordinary.
There was none of that dislike to a cap and gown which
has become so marked a feature in modern academical
life, and which finds its expression in avoiding the use
of them as far as possible, or in going about in ragged
gowns and boardless caps, or bare-headed. It is analogous
to the dislike to uniform that prevails in the army and
navy in this country, and among servants. The College
servants usually wore their livery in the public streets and
all day long; now they are rarely seen in it except when
waiting at table. 'Dons' were never seen out of doors
without cap and gown except in the afternoon; they
always wore them in the morning, and when going out
to dinner or to places of public entertainment in the
evening.* The undergraduates observed the same

* In the former half of the nineteenth century the venerable
Dr. Routh, President of Magdalen College, Oxford, wore his gown
all day long whether indoors or out, and at the beginning of the
Long Vacation people used to watch the President step into his
carriage in his unwonted hat and coat to go to his country living

custom as did their seniors, so that they were rarely
seen out of doors, as I mentioned just now, save in
square caps or tall hats. With care we used to make
a hat last for a year, finishing off the old one in Lent
and getting a new one for Easter. I am afraid that
the Lenten headgear sometimes presented a somewhat
forlorn appearance, but there was safety in numbers.
Straw hats with special ribbons were always worn in
the boats even while races were being rowed.

Knickerbocker suits did not come in until long after,
and at first it was not thought good form to wear them
with a cap and gown.

There was in those days very little smoking; what
there was was practised with a decent reserve—never,
indeed, but in private rooms or on country roads, much
less in College quads or while wearing cap and gown. And
it is observable that in the earliest rules of discipline there
is no mention of smoking, because it was never contemplated; so, again, in the old Castle Council-book there
are no reports of smoking peccadilloes dealt with by
the Censors, because none occurred. There were some
riotous and intemperate men occasionally at the Halls
as well as at the Castle; but in the matter of smoking
they seem to have practised that reserve to which I have
referred, and which was then universal among gentlemen.
It is true that one of the 'Verdant Green' pictures
represents the unfortunate youth being 'assisted to his
rooms' by two gentlemen in caps and gowns, one of
whom has a cigar in his mouth, but this occurred in
the course of a private entertainment, and was not
a public exhibition.

There was too much 'ragging' going on at the

Castle,* but I do not remember much at the Hall in my
time, though there was a case in which the attacking
party were held at bay by means of a red-hot poker,
and I have been told that some time before a similar
weapon was used at the Castle with such effect that
the ' ragger ' had to keep his bed for some time, though
the precise nature of his *æger* was effectually concealed
from the knowledge of the authorities.

I have referred to the pleasure I had in personal
friendships formed with men of my own time. The
principal friends of my first year were P. R. S. Bailey,
W. H. L. Rusby, and C. J. Naters, all of the Castle,
and Edward Tapsfield, of Hatfield Hall; then came
Alfred Cooper and E. G. Marshall, of Hatfield, and
J. M. Thompson and Henry Bradley, of Cosin's Hall.
Of these eight, only Rusby, Naters, and Marshall are
now living. Bradley died at Cosin's Hall after a few
days' illness, and was buried in the Cathedral grave-
yard. Archdeacon Bland referred to his early death
in a touching manner in the following Sunday morning's
sermon, which was printed by request.

There were choral societies at the Castle and at
Hatfield, at which part-music was practised for its own
sake. There had long been an annual concert at the
Castle in Michaelmas term, but at Hatfield we had no
regular concerts until many years later, when an annual
concert in Epiphany term was established. A general
University concert is usually given in the ' June week,'
and the unattached students give concerts from time to
time. At the end of my time—in the summer, that is,
of 1861—we practised for a performance of Sterndale

* See above, p. 43.

Bennett's 'May Queen,' in which Dykes, Greatorex, Matthew Brown, and others who were not members of the Hall, took part. The soprano solos and upper parts in the choruses were taken by Mrs. Barmby and other ladies, among whom was Mrs. Ellicott, who had accompanied Dr. Ellicott, now Bishop of Gloucester, when he came to examine for the Licence. There were also three boys, trained by Matthew Brown and brought by him to sing at our choral practices and at the choral service in chapel, which we then had only on 'surplice nights.'

Of our studies I do not know that there is much to be said, beyond what has been said already. There were then, as there always have been, and, it is to be hoped, always will be, some men who had a real pleasure and interest in their work, and who did not calculate how few hours a day they need 'put in,' or regard their work as a vexatious condition attached to their residence and the passing of their 'finals,' but read whenever they could, allowing reasonable but not closely calculated times for recreation. I was five-and-twenty when I came up, having resided for nearly four years at St. Thomas's Hospital, and being then a legally qualified medical practitioner, so that I brought with me some experience of life in its more serious aspects, and was past the age at which we commonly delight in what an early rhymer calls 'layks and plays.' So I never cared for boating, cricket, or the beagles; but, then, I had not acquired a taste for games when a boy, for when I was at school neither the system of compulsory games, nor the idea of play as an important if not the most important part of education, had come

in, so that in this direction my education had been sadly
neglected.

On coming to Durham I soon procured a copy of
Dr. Raine's 'Brief Account of the Cathedral,' then on
sale at Andrews's, and I acquired some interest in the
building beyond my great admiration of its general
effect. But I cared far more for part-singing than for
any pursuit other than that of the prescribed course of
study, to which I added Hebrew as a voluntary subject.
I think I learned to read music fairly well, but I had
neither voice nor ear of more than ordinary quality.
In connexion with music in the University, I may refer
to a notice of Matthew Brown in the *Durham University
Journal* of July 5, 1886, p. 72, and a letter in that of
the October following, p. 87.

Such are some of the reminiscences of my undergraduate days that occur to me now, besides what I
have mentioned in the ' Brief Lives.' Durham was
then, in respect of its principal buildings and scenery,
much the same as it is at present. Many old houses,
however, have disappeared, and new houses or public
buildings have taken their place. The suburbs of
Western Hill and of Neville's Cross scarcely existed,
nor had 'Wharton's Park' been presented and laid out.
The main line of rail did not pass within two or three
miles, and there was always the vexatious ' change at
Leamside.' ' Neptune ' wielded his trident on the top
of the old pant ; Lord Londonderry did not prance in
front of him. The beautiful ' Banks ' that surround
the Cathedral and College were there, and were illumin-
ated by coloured lights and fireworks at the end of the
Regatta. In more recent times they have been made

still more beautiful under the direction of Dr. Tristram, who has inspired the Chapter to pay more attention than ever in the way of planting and 'wild-gardening.' They still retain their sylvan character, and afford the same charming views of wood and water and venerable buildings that they did half a century ago.

CHAPTER VII

THE COLLEGE OF MEDICINE, NEWCASTLE-UPON-TYNE

§ 1. History.

The scientific study of medicine in Newcastle seems to go back for at least 174 years, for in 1730 the Incorporated Company of Barber Surgeons and Wax and Tallow Chandlers, which had existed since 1442, built a new hall, at which bodies were dissected and lectures on anatomy were delivered. In 1786 there was a society of physicians and surgeons, forty-eight in number, called the Philosophical and Medical Society. In 1800 this society was dissolved, and its property was transferred to the Medical Book Club. In 1834 the Medical and Surgical Society was formed, and in 1848 the Newcastle and Gateshead Pathological Society, now the Northumberland and Durham Medical Society. These societies, however, existed solely for the benefit of practitioners already qualified, not for the education of their juniors.

But in 1831 it was proposed by Mr. T. M. Greenhow, an eminent surgeon of Newcastle, to establish an insti-

tution for the promotion of literature and science,
including a school of medicine in all its branches. This
scheme, however, was not carried out. Nevertheless, in
the following year (1832), the year in which the Act
for establishing the University of Durham received the
royal assent, the school of medicine that was destined
to be connected with it was formed and began its work.
Six gentlemen combined, and in 1832-33 and 1833-34
gave two sessions of medical instruction in a large room
over the entrance of Bell's Court, Pilgrim Street.
After these two sessions the lecturers engaged the
Barber Surgeons' Hall.   They enclosed the vacant
space under the hall, and fitted up a lecture-room, dissecting-room, and a room for chemistry and materia
medica.   The designation of 'Barber Surgeons' was
now dropped, and the place was called simply Surgeons'
Hall.   Then, on October 1, 1834, the Newcastle-upon-
Tyne School of Medicine and Surgery was formally
opened, and the real work of medical education was
placed on a permanent basis.   The great difficulty was
the lack of subjects for dissection.   The first body dissected was that of Samuel Morgan, an old cutler and
instrument-maker in the town who had made much
money through the patronage of the medical profession,
and so, in token of gratitude, he sold his body to Mr. J.
Fife for the moderate sum of £10.   In 1840 the school
got possession of the dead body of an old Irishwoman
named Sophia Quinn, but there was an 'Irish row' in
consequence: the police and the Mayor demanded the
body, and carried it off in triumph.   The case went to
the sessions, and cost the school about £100.   In
1850-51 internal dissensions led to a 'schism' among

the members of the staff, and they divided into two
sections in June, 1851. The majority reorganized the
old school under the name of the Newcastle-upon-Tyne
College of Medicine and Surgery ; the minority formed
a new school under the above title, but substituting
' Practical Science' for 'Surgery.'   In 1850-51 the
Barber Surgeons' Hall was demolished to make way
for the North-Eastern Railway Company's buildings at
the Manors, and in August, 1851, the lecturers of the
old school obtained from the Corporation at a nominal
rent the premises at the Manors remaining on the
ground previously held by the Barber Surgeons after
the hall had been pulled down, and the session of
1851-52 was held in some temporary buildings erected
on that site.

   Meanwhile, in the same year (1851) the North-Eastern
Railway Company were building a new Surgeons' Hall
at the top of Victoria Street in compensation for the
old one destroyed at the Manors. The foundation-
stone was laid on February 6, and the Warden and
some chief officers of the University were present.
There had been some informal communications between
the Medical School and the University in the autumn
of the previous year, with a view to a connexion between
the two.   Hence, probably, the presence of the University authorities on this occasion.   As the new
Surgeons' Hall approached completion, the question
arose which of the two rival schools was to occupy it.
The old school declined to compete, and the new hall
became the seat of the new school. Negotiations for
the connexion of the Newcastle School with Durham
were going on in 1851, until they were brought to a

temporary suspension by the disruption in June above referred to. In October they were renewed, but only between the old school and the University, the new school offering vigorous but unavailing opposition. And the negotiations resulted, on the 17th of December following, in the actual connexion of the old school with the University, and its receiving the title of the ' Newcastle-upon-Tyne College of Medicine, in connection with the University of Durham,' which was changed in 1870, when the connexion became closer, to the ' University of Durham College of Medicine, Newcastle-upon-Tyne.' The temporary buildings at the Manors being totally inadequate, Westmorland House, in Orchard Street, Westgate Road, was bought. More buildings were erected in the garden behind the house, and the whole of the premises were fitted up as a medical school complete in all respects, and opened in 1852.

In this same year regulations were framed by the University for students in medicine. By the terms of the connexion between the College and the University students of the former were enabled to proceed, in the first place, to a Licence in Medicine in the University of Durham, by which they became entitled to practise their profession on the same footing with those who had passed the examinations of any other qualifying bodies, and to proceed afterwards, on fulfilling the conditions of residence and examinations required by the University, to the degrees of Bachelor and Doctor in Medicine.

In the same year provision for collegiate residence was thought desirable, and a house for the reception of

13—2

students, No. 1, Leazes Terrace, was opened as ' Neville Hall.' The collegiate life, however, did not attract a sufficient number of medical students to enable this Hall to be successfully carried on, and it was closed in 1856.

In the spring of 1856 the new School of Medicine petitioned the House of Commons against granting to the University the power of sending a representative to the General Medical Council, the formation of which was then under consideration by the Government.

This appears to be the last recorded instance of hostility on the part of the rival establishment, and in 1857 peace was made between the new school and the old, the museums were amalgamated, and the staffs of lecturers combined, to the great advantage of all concerned, and so the six years' ' battle of the schools ' was happily ended.

From the amalgamation of the two Newcastle schools to the present time medical education in that centre has prospered.

In 1856 the old College had instituted a system of practical examination in the dissecting-room, in the laboratory, and at the bedside, in addition to written papers and *viva voce*, and it is said to have been the first of the examining bodies in the United Kingdom to adopt this most complete method. The first medical examination of the University was held in 1857, the examiners being Dr. H. W. Acland, Regius Professor of Physic at Oxford, and John Erichsen, F.R.C.S., Professor of Surgery in the University of London, with two lecturers of the Newcastle College.

The Oxford and London examiners spoke in Convocation in the very highest terms of the fitness of the University of Durham and the Newcastle College to carry out medical education.

On October 3 of the same year the first session of the united schools at Newcastle was opened in the presence of a large assembly.

In the Medical Act of 1858 the University occupies the same position as the other English Universities. It elects a member of the General Medical Council, and its licentiates and graduates are entitled to be registered as qualified practitioners. It was represented by Dr. Dennis Embleton at the first meeting of the Council.

In 1867 a committee of the General Medical Council visited the College, and reported favourably, and at their session held in June, 1869, they placed Durham on the same footing as Oxford and Cambridge in respect to the tests of preliminary education for medical students afforded by the examinations.

In 1870 the College was taken into closer connexion with the University, the chief provisions of the new connexion being that the College should in future be called the Durham University College of Medicine, Newcastle-upon-Tyne; that the Readership in Medicine should be constituted a Professorship; that the College should elect a representative to sit in the Senate of the University; and that residence at the College should be allowed to count as residence in the University towards a degree in Medicine or Surgery.

In 1877 the regulations for the degree of Bachelor in Medicine were altered, so that one year only of the four years' study then required by the General Medical

Council need be spent at the Newcastle College; the other three might be either there or at one or more of the schools recognised by the licensing bodies.

In 1888 the College was again obliged by the requirements of the North-Eastern Railway, but greatly to its own advantage, to shift its quarters. The site of the College being wanted for the extension of the Central Station, a site was obtained in Northumberland Road, and a building was erected at a cost of £30,000. This building will be described in a later section.

In 1890 the General Medical Council resolved that the course of professional study after registration should occupy at least five years, and announced that 1892 would be the last year of entrance on the four years' curriculum, and the commencement of that of five years. As a consequence, in 1891 and 1892 the numbers of students in the College rose to 232 and 252.

In 1902 the General Medical Council issued an official report in which they expressed the opinion that ‘ the Final Examinations for Degrees in Medicine and Surgery of the University of Durham are of a high standard, and that they are “ sufficient.”’

From the first the students have obtained their hospital training at the Royal Infirmary. This institution was founded in 1751, augmented in 1800, and again in 1854. Latterly it has contained 280 beds. The new infirmary now being built will contain many more, and will have all the latest improvements. Thus, it will afford incalculable advantages to the College of Medicine as well as to those for whose benefit it is primarily intended. The foundation-stone was laid, June 30, 1900, by His present Majesty the King, then Prince of Wales, in association

with which ceremony Dr. George Hare Philipson, Pro-
fessor of Medicine in the University, President of the
College of Medicine, and Consulting Physician to the
Royal Infirmary, received the honour of knighthood.

§ 2. BUILDINGS.

The foundation-stone of the present buildings was
laid November 3, 1887. The formal opening of them
took place October 2, 1889. The architects were
Messrs. Dunn, Hansom and Dunn, of Newcastle-upon-
Tyne.

The building is designed in the Elizabethan style.
Externally the materials used are red-pressed bricks
from Normanby, with the architectural features in terra-
cotta, supplied by Messrs. Doulton of Lambeth. The
principal elevation, facing Bath Road, is divided by a
central tower, in which is an oriel window, reaching
almost to the top, supported on corbels, on which are
sculptured the arms used by the College. The entrance
is arranged as a recessed porch of Renaissance design,
enriched with heavy carvings executed in Bath stone
and a highly ornamental screen of carved oak.

Immediately facing is the grand staircase, of solid
oak, very spacious and massive in design. This is
partly hidden by an arrangement of arches, resulting in
a very striking effect; and extending right and left on
either side of the staircase are the corridors leading to
the council-room, lecture theatres, etc.

The dissecting-room, which is on the ground-floor,
but in another wing apart from the main building, has
been pronounced by competent judges to be the most

perfect yet erected.   The roof is of glass, on the 'ridge and furrow' principle, by which means top light is obtained only from the north.   The walls are built of white glazed bricks, which absorb nothing and are easily washed, and which brighten up the room and make the light all that can be desired.   The anatomical theatre immediately adjoins this, and is also perfectly lighted from the top.   On the upper floor of the main building the first thing to be noticed is the large examination-hall, which is a noble apartment, well lighted by long mullioned windows, some of which are in the form of oriels, occupying the whole of the north and west sides.   The ceiling is coved and divided into panels by mouldings and ornaments Elizabethan in character, having the leading names connected with the College inscribed upon them.   A panelled oak dado, fitted up with shelves for books, goes round the room, and a fine effect is produced by the overmantel of the fireplace, which is also of oak, stained dark, on which the arms of many of the members of the College are carved and emblazoned.   This hall opens into the museum, which is lighted both from the top and the sides, and is surrounded by a gallery, affording additional accommodation for the specimen cases.   The heating and ventilation are effected by steam, and work in a most satisfactory manner.

CHAPTER VIII

THE COLLEGE OF SCIENCE

§ 1. History.

(BY PROFESSOR G. A. LEBOUR.)

WHAT was first known as the College of Physical Science was founded at Newcastle-upon-Tyne in 1871. It was the result of many movements, and its real founders were many besides those whose names became publicly associated with its inception. Scientific education had been in the air for some time, and the more far-seeing amongst British manufacturers and professional men connected with mining and engineering had begun to recognise that England was decidedly behindhand as regards early training in science—behindhand very markedly compared with Continental nations, and behindhand even when compared with Scotland. Oxford and Cambridge represented then as now the highest culture in Theology and in Arts. Mathematics were studied in both, and transcendently so in Cambridge, but, as an end in themselves, scarcely as the handmaiden of the other sciences. Professorships of Mechanics, Natural Philosophy, Geology, Mineralogy, and Chemistry, were in existence, but the laboratories in which research in these subjects was conducted were scarcely frequented by undergraduates, and the lectures of the Professors and Readers were, in general, not much better attended. The School of Mines in London, founded in 1851, had provided a sound scientific education—from which, however, mathematics was oddly enough omitted—to a limited number of young men, most of whom, however, intended to devote themselves to mining and metallurgy. Its success as regards the eminence of its teachers and the reputation of its ' Associates ' was great, but the numbers attracted by it were very small. The Owens College at Manchester, the earliest of the true University Colleges in England, after passing through a period of discouraging depression, was entering into the really successful career which has now caused it to develop into a full-blown University. Durham had not been very successful in its early attempts to establish a School of Physical Science in the University city.*

There was thus a want felt in the whole country, but more especially in those parts of it where the local industries depend largely—one might say wholly—on scientific knowledge. So long as foreign competition did not make itself keenly felt, the golden ' rule-of-thumb,' combined with shrewdness and business capacity, had done its work sufficiently well. But things were by this time somewhat different. The processes which had brought fortunes to the manufacturers in such districts as those of the Tyne, Wear, and Tees were sometimes improved upon abroad ; men who were excellent colliery

* See above, pp 54, 56, 134.

' viewers ' at home found themselves occasionally beaten elsewheɪe by foreigners who had studied at Freiberg or at the École des Mines.   Worst of all, money, it was felt, might be lost by the lack of that particular form of education which Germans and others prized, but which Englishmen up till now had cared little for. The more intelligent of the inhabitants of Durham and Northumberland had no desire to become savants ; but if science was necessary for carrying on their mines or their works, they would, perhaps rather reluctantly, learn some themselves, or,-at all events, see that their children should have the opportunity of learning some.   . Amongst mining engineers, the late Mr. E. F. Boyd, of Moor House, Leamside, near Durham, was, in North-eastern England, probably the most ardent advocate of scientific training.   In his position of President of the Institute of Mining and Mechanical Engineers he had the opportunity of urging his views upon his profes-sional confrères, and he made full use of it.   As mining adviser to the Dean and Chapter of Durham he was friendly with most of the Canons of the Cathedral, and more especially had· the ear of the lately-appointed Dean, Dr. Lake, whose liberal bias in education as in other matters led him to look with favour upon Mr. Boyd's aspirations.   As Warden the Dean was able to interest the University in the new ideas, which at first probably did not go much beyond an enlarge-ment of the science side of the University within its own precincts at Durham.

During this time busy neighbouring Newcastle had caught the said new ideas in various ways and in various quarters. Mr. Boyd, oscillating between Durham

and the Coal Trade Buildings in Newcastle, was an
active intermediary, and fanned the growing flame.
The members of the Mining Institute followed his
lead and that of the late Mr. Nicholas Wood will-
ingly, and began to call for a School of Mines for
their apprentices and successors. 'Applied science
strictly' was their cry. But next door to the Coal
Trade Buildings, with their practical engineers, were
housed two other institutions of different aims. First
stood the ancient, nearly centenarian Literary and
Philosophical Society of Newcastle, where a goodly
library of many thousands of volumes had accumulated,
and where courses of lectures on subjects both literary
and scientific had been delivered regularly for many
decades; secondly came the Natural History Society
of Northumberland and Durham, with its precursor, the
Tyneside Field Club, publishing joint Transactions of
recognised value in the world of pure science, and
possessing important collections. Literature and pure
science, represented by such men as Dr. Hodgkin,
Dr. Spence Watson, the late Albany and John Hancock, besides many others well known to the world in
general, claimed to join in the clamour for an education
which in certain directions would be additional to what
the older Universities had hitherto provided. Why
not, they said to their engineering neighbours, add
natural history and all that is covered by that term in
its widest sense, and all literature as well, to the applied
science which you wish to have taught? Why not
make a complete University College at our doors, where
everything (save theology) will be taught? Thus,
many forces were working to one end. Meetings, private

and public, were held ; county magnates and municipal
magnates united with members of Parliament to stir
up the somewhat sluggish desire for higher education
amongst the middle classes; money was subscribed, and
that having been done as fully as for the time being
seemed possible, committees settled down to count
that money and to see what sort of coat could be
cut from their cloth. The money, some £20,000 or
so, was given quickly, but nothing grandiose could be
done with such a sum, supplemented though it was
by a handsome annual grant from the University of
Durham and by the honour of being recognised as, in
some not very definite or formal way, forming part of
that University. The friends of literature generously
conceded that, at starting, the proposed institution had
better profess a few branches of science well, and let
literary subjects follow when more firmly established
and when means were larger. The naturalists likewise
agreed to be content, in the early stages, if geology only
—a necessity for the miners—were at first taught.
The subjects finally selected as those on which to begin
were mathematics, physics, chemistry, and geology, and
men eminent in these were at once advertised for and
appointed as Professors.

The next step was the important one of finding
premises in which the teaching could be carried on.
The sum subscribed rendered adequate building impossible. The numbers of students to be expected at first
would probably not be overwhelmingly large, and
laboratory work was in those days very different in its
requirements both as to space and appliances from what
it has since become. There were vacant rooms in the

Coal Trade Buildings,* and chemistry need merely be
continued where it had for years been taught, in the
adjoining Medical College. It is historically useful to
record exactly the nature and the apportionment of the
space with which the College opened its doors to its
earliest learners in October, 1871.

The Mathematical Professor was provided with a
class-room and adjoining small study on the attic floor
of the Coal Trade Buildings. On the same floor the
Professor of Geology was furnished with exactly similar
accommodation.   On the ground-floor of the old
College of Medicine next door, in Orchard Street, the
small and incredibly many-angled chemical laboratory
of the senior institution, with a cupboard-like, sky-lit
closet for the Professor of Chemistry, was henceforth to
do double duty and serve both Colleges.   Lastly, three
underground basement rooms—cellars, in fact, beneath
the Wood Memorial Hall, and adjoining both the
College of Medicine and the Coal Trade chambers—
were converted into a private sanctum for the Professor
of Physics, which was more of a dark store-room than
anything else; a so-called physical laboratory, which
was little better than a passage; and a fairly large
lecture-room common to both physics and chemistry.
The rooms just enumerated were all that the new
College started with, and these were merely rented from
three different owners, viz., the Coal Trade Chambers
Company, the Wood Memorial Hall Trustees, and the
College of Medicine.   It is true that the Wood
Memorial Hall, in which the library of the North of

* Sometimes called the ' Neville Hall,' as being on the site of an
old mansion of the Nevilles; not to be confounded with ' Neville
Hall,' p. 196.

England Institute of Mining and Mechanical Engineers, then comprising a few hundred volumes only, was at the disposal of the students for study and reading. The Literary and Philosophical Society was next door, and to members of the staff and to those few amongst the students who were members its excellent and, at that time, up-to-date collection of scientific books was a veritable boon. Meetings of Council or House Committee were held in one of the first-floor board-rooms of the Mining Institute, and prize gatherings or other semi-public functions took place in the Wood Memorial Hall itself. This fine hall had, happily, been opened a short time before, and gave a useful, if borrowed, dignity to the small beginnings of the College of Physical Science. In one of the many speeches he delivered in it, Dean Lake said it was a relief to him, when anyone asked him where the new College was, to wave his hand in a vague way so as to include the Hall and its surroundings, and say 'There !' with a flourish.

As time wore on, one large and two small rooms on the attic floor of the Coal Trade Buildings were added for the purposes of natural history, and one of these was even sometimes called 'the Museum.' Then a structure of glass—a greenhouse, in fact—was added to the chemical laboratory in a yard belonging to the Literary and Philosophical Society—a fourth landlord! —and a little triangular area between the Wood Hall basement and the College of Medicine was covered in with a glazed roof and used for practical work in physics. Still later an upstairs room of fair proportions was converted into a physical laboratory. The additions mentioned completed all that the Science College could ever boast of in the way of working accommodation before it entered its new building at Barras Bridge in 1888. For seventeen years, though Chairs and lectureships increased in number, though apparatus and specimens were constantly being added, and though practical work was required in subjects which had formerly been regarded as sufficiently dealt with by means of mere book-work and lectures, no more space was available.

This period, from 1871 to 1888, may be regarded as the first in the history of the College. Much of importance to itself had happened during these years, and first may be considered the gradual closing of the bonds of union between it and the University.

As already hinted at, the connexion between the University and the College of Physical Science at Newcastle was in the beginning slender. Its most important features were the annual grant from the University chest, from which the stipends of the two senior professorships were paid (Mathematics and Physics),* and the fact that the Warden presided at the College meetings and gave its managers the inestimable advantage of enthusiastic and untiring co-operation in all things. Very soon after the foundation a new departure in favour of the College was taken by the University in granting the title (not a degree) of Associate in Science to its students, upon examination by external and home examiners jointly at the end of a two years' course in science. Then after a longer interval a degree was granted, namely, that of Bachelor of Science, which could be claimed by examination by

* More followed later.

Associates of two years' standing.*   This degree, it may
be noted, did not, and does not, give a vote in Convocation, so that the holder, though a graduate of the
University, cannot take part in its legislative functions.
It was not till 1881 that the further degree of Master
of Science was added, which placed the holder (in his
faculty) on the same footing as the Master of Arts.
Later still (in 1888) the set of degrees was completed
by the establishment of a Doctorate in Science.   It is
specially to be remarked that of these degrees in science
none could be, or can be up to the present time,
obtained except by a student who has matriculated at
the Science College and has studied there at least two
years.   In this way the Newcastle Science College
became actually, though not, perhaps, by any formal
instrument, a College of the University of Durham,
since through it alone could the degrees in one of its
faculties be obtained, with the exception, of course, of
honorary and *ad eundem* degrees.

The Faculty of Science of the University was thus
the direct outcome of the establishment of the Newcastle College of Science, just as the Faculty of Medicine
was due to the existence of the Newcastle College of
Medicine.   But whereas the Professors holding Chairs
in the former College are not, as some of the medical
Professors are, either appointed or paid by the University, they have not the title of Professors in the
University.   On the other hand, the Principal of the
College of Science is *ex officio* a member of Senate, and
all the Professors and some of the Lecturers are members
of the body known as the Board of Faculties.

* Afterwards altered to one year.

14

It may be mentioned here that the title of Associate in Science is about to be abolished.

From the beginning the authorities of the Science College consisted of—

First, a very large body (the Governors) representing all local corporations and societies, graduates, subscribers of a certain amount, peers of the six Northern counties, etc., meeting once a year.

Secondly, a Council, smaller in number than the Governors, but, still, rather cumbersomely large, presided over by the Warden, and meeting about once a month. The Professors of the College are consultative members only of this, its higher executive body.

Thirdly, a House Committee, consisting of certain members of the Council and of all the Professors of the College, meeting once a month to transact most of the current affairs and to prepare the business for the Council.

Fourthly, a Finance Committee, consisting of the lay members of the House Committee, with representatives of the professorial body.

Fifthly, the Board of Professors, which deals with much of the academic and internal work of the College, and from whom recommendations are received by the other bodies. This is the only purely academic body, and it is presided over by the Principal, or in his absence by the Vice-Principal.

From these various administrative bodies we may proceed to consider the growth of the College, as shown by comparing the four subjects of 1871 with the twenty or thirty taught in 1904.

Subjects in 1871.

Mathematics (one Professor).
Physics (one Professor).
Chemistry (one Professor).
Geology (one Professor).

Subjects in 1904.

Mathematics (one Professor and two Lecturers).
Physics (one Professor and two Lecturers).
Chemistry (one Professor and five Lecturers and
  Demonstrators).
Metallurgy (one Lecturer and one Demonstrator).
Geology (one Professor and one Lecturer).
Crystallography and Mineralogy (two Lecturers).
Natural History (one Professor and one Lecturer).
Mining and Surveying (one Professor and one Demon-
  strator).
Agriculture and Rural Economy (one Professor and
  five Lecturers and Assistants).
Engineering (one Professor and three Lecturers and
  Demonstrators).
Electrical Engineering (one Lecturer).
Botany (one Professor and one Assistant).
Classics and Ancient History (one Professor).
English Language and Literature (one Professor).
Modern History (one Lecturer).
Modern Languages (one Lecturer and two Assistant-
  Lecturers).
Logic and Political Economy (one Lecturer).
Law (one Lecturer).
Education (one Professor, one Normal Mistress, three
  Assistant-Lecturers and Instructors).

Art (one Headmaster, three Assistant-Masters, one Teacher of Architecture).

In addition thirteen Technical Lecturers on Ambulance Work, Building Construction, Carriage-building, Materia Medica, Plumbing, Sanitary Science, Telegraphy, and Typography.

It must not be supposed that so great an increase was at first very rapid. The extremely limited space at the command of the College for the whole of the first period of its existence (1871-1888) militated against this. In those years natural history was added, next geological surveying—both in 1873; then mining and, for a short time only, modern history. Modern languages were included almost from the very first, and occasional volunteer courses of lectures on special subjects were also given from time to time; but the subjects mentioned are the only subjects dealt with in the old Neville Hall and old College of Medicine rooms.

Before leaving this early period of small things, perhaps, but of much hard and, judging by results, as we are now able to do, in many ways excellent work, a word or two must be said respecting the members of the staff who did the work in those somewhat thankless days, and did it well.

The first Professor of Mathematics, a brilliant teacher, was WILLIAM STEADMAN ALDIS, one of the last whose Nonconformity was a bar to the awards which a brilliant Senior Wrangler and Smith's Prizeman can always claim. Professor Aldis is still living, we are happy to know; he resigned his professorship and the principalship which he then held, and which will be referred to later on, in 1883.

The first Professor of Physics, still, happily, living also, and still figuring in the calendars as Honorary Professor, was ALEXANDER STUART HERSCHEL, the son of Sir John and grandson of Sir William Herschel, the astronomers, and himself renowned for his researches on meteorites and many other points connected with astronomical physics. He resigned his Chair 1886, having been elected a Fellow of the Royal Society in 1884, and received the honorary degree of D.C.L. and the honour of having the new physical laboratories of the College named the Herschel Laboratory after him. He was a profuse donor of apparatus and appliances during his tenure of the Chair.

The first Professor of Chemistry, previously Reader in Chemistry in the University of Durham and Lecturer in the College of Medicine, was the only member of the original staff with local connexions. He was ALGERNON FREIRE MARRECO, partly of Portuguese and partly of English descent, a heaven-born teacher beloved of his students and friends, and the terror of all evil-doers— even, perhaps, venial evil-doers—on whom his biting tongue played like a whip. This quite remarkable man, a master of his subject and of many things beyond it, died, after a painful illness, in 1882, at the early age of forty-seven. His funeral, to which, by his request, no one was invited, was one of the largest and most impressive ever held in Newcastle. An annual medal commemorates his name.

The first holder of the Geological Chair, Professor DAVID PAGE, was a good deal older than his three colleagues when he entered the College. He was already to some extent disabled by locomotor ataxia, and the manner in which for eight years he fought against his infirmities and carried on his teaching in spite of them was truly heroic. He succumbed to his terrible malady in 1879. As the author of the first really popular, and at the same time good, text-books of geology, Dr. Page must always be remembered gratefully. As a lecturer, excellence of method and clearness of statement were his most prominent characteristics. A touching poem entitled ' Disabled ' was read at his burial, and is proof that his literary powers were by no means limited to the writing of text-books.

The other later Professors and Lecturers in the old rooms include the late Dr. HENRY ALLEYNE NICHOLSON, F.R.S., who was the first Professor of Natural History (1873), at that time in the two Colleges of Medicine and Science jointly. He came to Newcastle from Dublin and Toronto, where he held similar Chairs, and in 1874 left to take up the Professorship of Civil and Natural History, as it is quaintly called, at St. Andrews. Subsequently Professor Nicholson was elected to the Chair of Natural History in the University of Aberdeen, in the enjoyment of which he died in 1899. Amongst his numerous publications, his great ' Treatise on Palæontology ' holds the first place.

In the early days the whole of the business portion of the College work, such as account-keeping, minuting the doings of the various meetings, interviewing students and parents, etc., was in the hands of the first Secretary, the late Mr. THEOPHILUS WOOD BINNING, Secretary to the Mining Institute and Coal Trade Association of Northumberland and Durham, whose clerks and offices were generously also placed at the disposal of the

College. As time went on, the more academic portion of this labour was by degrees taken up by Professor Aldis as Senior Professor. It was felt that the duties of the latter had been in this way very considerably augmented, and he was in 1879 given the title of Principal. So long as Professor Aldis remained on the staff this arrangement continued. On his resignation in 1883, a brief interregnum occurred, during which the duties attached to the principalship were carried on by Professor Herschel, who acted until the appointment of the second Principal (like the first, Professor of Mathematics as well). Principal Garnett, when thus appointed, stipulated that the Council of the College should at the earliest opportunity take active steps to remove the College to more suitable buildings, and for the first two or three years of his tenure of office several existing buildings were visited with a view to their adaptability to College purposes. It may be of some interest to mention some of these suggested localities. Singleton House, a mansion facing Northumberland Street, and now converted into a row of shops, was among the most likely places examined. This house belonged to the Corporation of Newcastle, and had for many years been given rent-free to the late distinguished surgeon, Sir John Fife, as an acknowledgment of his public services in quelling some street riots. Then the old College of Medicine buildings, about to be vacated by its owners, were for a time thought of. The large brewery near Bath Lane was also considered. Even Bamburgh Castle and the fortress-like county gaol at Morpeth, now partly dismantled, were surveyed, as well as two or three more or less suitable old mansions in the centre of

Newcastle. The Northumberland county cricket field behind Singleton House, on part of which the present College of Medicine has been erected, was thought a possible site.

Ultimately an excellent piece of ground known as Lax's Gardens was selected and bought at what must now be looked upon as a very cheap rate. The area was considerably larger than the College required, so that it was reasonable to suppose that, when proper roads should be made, some portions of the unoccupied land would be saleable at remunerative prices for building or other purposes. This anticipation was more than realized, and the wisdom of the selection became very evident, as in a few years the value of property in the northern parts of Newcastle speedily increased. As a matter of fact, the new College soon found itself in the fortunate position of possessing its freehold site practically for nothing, and of still having land to dispose of either for possible extensions in the future or further sales.

The architect commissioned to design the new building was the late Mr. Johnson, well known in the North of England for many handsome ecclesiastical and other structures. The finances of the College, crippled by the purchase of the site, did not permit of the entire proposed plan being proceeded with at once. This plan comprised four sides of buildings surrounding a not quite rectangular quadrangle; the west front (towards the Leazes) and the back (facing St. Thomas's Church) were each provided with a fine central tower. In 1887, the first Jubilee year, a great international exhibition had been held in Newcastle on the Town Moor. This, largely owing to the splendid weather that summer, proved highly successful financially, and the surplus received by the promoters was handsomely handed over to the College and devoted to the erection of the eastern façade with its tower. Only the west front now remains to be completed, and, at the time of writing, this is rapidly growing, with its high tower and an elevation more highly decorated than that of any other part of the College. In this portion the plans provide for museum, library, offices, council-rooms, refreshment-rooms, common-rooms, and more especially a great hall, in which large meetings or College functions can be held with comfort.*

Although the building of the Science College is now, therefore, nearly completed, it must not be thought that this is due to any great wealth with which the institution has been endowed. It has a large staff of teachers of all grades, it has now large numbers of students, it is intensely busy, its connexion with the University has become so close that once a year at least Convocation for the granting of degrees is held within its walls; but every student costs a great deal more than he pays, the deficits in each year's balance-sheets are large and show little tendency to decrease, and it is still in debt, though less so than it was. It spent its early money in acquiring land and beginning to build. The second and third wings were built with borrowed money, or almost altogether so. This is not the case with the new front. For this portion of the work a special subscription has been gathered, with the object of honouring the memory of Newcastle's great citizen, the late Lord Armstrong, and when completed the

* A more detailed account of the buildings will be found below.

College will be known in consequence as the Armstrong College, or, as some wish, the Armstrong College of Science.

The difference of opinion as to the new name just adverted to brings us to the consideration of one phase in the development of the College which has not yet been touched upon. This is the introduction of education and literature among the subjects taught there. It is certainly now no longer a College of Science pure and simple. Attendance within its walls will now no longer only qualify an undergraduate for degrees in Science. The degrees in Literature instituted in the University in 1895 can be obtained as well. The 'humanities,' as the Scotch have it, are taught here, and modern literature and history, and a student may obtain the B.Litt. degree from study here, but not the B.A. degree. The Arts degrees are still confined to those who study and keep academical residence at Durham, as is also the case with those in Theology.

Where so much building in detached portions has taken place, some ceremonies of stone-laying and opening have necessarily to be recorded. The first and last of these, namely, the foundation-stone-laying of the first portion and that of the last, are connected with the name of Armstrong. The first stone Sir William Armstrong laid in 1887. The last, that of the Armstrong College eo nomine, was laid by the largest subscriber to the fund, Alderman Gibson, this year (1904). The second stone commemorates the opening of the first wing in 1888 by Her Royal Highness Princess Louise, who was accompanied by her husband, the present Duke of Argyll. The third stone was laid by the Earl of Durham in 1891, and is that of the so-called Exhibition Tower already referred to.

In so new a building belonging to so young an institution not many objects of memorial interest can be expected. There are a few, however. In the top room of the existing tower to the east of the quadrangle are portraits of most of the former members of the staff, including Professor Marreco, Professor Herschel, Professor Page, Professor Merivale, Mr. H. B. Brady, a benefactor to the biological side of the College, and a few others. In the temporary library is a fine bust of Principal Garnett, by Frampton, and a portrait of Dean Lake, in a sense the founder of the College, In the north corridor are memorial tablets to two old students: one to Mr. Oliphant, who was killed whilst helping at the defence of the British Legation at Pekin in 1900 ; the other to Mr. Clarence Lindsay, burnt to death in the diamond-mines at Kimberley, of which he had just been appointed manager, in attempting an heroic rescue.

We may now leave the subject of buildings and return to men. In 1893 Principal Garnett, having seen three-quarters of the new College built, resigned, and went to London as Director of Technical Education and Secretary of the Education Committee of the London County Council. He has quite recently been promoted to be Adviser in Education to that Council. In Newcastle he not only, by the great energy which characterized him in all things, succeeded in making a large and increasing College out of a very small and somewhat stagnant one, but he had set an example in principalship which it was difficult for any successor to follow. The late holder of the post, however, the Rev. Dr. Henry Palin Gurney, found no difficulty in doing so, as the continued increase of staff and students and the completion of the buildings amply testify. In an informal address once given at the College, a speaker ventured to characterize as follows: of the three Principals who have so far steered the fortunes of the College, the first, he said, might be called William the Teacher; the second, William the Builder; and the third, Henry the Arch-Builder.

In the list of subjects given at p. 211, mention has been made of Education as a subject with the Professors, Lecturers, etc. A Normal Department has now for several years been attached to the College, under the direction of Professor Mark Wright, M.A. This is a large Day Training School. The students in this department combine their own professional subjects with the studies of the rest of the College, and compete for the same prizes and degrees. Some excellent results have been obtained by pupils in this department.

§ 2. BUILDINGS.

(BY THE LATE PRINCIPAL GURNEY.)

The Durham College of Science stands in its own grounds of about 6 acres between the Leazes Common and Barras Bridge.

The first portion erected was the north-east wing, the foundation-stone of which was laid by the late Lord

Armstrong on June 15, 1887, and which was opened by
H.R.H. the Princess Louise on November 5, 1888.

The principal entrance to this wing lies at the north-
west extremity, where a door leads to a circular staircase contained within an octagonal tower.   On the
other side the tower opens on to the principal corridor,
which is carried round the greater portion of the quadrangle.   Beneath is a basement corridor, through
which various ventilating shafts, etc., pass.

Next the tower is the Herschel Physical Laboratory,
built without iron girders, and having the tables supported on brick piers independent of the floor.   The
adjoining Armstrong Electrical Laboratory is similarly
furnished, the heating apparatus being also constructed
of copper.   Opposite is the women's common-room.

From the electrical laboratory a door opens into the
preparation-room, beyond which is the physical theatre,
which accommodates 200 students.

A passage from the principal corridor leads to the
private room of the Professor of Chemistry, which communicates with his private laboratory, beyond which
are a room for gas analysis, a laboratory for advanced
students, and the chemical lecture-room.

Opposite the latter a stone staircase leads to the
Johnston Chemical Laboratory, one of the most
spacious and handsome in this country.   More than
100 students can work at one time.   Water, gas, and
vacuum are supplied to the benches, and fume-closets
and facilities for distillation and evaporation are also
provided.   The fireproof combustion-room and the
balance-room lie between the laboratory and the upper
part of the physical theatre.   Crossing this by a gallery,

we enter the apparatus-room, above the preparation-room, and beyond it there is a physical laboratory for advanced students, between which and the private room of the Professor of Physics will be found the physical lecture-room. This is entered from a passage communicating with the circular staircase. Ascending this to the second floor, a passage brings three lecture-rooms intended for the department of agriculture, and three others used for physics, one being a large dark-room for optical experiments.

The foundation-stone of the south-east and south-west wings was laid by the Earl of Durham in December, 1892, and the buildings were opened by the Mayor of Newcastle-on-Tyne in October, 1894.

The south-east wing contains the chemical theatre, above which are five private laboratories, and, on a still higher floor, a large room which has been used as the College library. Adjoining this block is the great gateway in the Royal Jubilee Exhibition Tower, affording access to the quadrangle, and surrounded by four sentinel towers rising to a height of about 96 feet. The tower contains six rooms on three floors, which have served temporarily as laboratories, lecture-rooms, and private rooms for Professors. It forms the Newcastle memorial of the Jubilee of the reign of Her late Majesty Queen Victoria, the cost of its erection having been defrayed out of the surplus of the Royal Jubilee Exhibition held in Newcastle in 1887. The gateway forms a noble carriage-way, the roof being groined in stone, with red brick filling the spandrels.

Between the north-east wing and the gateway is the boiler-house, with three boilers and all their fittings,

feed-pumps, measuring-tanks, etc. Adjoining the gateway on the other side is a metallurgical laboratory,
with wind, muffle, and assay furnaces. Next is the
engine-room, where electricity is produced for lighting
and power. This chamber occupies the south corner
of the building, and adjoining it, forming the ground-
floor of the south-west side of the quadrangle, is the
George Stephenson Engineering Laboratory. This is
123 feet long and 44 feet wide, supplemented throughout the greater part of its length by an annexe 9 feet
wide. It is well equipped with experimental engines,
lathes, testing-machines, etc. Below lies an underground gallery used for photometric work ; above it is
the engineering drawing-room ; adjoining it, filling the
first floor of the south corner, is the engineering lecture-
room, between which and the Jubilee Tower lies the
mineralogical lecture-room.

The whole of the upper floor of the south-west wing
and of that portion of the south-east wing which lies
to the south of the Jubilee Tower is devoted to the
study of the fine arts. One of the shops in the College
annexe is also used for ornamental metal-work.

The section of the building now proceeding forms
the north-western side of the quadrilateral on which
the plan is based, and includes the principal front—
nearly 100 yards in length—towards the Castle Leazes,
the Sir Lowthian Bell Tower, and the Great Hall.

The chief entrance, in the centre of the elevation,
gives access to a spacious vestibule which communicates
with the north and south wings, the principal staircase,
and the large hall which is used for lectures and
examinations.

The entrance-hall is paved with marble blocks, and arranged in two bays, with a semi-domical ceiling carried on coupled columns.

The staircase is largely constructed of Hoptonwood stone, with a massive balustrade supported on a series of columns.

The northern half of the ground-floor is occupied by the Principal's room, which adjoins the Council-room, the students' common-room, which is about 42 feet square, and the junior staff room. In the southern half are the porter's, secretary's, and clerks' offices, and the electrical engineering laboratory and lecture-room. The public lecture and examination hall is accessible from corridors on the north, south, and west sides, and on the east side it is lighted by windows divided by stone mullions and transoms, and filled with glass bearing heraldic shields. The walls are panelled in oak, and the ceiling is relieved with decorative panels.

In the basement are dining-rooms, cloak-rooms, and lavatories. On the first floor is a library, 60 feet by 45 feet, and class-rooms for mathematics, naval architecture, classics and literature, Professors' and preparation rooms.

On the second floors are the botanical laboratories, museum, lecture and preparation rooms, together with class-rooms for languages and history.

The fourth floor is largely given up to laboratories and a museum for zoology.

The floors are of fireproof construction, and the class-rooms generally have dados of wood, while those of the laboratories are of tiles. The whole is warmed by a steam atmospheric apparatus, and the vitiated air extracted from each room by fans driven by electric motors placed in the tower.

The tower is to be 120 feet in height. The lowest stage comprises an open portico of the Ionic order, with a straight pediment protecting a shield bearing the College arms, with cherub supporters and scroll-work. The three stages immediately over the entrance have tiers of columns which support an arched pediment deeply recessed and containing a large shield bearing the University arms, and above it, on either side, the arms of Lord Armstrong and of Sir Lowthian Bell, the donor of the tower. The angles of the tower are enclosed in massive masonry, and form a pedestal, continued through the ground and first floors, on which are placed seated figures of Science and Art. The upper stages of the tower are pierced with windows having broken pediments, and are surmounted by an open carved balustrade. The angles, octagonal on plan, terminate in turrets.

The cost of the third section of the buildings, erected from the designs of Mr. W. H. Knowles, F.S.A., architect, of Newcastle, was £53,000.*

* The hand that wrote this account is now at rest On August 13, 1904, Dr. Gurney met with a fatal accident while on a mountain excursion in the Alps, to the great loss of the University and the deep sorrow of his friends.

APPENDIX I

EXTRACTS FROM THE DURHAM ABBEY ROLLS RELATING TO DURHAM COLLEGE, OXFORD

1278. Burs. (485*): Clerico de Burdon versus Exon. [*sic;* read 'Oxon.'] 5 marc.

Burs. (486): Garcioni eunti apud Exon. [*sic*] pro liberatura fratrum, 6*s.* 8*d.*

1292. Burs. (492): In liberatura facta fratribus Oxon., 24*li.* 3*s.* 11*d.*

1299 Burs (497): Cuidam scolari, 7*s.*

Soc. Oxon per man M'ri Rab . . . [?] 66*s.* 8*d.*

Burs. (499) : Cuidam portanti pecuniam sociis Oxon , 12*d.*

c. 1310. Burs. (510): D'no Gilberto de Elwyk versus Oxon., 16*li.*

1310-11. Burs. (508): Sociis commorantibus apud Oxon., 13*li.* 6*s.* 8*d.*

Henr. de Castro versus Oxon. per duas vices eundo et redeundo, 30*s.*

Gilb. de Ellewik versus Oxon., 10*s.*

Ricardo Crakale versus Oxon. Anno, etc., x° et xj°, 4*li.*

Consanguineis d'ni Ep'i versus Oxon., 26*s.* 8*d.*

1313-14. Burs. (512): Scolaribus Oxon. commorantibus, 16*li.* 13*s.* 4*d*

Cuidam versus Oxon. querenti pannos Emerici de Linne Regis. . . .

c. 1320. Burs. (514): D'no Uthredo versus Oxon., 40*s.*

c. 1330 Burs. (519): D'no Suppriori versus Oxon. pro incepcione d'ni T. de Lunde, 40*s.*

D'no T. de Lunde pro incepcione sua, 6*li.* 13*s.* 4*d.*

Burs. (518): Sociis studentibus Oxoniis in pensione de Aluerton, 10*li.*

---

* The references in parentheses are to the pages of the ' Durham Account Rolls ' published by the Surtees Society.

226

1333-34. Burs. (525): Cuidam garcioni venienti de Oxon. cum literis d'no R. de Graystan Ep'o, 2s.

Burs. (522): In exp. 2 sociorum Oxon. student., 13*li.* 6s. 8*d.*

c. 1335. Burs. (530): Studentibus apud Oxon. in pens. de Aluerton, 20*li.*

1335-36 Burs. (527): Scolaribus Oxon. commorantibus, 20*li.*

c. 1341. Burs. (542): In solucione facta d'no Ric'o Harpyn versus Oxon et pro mora sua ibidem causa convalescenciæ recuperandæ, 40s.

Sociis studentibus ibidem in pensione de Aluerton, 10*li.*

Burs (541): In exp. garcionis Hostillarii versus Oxon. cum 1 equo ad querendum D'nm W. de Hawtwisill, 3s.

1342-43. Camer (170): Fratribus commorantibus Oxon. et Staunford, et fratribus de claustro visitantibus amicos, 69s. 2½*d.*

1347. Celer. (42): Sociis commorantibus apud Oxon ex præcepto Supprioris et Conventus, 5s.

1347-48. Hostill. (119, here in full from Roll): Sociis nostris studentibus Oxon. ad fest. S'ci Michaelis et S'ci Cuthberti in Marcio, 13s. 4*d*   Et sociis nostris studentibus Stanford, 6s.

1348 Hostill (119, here from Roll): Sociis nostris studentibus Oxon , 13s 4*d.* Cognato d'ni Joh'is Baty eunti versus Staunford, 4*d*

1348-49. Burs. (549): D'no Uthredo cum uno socio student. Oxon., 13*li.* 10s.

c. 1350. Sacr. (381). Clericis Oxon. studentibus, 20s.

Celer. (44): In sociis commorantibus Oxon. ex præcep. Supprioris et Conventus, 5s.

1350-51 Burs. (552): D'no Uthredo et socio suo studentibus Oxon , 6*li* 6s. 8*d.*

1351-52. Hostill. (120, here from Roll): Sociis existentibus Oxon. per tempus compoti (the year), 10s.

Elem (207): Scolaribus Oxon. et Staunford studentibus [included with other expenses].

1352-53 Elem. (207): Scolaribus Oxon. ['et Staunford' erased] studentibus, per præceptum Prioris, 20s.

Burs. (553): D'no Uthredo et sociis suis Oxon. studentibus, 4*li.* 16s.

Duobus monachis incipientibus in theologia apud Oxon. ex dono d'ni Prioris, 40s.

1354-55. Elem. (208): In pensione studentium Oxon., 20s. Et in curialitate facta sociis nostris de consanguineis monachorum ibidem studentibus, 33s. 8d.

1355-56. Hostill. (121, here from Roll): Sociis Oxon. studentibus per tempus compoti (the year), 13s 4d. Item d'no Petro de Dunelm. eunti apud Staunford, 3s. 4d.

1356-57. Sacr. (383). Clericis studentibus Oxon., 20s.

Hostill. (124, here from Roll): Sociis Oxon., studentibus per tempus compoti (the year), 40s. Item eisdem ex dono d'ni Prioris, 20s. Item Petro de Stapilton versus Oxon., 2s.

1357-58 Hostill (124, here from Roll): Sociis Oxon. studentibus per tempus compoti ex precepto d'ni Prioris, xls. Item eisdem ex curialitate Hostillarii, 16s. 8d. Item d'no Uthredo ex precepto d'ni Prioris, 13s. 4d. Item consanguineo d'ni Hugonis de Falowden versus Oxon., 3s. 4d.

Burs. (559) [dated '*c.* 1357?']: D'no Uthredo et sociis suis Oxon. studentibus, 10*li*. Et eidem d'no Uthredo incipienti in Theologia apud Oxon., 13*li*. 6s. 8d Et in expens unius garcionis Bursarii cum uno equo versus Oxon. pro monachis reducendis, 3s. 4d. Et Johanni Tonis [?] et Willelmo Lascels deferentibus literas Abbatibus de Ebor., Selby, et Whytby, pro negociis tangentibus incepcionem d'ni Uthredi in Theologia, pro expensis suis diversis vicibus, 3s. 4d.

1359-60. Burs. (561) [dated '*c.* 1358']: D'no Uthredo et sociis suis Oxon studentibus, 13*li*. 6s. 8d. Et eisdem pro expensis suis a retro existentibus de anno elapso, 66s. 8d. Item eidem d'no Uthredo pro expensis factis ad incepcionem suam in Theologia ultra summam sibi solutam in anno præcedenti, 14*lt*. Et in expensis ij garcionum cum ij equis versus Oxon. pro d'no Uthredo et sociis suis reducendis, 7s. 4d

Sacr. (384): D'no Uthredo versus Oxon., 20s.

c. 1360. Burs (563): D'no Uthredo et sociis suis Oxon. studentibus, 13*lt*. 6s. 8d. Item eidem d'no Uthredo per manus Henr. de Weland, Rob'ti de Walworth, terrarii, et Joh'is de Tikhill, 15*li*. 13s. 4d. Item eidem d'no Uthredo per manus d'ni Rob'i de Rokes socii Aulæ de Marton [Merton], 6*li*. 16s. 8d. Item d'no Uthredo, versus capitulum generale pro expensis suis, 5s. 8d.

1360-61. Burs. (562): Cuidam monacho de Abyngton incipienti in Theologia apud Oxon., 40s.

Sacr. (385): Studentibus Oxon., 20s.

1360-70? Camer (176, here from Roll): Student., Oxon., 10s.?

Burs. (566): In exp. D'ni Uthredi et socii sui versus Alnewyk ad sepulturam d'næ de Percy, 7s. 3½d.

1362-63. Sacr. (385): Succentoribus, Magistro Infirmariæ, studentibus Oxon., et Episcopo Elimosinario, 26s.

Camer. (178, here from Roll)· Studentibus Oxon. de debito eiusdem Ade (de Derlington, Camerarii), 60s. Item d'no Vthredo de debit. eiusdem licet non contineatar in debitar. dicti d'ni Ade, 10s.

1363-64. Burs. (567): D'no Utredo pro expensis suis versus capitulum generale, 73s. 4d. Sociis scolaribus Oxon. studentibus, 13li. 6s. 8d.

1364-65. Burs. (568): In exp. d'ni Uthredi et Burs. apud Aluerton ad loquend. cum d'no ep'o, 5s. 10d.

1365-66. Burs. (568): D'no Uthredo et sociis suis Oxon. studentibus, 13li. 6s. 8d.

1366-68. Burs. (569): D'no Uthredo [ut supra] 13li 6s. 8d., eidem pro. exp. de Oxon. usque Dunelm., 50s

1367-68 Host. (128): Consanguineis monachorum et aliis scolaribus versus Oxon., 14s. 8d D'no Uthredo versus Oxon. ex curialitate, 13s. 4d

Elem. (208): In pensione studentium Oxon., 20s.

1370-71. Burs. (576): In exp. d'ni Uthredi Supprioris existentis apud Ebor. per 6 dies in convocacione cleri, et eciam eundo et redeundo, 43s. 3d.

In exp. d'ni Uthredi supprioris apud Aukland et Stokton, 2s 9½d.

1372-73 Elem (210): In pensione studentium Oxon., 20s.; in curialitate facta eisdem et sociis euntibus et comorantibus ad cellas per tempus compoti, 21s. 8d.

1373-74. Burs. (579): In exp. Adæ Jolilok a Dunelm. usque Oxon. et redeund, 22s

In solucione facta d'no Joh'i de Acley et sociis suis Oxon. studentibus, 13li. 6s. 8d.

Cuidam nuncio d'ni Regis portanti unam literam d'no Priori pro d'no Uthredo, 3s. 4d.

1374-75. Burs. (581): In exp. Stephani del Kiln versus Oxon. cum literis ad citand. confratres ad eleccionem, 8s. 1d. [sc. Prioris, Rob. Beryngton de Walworth]

1375-76. Burs. (582): In solucione facta d'no Joh'i de Acley et
sociis suis Oxon. studentibus pro secundo termino
anni 74^{ti}, 6li. 13s. 4d ; do., pro anno 75$_{to}$, 13li. 6s 8d.
Item d'no Joh'i Gouer Oxon. studenti, ex dono d'ni
Prioris, 40s.   Item in curialitate facta d'no Joh'i de
Acley et sociis suis, et aliis ad extra missis per
tempus compoti, 13s. 4d.

1377-78. Camer. (181): Fratribus nostris Oxon. studentibus, 20s.
[as frequently among ' Pensiones ']

1378-79 Feretr (422) : In pensione scolarium Oxon. studentium, 20s.

1379-80. Burs. (588): In solucione facta d'no Joh'i de Acley, suppriori, in subsidium expensarum suarum circa reparacionem domorum et murorum loci in quo fratres
nostri inhabitant Oxon., ex præcepto Prioris, 8li.

Burs. (589): In exp. d'ni Uthredi et sociorum suorum in
Houdenschire visitand., 44s. 1½d In exp. d'ni Joh'is
de Beryngton a festo S'ci Hillarionis Abbatis, de
Dunelm. usque London et Northampton pro centum
libr. per Regem debitis adquirend., ac eciam pro
collegio Oxon. per Ep'm fundando, et aliis negociis
ecclesiam tangentibus expediendis, usque in vigiliam
Nat. D'ni, per 9 septimanas, 9li. 18s. 2d.   In uno
pipe de Malvesin dat. d'no Archiep'o Cantuar. Can-
cellario d'ni Regis pro amicicia sua nobis adquiranda
in conformacione [sic] cartarum nostrarum, 7li. 6s. 8d.
In duobus paribus caligarum dat butelariis suis, 5s.
D'no Thomæ de Newneham uni de duodecim Can-
cellariis Regis pro examinacione cartarum nostrarum,
40s.   In donis datis diversis ministris et clericis
Theserarii, 6s. 8d.

[Other law and travelling expenses follow, relating
partly, perhaps, to the above business.]

Feretr. (422): Studentibus Oxon., 20s.

1380-81 Burs. (591): D'no Rob'to de Blaclaw et sociis suis Oxon.
studentibus, 13li. 6s. 8d.

In exp. Magistri Uthredi versus Lond. ad tractand. cum
Ep'o et consilio suo pro Collegio Oxon., 40s.

Feretr (423): Scolaribus Oxon. pro pensione, 20s.

1381-82. Burs. (592): In solucione facta Rob'to Blaclaw et sociis
suis studentibus apud Oxon., 10li., et non plus, quia
aliqui eorum fuerunt domi causa pestilenciæ.

In exp. Magistri Uthredi versus Ebor. et Kawod pro
negociis monasterii, 39s. 3½d.

1382-83. Sacr. (390): Uni novicio celebranti primam missam apud Oxon., 6s. 8d.

1383-84. Feretr (425): In pensione soluta scolaribus Oxon., 20s.

Burs. (593): Scolaribus Oxon., 13li. 6s 8d.

Willelmo Palfreypage versus Oxon. cum equo Magistri Uthredi, 6s. 8d.

In exp. Magistri Uthredi pro visitacione facta in Howdenschire, 46s. 10d.

1385-86 Feretr. (441): Scolaribus Oxon., 20s.

1386-87. Feretr. (442): Scolaribus Oxon. ex dono, 3s. 4d

Clerico feretri usque Oxon., 2s.; uni pauperi scolari, 12d.

1388-89 Burs. (596): D'no Uthredo, Priori de Finchall, pro excambio de Donwelmedow et Aldestonfeld, 20s.

1389-90 Feretr. (444): Dona minuta Sociis Oxon., 3s 4d.

1397-98 Feretr. (446): Scolaribus Oxon., 20s. [also in 1398-99].

1399-
1400   { Burs (602): Scolaribus Oxon. ad festum S'ci Michaelis, 3s. 4d

Feretr. (448): Scolaribus Oxon., 20s.

1402-03. Feretr. (455): Scolaribus Oxon. (20s)

Elem (220) Pro pensione scolarium Oxon., 20s

Joh'i Fyssheburn Oxon. commoranti, 3s. 4d.

Camer. (182): In solucione iiij^or sociis Oxon. studentibus, pro eorum femoralibus, 16s

1406-07. Elem. (222): In donacione ad ædificacionem capellæ in Collegio Oxon., 8li.

1407-08. Camer. (183): Pro pensione Oxon. pro concordia, 30s. 8d

Elem. (223): Ad ædificacionem capellæ Oxon., 22li. [also in 1408, 118s. 4d].

1409-10. Sacr. (402): Scolaribus Oxon., 20s.

1409-10. Min. Carb. (708): In exp. servientis Elemosinarii versus Oxon., ex præcepto dicti Prioris, 5s

Min Carb. (709): Joh. Burneby versus Oxon., 3s. 4d.

1410-13 Sacr. (403): Fratribus versus Oxon. et cellas, 15s.

1414-15. Sacr. (405): D'no Tho. Hesilrig celebranti primam missam, 6s 8d D'nis Thomæ Hesilrig et Willelmo Lasyngby versus Oxon., 6s. 8d.

1416-17. Burs. (613): In 4 uln. de blewmedled empt pro clerico Prioris Oxon , 7s. 9½d.

Comm. (287) · D'no Will'o Ebchester versus Oxon., 20d.

Terr. (301): Roberto Horneby versus Oxon , 3s. 4d.

Hostill. (140): In solucione facta Rob'to Horneby versus Oxon. et Rob'to Clifford versus Stanford, 6s. 8d.

1419-20 Elem. (228) : De quibus [corn and hay bought] deliberat.
sunt custodi Collegii Oxon. 2 quart. et di. avenæ et 1
fothir et di. feni pr., 10s.

1420-21 Feretr. (463) : D'nis Will'o Ebchest., 20d., et Rob'to
Moreby ex curialitate, 20d. ; d'nis Thomæ Ponte-
fract, 20d., et Thomæ Hexham ex cur., 20d ; et
eisdem pro expensis versus Oxon., 3s. ; Will'o
Ebchest. in principio bacallar in Theologia, 6s. 8d.

Elem. (228) : Delib fuerunt Will'o Ebchester custodi collegii Oxon., 2 qr et 1 fother di. feni.

1422-23. Feretr. (464) : Quatuor noviciis versus Oxon. pro cariag.,
6s. 8d , et ex curialitate, 6s 8d.

1425-26. Feretr. (465) : D'nis Joh'l Byrtley et Thomæ Lewyn versus
Oxon. pro expens., 3s. 4d.

1427-28 Min. Carb. (709) . Joh. Burneby versus Oxon., 3s. 4d

1431-32. Elem. (231) : D'no Ric. Barton tunc gardiano collegii
nostri in Oxon. in precio unius plaustrat. feni, 3s. 4d.

1437-38 Elem. (233) : Thomæ Brogham, Will'o Fysshborn, et
Will'o Hesleden ex curialitate versus Oxon., cuili-
bet 20d.

Feretr. (469) : Thomæ Brogham, W. Fysshborn, et Will'o
Hesilden versus Oxon. ex consuetudine pro vectura, 5s.

1440-41. Burs. (627) : In exp. Magistri Will'i Ebchestre et Joh'is
Gatesheued, Bursarii, versus Oxonias et generale
capitulum, 8li. 19s 11d.

1441-42. Camer. (184) : Ricardo Sherburn et Thomæ Cave pro
vectura sua versus Oxon., 10s.

1446-47. Burs. (631) : Joh'i Wynyarde versus Stamford et Oxon. ad
citand. fratres ad comparend. in eleccione Prioris
[sc. Will. de Ebchester], 7s 8d.

[Citations for the same to Coldingham, Holy Island,
and Farne.]

Feretr. (473) : Will'mo Seton et Ric'o Billingham pro
expensis versus Oxon. per ordinationem in Marti-
logio scriptam, 3s. 4d. Item eisdem ex curialitate,
3s 4d.

1456-57. Feretr. (476) : Pro vectura d'nor. Rob. Ebchester et Rob.
Wardall versus Oxon , 3s. 4d. ; et eisdem ex curialitate, 3s. 4d.

Camer. (192) : Pro uno equo conducto de Joh. Coken
versus Oxon. et ibidem pro nimio labore mortuo,
5s. 7d.

1457-58 Hostill. (151) : In 3 dd. et di. cirothecarum empt. apud Oxon. et dat. servientibus, 8s. 7d.

1459-60. Feretr. (478) : Duobus noviciis vz Will'o Yowdall et Will'o Lawe pro vectura sua versus Oxon., 3s. 4d. ; et eisdem ex curialitate, 3s. 4d.

1470-71 Hostill. (155) · In donis datis d'no Rob'to Ebchestr Custodi Collegii Oxon ad suam incepcionem, 13s. 4d.

1478-79 Elem. (247) : In regardis datis Gardiano collegii Dunelm et d'no Thomæ Rowland, 10s.

1485-86. Elem. (249) : Solvit d'nis Thomæ Swalwell et Henrico Thew ex curialitate versus Oxoniam, 9s 11d.

Hostill. (157) : D'nis Thomæ Swalwell et Henrico Thewe versus Oxon. ex curialitate, 10s.

1488-89 Feretr. (480) : Dompni Tho Dukett et Rob Todde pro vectura sua versus Oxon., 3s. 4d. ; eisdem ex curialitate, 3s 4d.

1493-94. Burs. (652) : Sol. pro vectura d'ni Will'i Cathorne versus Oxon., 6s. 8d

1498-99. Burs. (655) : Sol. in expens. d'ni Will'i Cathorne Custodi [sic] collegii in Oxon., et d'ni Thomæ Swalwell, cancellarii Dunelm , cum aliis, equitantibus in visitacione usque Whytby, Ebor., Selby, et Monkburton, 40s. 9d., ut patet per papirum Ric'i Wren. Et in expens. d'ni Will'i Caythorn custodi [sic] Collegii in Oxon. cum aliis equitantibus usque Northampton ad generale capitulum ordinis S'ci Benedicti tentum ibidem hoc anno, 4li. Et in Expensis Rob'ti Selby equitantis usque Whytby, Ebor., Selby, Monkburton, ad citand prædictas fratres, 8s.

Et sol. pro factura d'ni Will'i Caythorne Doctorem Theologiæ, 13li. 6s. 8d.

1500-01. Burs. (656) : Pro vectura . . . d'nor. Ric'i Caly et Henrici Thewe versus Oxoniam, 13s 4d.

1501-02. Burs. (657) : In expens. d'ni Thomæ Swalwell et d'ni Ric'i Caly bis equitancium ad Regem pro eleccione d'ni Ep'i [sc. Will. Sever] Et sol. in exp. d'nor. Will'i Bukeley et Hugonis Whiethede equitancium versus Oxon., 10s

Feretr. (480) : Henrico Thew equitanti versus Oxon,, 2s. 4d.

1516-17 Commun. (292) : Sol. d'no Wylli'o Wylome, d'no Wyll'mo Hulome, et d'no Stephano Merlay versus Oxon., 10s.

1525-26 Feretr. (482) : Tribus confratribus equitantibus Oxoniæ, 5s

APPENDIX II

REV. C. THORP'S SCHEME OF A NEW UNIVERSITY

[One leaf, printed on both sides, 8 inches by 10 inches   F. Humble, Printer, Durham.]

THE UNIVERSITY OF DURHAM.

DURHAM COLLEGE.

The Government to be vested in the DEAN AND CHAPTER, the BISHOP being VISITOR.

A Chief Officer of the College or University to be appointed, with the title of WARDEN, to whom will be committed the *ordinary* discipline.

PROFESSORS —1. Divinity and Ecclesiastical History   2 Greek and Classical Literature   3. Mathematics and Natural Philosophy

READERS.—1. Law.   2. Medicine.   3. History, Ancient and Modern

To these may be added Readers in other Branches of Literature or Science, as opportunities offer or circumstances require.

TEACHERS of Modern Languages, especially French and German.

TUTORS.—1. Senior Tutor and Censor.   2. Junior Tutor and Censor.

Each to superintend the Studies of their respective Pupils, and to have the care of their general conduct.

STUDENTS.

1. FOUNDATION STUDENTS, having Lodgings and a Table provided for them, free of expence.

2. ORDINARY STUDENTS, maintained at their own cost, but

234

subject in all respects to the College Rules of Discipline, and to have every Academical Privilege in common with the other Students.

3. OCCASIONAL STUDENTS, to be admitted, under certain restrictions, to attend one or more Courses of Public Lectures, but without other Academical Privileges

4. DIVINITY STUDENTS, specially so called, who, though not actual Members of the College, may be admitted after due examination and inquiry, and subject to such conditions and regulations as the Chapter may hereafter prescribe, to attend, for a specified time, the Lectures of the Divinity Professor, and to pursue their Theological Studies under his direction, for the express purpose of qualifying themselves for Holy Orders

The course of study required to complete the Education of a Member of the College will extend to FOUR YEARS.

THE ACADEMICAL YEAR to commence in *October* and end in *June*, being divided into *Three Terms.*

Terminal and Annual EXAMINATIONS to be made in the presence of the Chapter, and the students classed according to their respective proficiency.

PRIZES to be instituted for the reward of special merit at the close of each Annual Examination, and for such particular Exercises as may be deemed worthy of public distinction.

The foregoing outline, subject to revision as to its specific statements, may suffice to explain the nature and design of the proposed Institution; for which the Dean and Chapter, with the aid and co-operation of the Bishop, are providing the requisite means of carrying it into effect.

It is intended that the College, or University, be opened in October, 1832.

Further information may be obtained from THE VENᴮᴸᴱ ARCHDEACON THORP, COLLEGE, DURHAM, who is appointed, provisionally, to the Office of WARDEN.

DURHAM,
December 9, 1831.

APPENDIX III

A PAPER ISSUED BY ARCHDEACON THORP
JULY 20, 1833*

July 20, 1833

PRELIMINARY ARRANGEMENTS.

STUDENTS WILL BE ADMITTED MICHAELMAS TERM, 1833.

The Academical Course will comprise 12 Terms, 3 Terms in each year (Michaelmas, Epiphany, and Easter), of about two Months each

The Age of Admission of Students for the Academical Course is from 15 to 21 Years.

Occasional Students of any Age will be admitted to attend particular Courses.

Students in Divinity, beyond the age of 21, will be admitted to read under the Divinity Professor, if found to be qualified by previous Attainment.

OFFICERS OF THE UNIVERSITY.

WARDEN:

The Venerable ARCHDEACON THORP, B.D., late Fellow and Tutor of University College, Oxford.

---

* Printed on the blank leaf following No. II.

PROFESSORS :

Divinity and Ecclesiastical History. . . .
Greek and Classical Literature. . . .
MATHEMATICS.—The Rev. JOHN CARR, M A., late Fellow of
Trinity College, Cambridge.
SENIOR TUTOR.—Rev. WILLIAM * PEILE, M.A., Trinity College,
Cambridge.
Junior Tutor. . . .

READERS, ALREADY APPOINTED:

Law.—WILLIAM GRAY, ESQ , M A., Christ Church, Oxford.
Medicine —WILLIAM COOKE, ESQ., M D.
History —THOMAS GREENWOOD, ESQ , M A., St. John's College,
Cambridge.
Moral Philosophy.—REV. JAMES MILLER, D.D., of St. Andrews.
Natural Philosophy.—CHARLES† WHITLEY, ESQ., M.A., Fellow of
St. John's College, Cambridge.
Bursarius.—REV. LUKE RIPLEY, M.A., late Student of St. John's
College, Cambridge.
Lecturer in Chemistry and Mineralogy.—J. F. W JOHNSTONE, ESQ ,
A.M., F.R.S.E.
Lecturer in Modern Languages —JAMES HAMILTON, ESQ.

The Students of the Academical Course and in Divinity are
required to attend for Examination in the Chapter Room, Durham,
on the 28th October next, at 10 o'clock in the morning.
All Letters relating to the University to be addressed to the
Warden, College, Durham.

THE CHARGES.

	£	s	d.
Admission of Students	2	o	o
Caution of Ordinary and Divinity Students (to be returned)	10	o	o
Caution of Occasional Students (to be returned)	5	o	o
Tuition each Term, to be paid terminally in advance	3	o	o
University Chest, Students (annually) ...	1	o	o
———— ———— Members on the Boards, not Students (annually)	1	o	o

* Read THOMAS WILLIAMSON.
† Read CHARLES THOMAS.

The following Gentlemen have been nominated to FOUNDATION STUDENTSHIPS: Messrs Cundill, Treacy, Pratt, Stoker, St Claire* Raymond, Hicks,† Dunn, Erskine, Wright, Marshall, Fairles, Thompson, Errington, Skinner, Wyatt, Watson, and Yarker.

CHARLES THORP, *Warden.*

Payments on account of the University may be made to W. C. CHAYTOR, ESQ , College, Durham, the Treasurer, or to his Account at Messrs. Coutts and Co., Strand, London ; Sir M. W. Ridley and Co., Bankers, Newcastle; or at any of the Durham Banks.

---

* Read St. Clere.   † Read Hick.

APPENDIX IV

'FIRST CALENDAR' (NOW SO CALLED) OF THE UNIVERSITY

[A tiny pamphlet of 20 pages, in 24mo., size about 4¾ inches by 3¼ inches.]

UNIVERSITY

OF

DURHAM.

———◆◇◆———

FOUNDED BY ACT OF CHAPTER

WITH THE

CONSENT OF THE BISHOP OF DURHAM,

28 SEPTEMBER, 1831.

————◆————

CONSTITUTED A UNIVERSITY BY ACT OF PARLIAMENT,
2nd and 3rd William IV., Sess. 1831-2.

————◆————

𝔇urham :
PRINTED BY FRANCIS HUMBLE, QUEEN STREET.

————

1833.

OF

DURHAM.

. Visitor:

THE LORD BISHOP OF DURHAM,

Right Rev. William van Mildert, D.D.

Gobernours:

THE DEAN AND CHAPTER OF

DURHAM.

4]   Dean:

The Right Rev. J. B. Jenkinson, D.D.,
    Lord Bishop of St. David's.

Prebendaries:

The Rev. D. Durell, M.A.
The Right Rev. the Lord Bishop of Bristol.
The Rev. R. Prosser, D.D.
The Right Rev. the Lord Bishop of Chester.
The Rev. J. S. Ogle, M.A.
The Rev. T. Gisborne, M.A.
The Rev. G. Townsend, M.A.
The Rev. W. S. Gilly, D.D.
The Rev. G. V. Wellesley, D.D.
The Ven. C. Thorp, B.D.
The Right Rev. the Lord Bishop of Exeter.
The Rev. S. Smith, D.D.

p. 5]

OFFICERS

OF

THE UNIVERSITY.

𝔚𝔞𝔯𝔡𝔢𝔫 :

The Venerable Charles Thorp, B.D., Archdeacon of Durham, late Fellow and Tutor of University College, Oxford.

𝔓𝔯𝔬𝔣𝔢𝔰𝔰𝔬𝔯𝔰 :

Divinity and Ecclesiastical History.—The Rev. H. J. Rose, B.D., late Fellow of Trin. College, Cambridge.

Greek and Classical Literature.—The Rev. H. Jenkyns, M.A., Fellow of Oriel College, Oxford.

Mathematics.—The Rev. J. Carr, M.A., late Fellow of Trin. College, Cambridge.

p 6]   #### 𝔖𝔢𝔫𝔦𝔬𝔯 𝔉𝔢𝔩𝔩𝔬𝔴𝔰 :

Rev. J. Carr, M A., etc., etc.
Rev. T. W. Peile, M.A late Fellow of Trin. College, Cambridge
Wm. Palmer, Esq., M.A., Fellow of Magdalen College, Oxford

𝔍𝔲𝔫𝔦𝔬𝔯 𝔉𝔢𝔩𝔩𝔬𝔴𝔰 :

William Gray, Esq., M.A., Christ Church, Oxford.
Wm. Cooke, Esq., M D.
Thos. Greenwood, Esq., M.A., St. John's College, Cambridge.
Rev. James Miller, D.D., of St. Andrew's.
Charles* Whitley, Esq., M.A., Fellow of St. John's College, Cambridge.
Rev. Luke Ripley, M.A., late Scholar of St. John's College, Cambridge.

Senior Tutor and Censor.—Rev. T. W. Peile, M.A., etc., etc.
Junior Tutor and Censor.—Wm. Palmer, Esq., M.A., etc., etc.

---

* Read ' Charles Thomas.'

16

p. 7] 𝕽eaders :

Law.—William Gray, Esq., M.A., etc., etc.
Medicine.—William Cooke, Esq., M.D., etc., etc.
History.—Thos. Greenwood, Esq., M.A., etc., etc.
Moral Philosophy.—Rev. J. Miller, D.D., etc., etc.
Natural Philosophy.—Chas.* Whitley, Esq., M.A.
Bursarius.—Rev. Luke Ripley, M.A.
Librarian.—Rev. P. George, M.A.
Treasurer.—William Charles Chaytor, Esq.
Lecturer on Chemistry and Mineralogy.—J. F. W. Johnston, Esq., A.M., F.R.S.E.
Lecturer on Modern Languages.—James Hamilton, Esq.

p. 8] 𝕸embers on the 𝕭oards:

The Rt. Hon. the Earl Grey, K.G., First Lord of the Treasury.
Sir Charles Grey, M.A.
W. L. Wharton, Esq., M.A., High Sheriff of the County of Durham.
John Stapylton, Esq., M.A.
Robert Ingham, Esq., M.A., M.P.
P. Selby, Esq., M.A.
Rev. James Ellice, M.A.
Robert Wharton, Esq., M.A.
George Hutton Wilkinson, Esq., M.A.

Rev. N. J. Hollingsworth, M.A.
Rev. W. N. Darnell, B.D.
Frederick Pollock, Esq., M.A.
T. Coltman, Esq., K.C.
Rev. C. J. Plumer, M.A.
John Pemberton, Esq., M.A.
Rev. Edward South Thurlow, M.A.
Rev. B. Bandinell, D.D.
Rev. Thomas Collins, M.A.
Rev. T. L. Strong, M.A.
Sir David Brewster, M.A.

p. 9]

Rev. P. Penson, M.A.
Mr. Serjeant Jones, M.A.
Rev. H. Douglas, M.A.
G. Stanley, Esq., M.A., M.P.
Rev. T. R. Shipperdson, M.A.
Rev. Luke Yarker, M.A.
Rev. Samuel Gamlen, M.A.
Rev. James Raine, M.A.
Rev. G. F. Rudd, M.A.
Rev. George Newby, M.A.
Rev. Mark Newby, B.A.
Rev. William Smoult Temple, M.C.

Rev. W. N. Andrews, M.A.
Rev. C. J. Wheler, M.A.
Rev. Thomas Ebdon, B.A.
Pudsey Dawson, Esq., M.A.
Rev. Percival Spearman Wilkinson, M.A.
Rev. John Raine, M.A.
Rev. R. G. L. Blenkinsopp, B.A.
Rev. J. A. Park, M.A.
Rev. H. G. Liddell, M.A.
Hon. and Rev. G. V. Wellesley, M.A.
Rev. Henry Wardell, M.A.

---

* Read Charles Thomas.

p. 10]   *Others with Temporary Privilege:*

Lord Mark Kerr.
Col. Shadforth.
G. T. Fox, Esq.
Mr. A. Wilkinson.
Mr. Donkin.
Mr. T. Griffith.
Mr. Elliott.
Mr. Burrell.
Mr. R. Burrell.
Mr. Stoker.
Mr. W. Green.

Mr. Barry.
Mr. W. Henshaw.
Mr. Hays.
Mr. Bouet.
Mr. Stafford.
Mr. Ornsby.
Mr. Brooksbank.
Mr. Bonomi.
Mr. E. Dunn.
Mr. Humble.

p. 11]

Mr. E. P. Humble.
Mr. Peele.
Mr. F. Wharton.
Mr. G. Andrews.
Mr. W. Binks.
Mr. W. J. Appleby.

Mr. J. Shields.
Mr. A. Smith.
Mr. Telfair.
Mr. Stimpson.
Mr. T. Brown.
Mr. T. Eggleston, Jun

Divinity Students:

Maughan Humble, B.A.
George Selby Thompson, B.A.
Robert Warren Furness.

William Cooper Maclaurin.
Phinehas Stubbs.

p. 12]   *Students of the Foundation:*

John Cundill.
St. Clere Raymond.
Henry Stoker.
John Treacy.
Robert Pratt.
Morton Eden Wilson.
Henry Press Wright.
George Marshall.
John Francis Erskine.
James Skinner.

Frederick Brewster Thompson.
Henry Humble.
Ralph Errington.
Thomas Maddison.
William Thomas Watson.
John Yarker.
James Watson Hick.
William Bramwell Ferguson.
George Hills.

16—2

p. 13]   𝔖tudents :

Thomas Garnett.   Thomas C. Price.
Hugh Martin Short.   Arthur Eveling Legard.
Richard Horn.   Matthias Stephenson.
Andrew Faulds.   John Headlam.
John Anthony Pearson Linskill.   John Gibson.
John Bennett.   Moorhouse Thompson.
Ralph Robinson.   George Hodgson.
James George Howard.   Francis Thompson.
George Heriot.   Richard Dalby Easterby.

p. 14]   *TERMS* 1833-4 :

Michaelmas Term ends 18th Dec.
Epiphany Term begins 18th Jan.
————————— ends 19th March.
Easter Term begins 19th April.
————————— ends 18th June

Students are admitted in any of the Terms.

The age of admission to the Academical Course is from 15 to 21, the Candidates being subject to due examination, in order to ascertain their fitness. Beyond this age, Students are admitted only by special leave.

p. 15]

Students of any age are admitted, under limitations, to attend particular classes, without being of the Academical Course, and without Academical Privileges.

Students under the Age of 26 are admtitted to the Divinity Course, after due inquiry and examination by the Professors before the Dean and Chapter.

Students, beyond the age of 26, are admitted only by special leave. *The Academical Course extends to Four Years.*

Nine Terms, or 3 years of residence, are necessary to the B A. degree, which will only be conferred after examination by the Officers or Fellows, in presence of the Dean and Chapter, at the usual Academical period.

Twelve Terms, or 4 years, must precede the examination which closes the Academical Course. The degree of M.A. will be conferred at the usual Academical standing.

p. 16]

Fifteen Terms, or 5 years of residence, the study of the two last years being under the Divinity Professor, will entitle a Student to be examined in Theology—and at this standing the Testamurs of attainment and character will be given. The degree of B.D. will be conferred at the usual Academical standing.

Students with a B.A. degree of Oxford or Cambridge, will read at least one year with the Professor, previous to examination for the Testamur.

Students, not having graduated, will be subjected to strict examination by the Professors, and to enquiry, before admission to the Divinity Class, and will read two years with the Professor of Divinity previous to examination for a Testamur.

The Terms of the Divinity Students will be of greater length than the Terms of the Academic Course.

The Professor of Greek will read with the Students of the Academic Course, as well as with the Divinity Students, on the Philology of S S. during the whole period of study.

The Professor of Divinity will also read with the Students of the Academic Course, as well as with the Divinity Students, in Theology, during the whole period.

p. 17] 𝔗𝔥𝔢 𝔓𝔯𝔦𝔫𝔠𝔦𝔭𝔞𝔩 𝔆𝔥𝔞𝔯𝔤𝔢𝔰:

	£	s.	d.
Admission of Students	2	0	0
Caution, deposit, of Students	10	0	0
Caution, deposit, of Occasional Students ...	5	0	0
Tuition each Term, to be paid terminally in advance...	3	0	0
University Chest	1	0	0
Detriment...		10	0
Servants		10	0
Library		10	0

The Students' Apartments are in the Archdeacon's Inn, on the Palace Green.

𝔑𝔞𝔱𝔲𝔯𝔞𝔩 𝔓𝔥𝔦𝔩𝔬𝔰𝔬𝔭𝔥𝔶:

The Reader delivers, during the October Term, a popular Course of Lectures on the History of the Sciences.

p. 18]

During the Epiphany and Easter Terms, his principal course, on Mechanics, Hydrostatics, Optics, and Astronomy—three Lectures in a week.

Also, during the Easter Term, on the alternate days, a popular course, on the application of Science to Manufactures.

TERMS:

For each of the Popular Courses   ...   One Guinea.
For the Principal Course   ...   ...   Three Guineas.

Anatomy and Physiology:

The Reader in Medicine delivers, during the October Term, his first part of a Course of Lectures on the above subject, to commence on Tuesday, the 12th, and to be continued on Thursdays and Tuesdays, at one o'clock; when the Importance of Anatomy and Physiology; the Origin, Phenomena, and Laws of Life; Osteology, etc, will be explained.

Each Friday, at 2 o'clock, will be more particularly devoted to Demonstrations, in allusion to the previous Lectures, explaining the application of Anatomy to the Practice of Surgery and Pathology.

p. 19]

During the Epiphany Term, he will deliver the second part of his Anatomical Course, on the same days

The principal subjects are, the Structure and Functions of the Vital Organs; the Brain and the Nervous System; the Component Parts of the Blood; the Absorbent System; the Muscles, and their Functions; the Heart and the Blood Vessels, the Thoracic, Abdominal, and Pelvic Viscera, the Organ of Hearing, Voice, Taste, and Smell; the Fœtal Circulation, the Teeth, etc., etc.

TERMS:

For each part of the Course, One Guinea and a Half.

Perpetual Tickets—Medical Students and Practitioners, Seven Guineas; Amateurs, Five Guineas.

Chemistry:

The Lecturer delivers, during the Epiphany Term, a Popular and a Practical Course.

Terms for Each—Two Guineas; or for both—Three Guineas

p. 20]   𝔐𝔬𝔡𝔢𝔯𝔫 𝔏𝔞𝔫𝔤𝔲𝔞𝔤𝔢𝔰 :

The Lecturer on Modern Language delivers, during Epiphany Term, a Popular Course of Lectures on the History of the Literature of Germany.

Terms...   ...   .   One Guinea.

Payments on account of the University may be made to W. C. CHAYTOR, ESQ., College, Durham, the Treasurer, or to his account at Messrs COUTTS and Co , Strand, London ; SIR M W. RIDLEY and Co., Bankers, Newcastle ; or at any of the Durham Banks.

Applications may be made to the Warden, to William C. Chaytor, Esq., the Treasurer ; or to the Rev. Luke Ripley, the Bursar.

FINIS.

APPENDIX V

Regulations of Discipline, &c.,

FOR THE

STUDENTS OF DURHAM.

[Printed by F. Humble, Queen Street, Durham; 4 pp., 8vo.]

1. Applicants for admission must present to the Warden a certificate of their age; the ordinary age for admission being from sixteen to twenty-one. They must also bring Testimonials to their character and conduct during the two previous years.

2. No one will be admitted until he has passed an Examination. The Examination usually extends to construing Greek and Latin, writing Latin—Arithmetic—the Elements of Geometry and Algebra—History (particularly that of the Old Testament) and Geography—the Evidences and Doctrines of Christianity.

3. At the time of Entering, the Applicant is required to subscribe his name to a declaration of obedience, adding his age, the address of his Parent or Guardian, and the date of his admission. He is required at the same time to pay Twelve Pounds as Caution money to the Treasurer. This money is returned whenever he ceases to be a Member of the College.

4. Immediately after admission, the new Student is shewn the Rooms assigned him by the Warden. The Furniture of the Rooms is supplied by the Establishment, and charged to the Student. No

248

Student is suffered to furnish his own Rooms, nor to add any thing to the Regulation Furniture, without permission of the Censor.

5. The Students are required to be present

> At Breakfast in Hall,
> At Chapel Prayers, or at Cathedral Service,
> at the times appointed,
> At Dinner in Hall,
> At Prayers in the Evening.

They are also required to attend such Lectures of the Professors and Tutors, and such other Lectures as the Authorities may direct

6 No day will count as a day of Residence, unless the Student has been present on all the occasions required; and if he absents himself on more than one occasion, he will be *liable* to lose a day for each non-appearance. The Censor, or other Officer under whose notice the irregularity has come, will signify the loss of the day by a cross in the Butler's Book. Ten such crosses will lose the Term.

> (1) Yet the Warden, Professors, Tutors, and other Officers will, in certain cases, give permission to be absent from Chapel, Lectures, &c , and the day will then reckon. They will also remit crosses on a satisfactory explanation being given.
>
> (2) Also, any one wishing to absent himself from Hall may make an entry in the Butler's Book of the person he is going to visit, or the place he is going to, and the reason of his absence. If the cause be approved, the day will reckon, but if disallowed, or if no entry has been made, the day is lost.
>
> (3) In cases of ægrotat, the day will always be *crossed*, but with a distinct (a red) cross. The Censors will judge, at the end of the week, from the medical certificates, and from their own knowledge of the Patient, how far such crosses should or should not be counted against the Term.

7 Students are expected to be in College before the gates are closed at night; a report of all those who come in afterwards is delivered to the Censor.

8. Any Stranger going out of College after the gates are shut, will be required to give the name of the Student from whose Rooms he comes. All Strangers must leave the College before Prayers at night.

9. At twelve o'clock the Servants will go round (and occasionally the Censor with them) to see that all lights are extinguished.

10. The Academical Dress is always to be worn in public, except

(1) On the River; and then the Cap and Gown must be worn down to the boat-house. In the boat, either the Academical Cap or a boating-cap may be used, but no hat.

(2) In going to a gentleman's house more than two miles distant from Durham; and of this notice must always be given beforehand, by entry in the Butler's Book. On any other reasonable occasion, a similar entry may be made, subject to the discretion of the Censor to disallow or approve.

11. All play with Dice and Cards, and generally all Betting and Gambling are strictly prohibited.

12. Students must not hire any Room or House in the Town, nor frequent Inns, Public-Houses, Cooks' or Confectioners' Shops.

13. It is forbidden to Students to go to the neighbouring Towns, (as Sunderland, Newcastle, &c.) or to hire Horses, Gigs, Chaises, or other Vehicles, without reasonable cause assigned, and notice given to the Censor, either verbally or by entry beforehand in the Butler's Book.

14. The Parent or Guardian of every Student will have the option of putting his Bills contracted out of College, under the control of the Tutor. In that case, the Bills must be made up and sent in by his Tradesmen to the Tutor three days before the end of each Term. The Tutor will forward them to the Parent or Guardian, and, if desired, will transmit the money to the Tradesmen. The Student will be expected to give his Tradesmen notice to send in their Bills, and will be held responsible if they are not delivered to the Tutor in proper time; or if they do not contain the whole amount of debt. If the Tradesman also shall appear to be in fault, all Students will be forbidden to deal with him.

C. Thorp, *Warden*.

APPENDIX VI

THE LECTURES OF THE LATE DR. JENKYNS

BY THE REV. DR. FARRAR

[*From the ' Durham County Advertiser ' of June* 29, 1882.]

THOSE who are old enough to remember Durham and its University a quarter of a century ago will know that the Professor of Divinity in the University at that time was Canon Jenkyns. He had held that office for a quarter of a century (from 1839 to 1864), with a reputation for learning and power of teaching then unequalled in England, and worthy to be compared with the great Professors of Germany. During that period there were no theological Colleges, and virtually there was no systematic teaching of Divinity in the old Universities of Oxford and Cambridge. Hence a flow of students set in northwards to learn theology from Dr. Jenkyns' lips, of thoughtful and studious men such as (to name no other) the new Bishop of Wakefield, Dr Walsham How. Dr. Jenkyns, when he came to Durham, brought with him a very high reputation for learning, accuracy, and good sense. He had won the highest honours at Oxford, and among the rest, what was at that time considered the blue ribbon, a Fellowship of Oriel. But when he came to Durham he was no idler; on the contrary, he was a very industrious student He worked hard constantly in preparation for his lectures, and organized the course of study for his pupils. Those lectures he never would write out at full nor publish The fastidiousness of the scholar prevented this. But the lectures were taken down in substance by his pupils, and, among others, by one who has lately passed away, the Rev. J. Low Low, Vicar of Whittonstall, who in 1842-43 was a student in Dr. Jenkyns' theological classes. At the recent sale of Mr. Low's library, the MS. notes of these lectures in four quarto volumes were sold, and were luckily obtained as the property of the University of Durham. As Mr. Low was both an attentive and intelligent student, the notes seem to be (approximately speaking) a trustworthy record of Dr. Jenkyns' teaching, and the more so as Mr. Low wrote down only what he heard, and did not attempt to intermingle with the report of the lectures materials which he had in his own reading collected from other sources.

Dr. Jenkyns' plan of lectures was adapted to a course of two years' study. In the one year the staple of his teaching was Church History, in the other Dogmatic Theology (the Thirty-nine Articles of the Established Church) and Forms of Worship (the ancient liturgies and the English Prayer-Book). The MS. volumes already spoken of contained these valuable lectures. In Church history the Professor, lecturing, as few teachers now have the chance of doing in this fussy and utilitarian age, to students who could construe Greek, and thought the time not to be lost which was devoted to theological study prior to meddling with pastoral work, used to venture to carry his pupils steadily through Eusebius. And, accordingly, one of these quarto volumes contains a very careful series of 270 pages of most valuable annotations on selected chapters of the works of that early authority. After Dr. Jenkyns had thus laid a solid basis for history, he bridged over the chasm between the period at which Eusebius ends, to the history of the English Church, by lecturing on three subjects, viz., the history of General Councils, the rise and fall of the Papal power, and the history of the Monastic Orders. He then proceeded to treat of English Church history from the earliest times, but especially of the period of the English Reformation, on which his careful study of original sources in editing the works of Cranmer enabled him to speak with a learning and authority which are rare. A second volume of Mr. Low's MS. notes contains the record (in 153 pages) of the interesting series of lectures just described.

We have already implied that the Articles of the Church of England formed the text-book of the system of theology which Dr. Jenkyns expounded to his pupils. The third of the volumes, written by Mr. Low, contains (in 229 pages) a full report of the series of lectures, necessarily from their subject more dry, but not less accurate, than the others.

The fourth MS. volume contains (in 170 pages) what perhaps was at that time the newest and the most original of Dr. Jenkyns' courses. We know that it was one on which he especially prided himself, and justly so. His lectures gave a luminous account of the history of forms of prayer and service-books from the earliest days of Christianity to the present time, and in the course of this account he was wont to carry his pupils through the Liturgy of the Church of Greece and the Ordinary and Canon of the Roman Mass, prior to entering upon the study of the Anglican Prayer-Book. He did so not only from the wish to develop the historic basis of the English Prayer-Book, but to exhibit in these earlier service-books, and eminently in the Roman Mass, the proofs, as he considered, of the abuses of those medieval and modern forms of doctrine on the Eucharist which are emphasized by that Church.

Yet though Mr. Low's MS. books furnish the outline and some-thing more of these various lectures, there were four other courses, on some of which it is known Dr. Jenkyns had bestowed especial pains, which are lacking. The present Divinity Professor (Dr. Farrar), who, though he had nothing to do with the purchase of the MS., feels intensely interested in the matter, has deemed it so desirable to try to complete the series by procuring suitable notes on these absent courses from old pupils, that he has printed and sent round to the chief of Dr. Jenkyns' old pupils the following circular letter, which we publish* in the hope that possibly it may catch the eye of some who can help to effect the object desired. It is as follows:

THE COLLEGE, DURHAM,
June —, 1888.

MY DEAR ——,

I take the liberty, though a stranger, of troubling you with a question on a literary matter. We have lately had the good fortune to procure for the library of the University four volumes, 4to., of MS. notes of the late Dr. Jenkyns' Lectures on Divinity, made by the late Rev. J. L. Low. The series, however, lacks notes on the following courses of Dr. Jenkyns' lectures, viz.:

1. That on the Epistles;
2. That on Bible Criticism;
3. That on the Interpretation of the N.T.;
4. The lectures delivered on Sundays at 5 p.m.

Now, as we desire to complete the set (not, of course, for publica-tion, but as a point of literary interest, and as supplying a chapter in the history of theological education here), I am venturing to write to several of the old Durham men, like yourself, to ascertain whether any of them possesses, and, if so, would be willing to lend,

---

* Dr. Farrar's leaflet is an overprint; see p. 251.

for the purpose of being copied, full notes of any of those courses. The especial value of Mr. Low Low's reports of the lectures is that, while thoroughly understanding, and therefore taking down correctly, what Dr. Jenkyns said, he has strictly adhered to his statements, and has not incorporated any remarks of his own drawn from other sources.

I may state, in reference to the lectures which were delivered on Sunday afternoons after Cathedral service (No. 4 of the above-named list), that Dr. Jenkyns told me that these had ranged over five topics. If you do not possess notes of these, can you remember what these five topics were? I know that he said that one was Evidences, and a second, Davison on Prophecy.

Again apologizing for this intrusion,

I remain,

Yours ——

A. S. F.,

Professor of Divinity in the University of Durham.

The writer who has drawn up the above account of this interesting literary acquisition would like to add a few remarks in reference to Dr. Jenkyns' teaching and work. He founds them not only on the careful perusal of the above described MS. notes, but on the circumstance that he had the privilege of hearing from Dr. Jenkyns a full account both of his plan of teaching and of the books which he studied to qualify himself for teaching.

The first particular to be named is the remarkable clearness and brevity with which Dr. Jenkyns expressed and compressed the information which he desired to convey. He possessed the rare gift of being able to lecture down to the capacities of the dullest of his class, and at the same time furnish material for informing and stimulating the minds of the highest. This was his peculiar natural gift; but, so far as it admits of analysis, the secret of it lay in three things—first, the adoption of Socrates' method of question and answer, the stating a difficulty, before supplying and criticising the answers to it; secondly, his complete and accurate mastery of every detail which bore upon the question (he spoke out of the abundance of his knowledge, and did not merely speak as a barrister who has got up a case); and, thirdly, his power of cool self-command, by which he never allowed himself to be diverted and led away by rhetoric or emotion, from the special subject and quantity which he had designed beforehand to embrace in his lecture.

The second feature is the remarkable fulness of his information, notably on liturgical matters, at a time when the grand series of modern works on the subject, which he that runs may now read, had not appeared. Hardly had Rock, and Palmer, and Neale, and

Maskell written, nor had the great German scholar Daniel edited his
' Codex Liturgicus.' Dr. Jenkyns approached the original sources,
and studied them with great assiduity. He often alluded to his
careful study of the work of Cardinal Bona on the Roman Mass.
The result is that one who is familiar with the active research
shown on each topic of theology in the works of modern writers is
startled to find that Dr. Jenkyns had previously attained to the
same erudition, and had communicated it to his pupils.

It need not be said that these MS notes will be preserved with
sacred care in the University Library, and will not under any
circumstances be allowed to be published. Dr Jenkyns had
naturally a very strong feeling on this subject. In late life, after his
resignation, on one occasion, when he thought that notes from his
lectures were about to be put forth, he consulted the writer of this
article for facts, with a view to get legal embargo, if necessary, to
forbid the publication. It may be a matter of regret that he did not
himself communicate his knowledge to the world But an English
Professor in a busy life has little time to write. His business is to
be the constant student and the assiduous teacher. These traits
Dr. Jenkyns exhibited. He lives, not in books, not even in MS.
notes, but in the living tables of the heart. He has lived and
acted through his pupils, and they have acted on others. The
stream has gone on fertilizing. He is partly forgotten. In a ripe
old age he was gathered to the grave as a ripe shock of corn is
brought home in its season. He lies buried in the most retired part
of a lonely village church in Hampshire ; but he sought (and doubtless found) his glory, honour, immortality, by patient continuance in
well-doing. He has rested from his labours, but his works still do
follow him.

APPENDIX VII

GRANT OF ARMS TO THE UNIVERSITY

To ALL AND SINGULAR to whom these Presents shall come Sir Charles George Young, Knight, Garter Principal King of Arms, Joseph Hawker, Esquire, Clarenceux King of Arms, and Francis Martin, Esquire, Norroy King of Arms, send Greeting: Whereas The Venerable Charles Thorp, Doctor in Divinity, Archdeacon and Canon of Durham and Warden of the University of Durham, on behalf of the Warden, Masters and Scholars of the said University, hath represented unto The Most Noble Henry Charles, Duke of Norfolk, Earl Marshal and Hereditary Marshal of England, that His late Majesty King William the Fourth by Letters Patent under the Great Seal of the United Kingdom of Great Britain and Ireland, bearing date the first day of June, One thousand Eight hundred and Thirty seven, was graciously pleased for himself, his heirs and Successors, to grant, constitute, declare and appoint, that the said Charles Thorp, and all persons who then were, or who should thereafter be duly admitted members of the said University, in pursuance of a regulation in the said Charter recited or according to such rules and regulations as might thereafter be made and established by the Dean and Chapter of Durham in manner therein mentioned, should be one body politic and corporate, under and by the name of 'The Warden, Masters and Scholars of the University of Durham,' and that by the same name they should and might have perpetual succession and a Common Seal, with power to break, alter and make anew such Seal from time to time at their will and pleasure: That being now desirous that Armorial Ensigns to be borne upon the Common Seal of the said body should be duly granted by competent Authority, He therefore requested that His Grace would be pleased to issue his Warrant for our granting such Arms as may be proper to be borne and used for ever hereafter by

256

the Warden, Masters and Scholars of the said University of Durham, on their Common Seal, Shields, Banners or otherwise, according to the antient usage and Laws of Arms. And forasmuch as the said Earl Marshal did by Warrant under his hand and Seal bearing date the sixteenth day of May instant, authorize and direct us to grant such Arms accordingly, Know ye therefore that We the said Garter, Clarenceux and Norroy in pursuance of His Grace's Warrant and by virtue of the Letters Patent of our several Offices to each of us respectively granted do by these Presents grant and assign unto the said Warden, Masters and Scholars of the said University of Durham and their Successors as Warden, Masters and Scholars of the said University, the Arms following that is to say, Argent, a Cross Patée quadrate Gules ; a Canton Azure, charged with a Cheveron Or between three Lions rampant of the First, together with this Motto ' Fundamenta ejus super montibus sanctis,' as the same are in the margin hereof more plainly depicted to be borne and used for ever hereafter by the Warden, Masters and Scholars of the said University of Durham, and their Successors, Wardens, Masters and Scholars of the said University on their Common Seal, Shields, Banners, or otherwise, according to the ancient usage and Laws of Arms. In Witness Whereof We the said Garter, Clarenceux and Norroy, Kings of Arms, have to these Presents subscribed Our names and affixed the Seals of Our several Offices, this eighteenth day of May, in the Sixth Year of the Reign of Our Sovereign Lady Victoria, by the Grace of God, of the United Kingdom of Great Britain and Ireland Queen, Defender of the Faith, &c., and in the Year of Our Lord One thousand Eight hundred and Forty three.

(Signed) CHARLES GEO. YOUNG, *Garter.*

J. HAWKER, *Clarenceux.*

FRAS. MARTIN, *Norroy.*

Sealed with the seals of the above three Kings of Arms, the seals contained in brass skippets with their coronets on the covers, and suspended by blue silk ribbons. Endorsed :

' Recorded in the College of Arms, London, this twenty-second day of May, 1843.

J. PULMAN, *Richmond Herald and Registrar.*

ALBERT W. WOODS, *Lancaster Herald, Heralds' College, London.*'

Stamped with Government stamp ' Ten Pounds, London, 15/4/43.'

The grant is contained in a purple morocco case stamped with ' V.R.' and royal crowns.

17

APPENDIX VIII

REGULATIONS FOR ACADEMICAL COSTUME
(June, 1904).

D.D.

Gown—Full dress: Scarlet cassimere, sleeves and front faced with palatinate purple silk, with soft black velvet square cap and black silk scarf
    Undress: Same as M.A., with black silk scarf.
Hood—Scarlet cassimere, lined with palatinate purple silk.
Convocation Habit—Scarlet cassimere, with palatinate purple buttons, to be worn under the gown at all Convocations.

B.D.

Gown—Same as M.A.
Hood—Black corded silk, lined with black silk.

M.A.

Gown—Black cord or corded silk, with long half-moon sleeve.
Hood—Black silk, lined with palatinate purple silk.

B.A.

Gown—Black cord, pointed sleeve, with cord and button
Hood—Black stuff, trimmed with white fur.

D.C.L

Gown—Full dress: Same as D.D., but faced with white silk; cap as D D.
    Undress: Same as M.A.
Hood—Scarlet cassimere, lined with white silk.
Convocation Habit—As above.

B.C L.

GOWN—Same as B.A.

HOOD—Palatinate purple silk, bound with white fur.

M D.

GOWN—Full dress· Same as D D., but lined with scarlet silk, faced
with palatinate purple silk ; cap as D.D.

Undress· Black corded silk, trimmed with black velvet
lace.

HOOD—Scarlet cassimere, lined with scarlet silk, faced with palatinate purple silk.

CONVOCATION HABIT—As above

M.B.

GOWN—Black cord, trimmed with gimp.

HOOD—Scarlet silk, lined with palatinate purple silk and bound
with white fur.

M.S.

GOWN—Same as M.B.

HOOD—Rose silk, lined with palatinate purple silk.

B.S. ·

GOWN—Same as M.B.

HOOD—Rose silk, lined with palatinate purple silk, bound with
white fur.

D.HY.

GOWN—Full dress: Same as D D , but lined with scarlet silk, faced
with palatinate purple and white silk ; cap as D.D.

Undress: Black cord, trimmed with velvet lace.

HOOD—Scarlet cloth, lined with scarlet silk, faced with palatinate
purple and white silk. ·

CONVOCATION HABIT—As above.*

B.HY.

GOWN—Same as M.B.

HOOD—Black silk, faced with palatinate purple and scarlet silk and
bound with white fur.

L S.Sc.

GOWN—Same as M B.

HOOD—Black silk, faced with broad black velvet and scarlet silk
and bound with palatinate purple silk.

D.Sc.

Gown—Full dress : Same as D.D., but faced with scarlet silk , cap as D.D.
Hood—Palatinate purple cassimere, lined with scarlet silk.
Convocation Habit—As above.

M.Sc.

Gown—Same as M.A.
Hood—Black silk, lined with palatinate purple silk and bound with scarlet silk half an inch wide both sides.

B.Sc.

Gown—Same as B A.
Hood—Palatinate purple silk, bound with white fur, and with a scarlet band half an inch wide next to the fur.

D.Litt.

Gown—Full dress : Same as D.D., but faced with old gold satin , cap as D.D.
Hood—Scarlet cassimere, lined with old gold satin.
Convocation Habit—As above.*

B.Litt.

Gown—Same as B.A.
Hood—Old gold satin, edged with fur.

Mus.D.

Gown—Full dress : Brocaded white satin, sleeves and front faced with palatinate purple silk ; cap as D.D.
Undress : Black silk, trimmed with broad black gimp.
Hood—Brocaded white satin, lined with palatinate purple silk.
Convocation Habit—As above *

Mus.B.

Gown—Same as undress Mus.D., without slit at back.
Hood—Palatinate purple silk, bound with brocaded white satin

L.Th.

Gown—Black with sleeves partly trimmed with velvet.
Hood—Black stuff, faced with velvet and bound with palatinate purple silk a quarter of an inch wide and velvet one inch wide.

A.Th.

GOWN—Same as L.Th., without velvet trimming.
HOOD—Black stuff, with purple silk edging.

A.Sc.

GOWN—Black, sleeves partly trimmed with velvet.
HOOD—Black stuff, faced with velvet and bound with palatinate ·
    purple silk a quarter of an inch wide.

PROCTORS' ROBES.

CAP—Black velvet.
GOWN—Same as M.A.
HOOD—Black velvet, lined with palatinate purple silk.

STUDENTS' GOWNS.

ARTS—Black cord, with short square sleeves
THEOLOGY—Black cord, with long pointed sleeves.
MEDICINE—The same as Arts, with gimp trimming on sleeves.
SCIENCE—The same as Arts.
EDUCATION—The same as Arts.

SCHOLARS' GOWN.

Same as Arts student's, but with no slits in sleeves.

---

* Doctors in Hygiene, Letters, and Music, can wear the habit if
otherwise qualified as members of Convocation.

APPENDIX IX

ATHLETICS

BY LEIGH SMITH, FELLOW OF THE UNIVERSITY

In treating of the history of athletics at the University it will greatly simplify matters to consider each separate branch of sport by itself, and combine the accounts at the end into one general verdict.

The chief branches of sport at the University are rowing, football (Rugby and Association), and cricket, while the claims of athletics pure and simple are recognised at a sports meeting held every summer term since 1884.

ROWING.

Of these branches perhaps the first in order of precedence is rowing Being the oldest sport in Durham, it has all the weight of tradition behind it. Its records go back as far as 1835; for does not the Museum contain a trophy won by a member of the University, R. B. Tower, at the regatta of 1835, the trophy being a silver medal bearing the excellent advice ' Detur dignissimo'? A record of this kind shows us that rowing must have been practically contemporaneous with the founding of the University, and we have ample evidence that it flourished with its growth; for the Grand Challenge Cup of the Durham Regatta—a regatta often called the Henley of the North, and believed to be one of the oldest, if not the oldest, rowing meetings in the country—was won by a crew from the University of Durham seven times between the years 1854-1862, and this at a time, too, when competition was not so purely local as it is now, but when crews from Cambridge and the South did not disdain to visit the Wear and match themselves

against the rowing talent of the North. True, later years did not
see the 'Varsity quite so victorious, but it was not for lack of keenness. That the rowing spirit was strong was evident from the fact
that letters—the first of a long series—began to appear in the
University Journal advocating a trial of strength at Henley and at
other regattas more cosmopolitan than that on the Wear.

An important step was taken in 1877, the year in which a
University boating club was definitely established; and that this
step was a good one was soon apparent at the regatta of 1881, when
a crew from the University carried off not only the Grand Challenge
Cup, but also the City and the Stewards' Cup. This was a great
triumph, and was followed, as often happens, by a rather lean time,
the only prize that came our way in the next few years being the
Lady Herschel Plate in 1886. The next year saw the commencement of that unhappy dispute over the date of the regatta, into the
merits of which this is not the place to enter. It is sufficient to
record that from 1887 to 1893 Town and Gown held separate
regattas, neither of which was wholly successful.

This period, however, was not without its honours for University
rowing. In 1888 a 'Varsity crew competed at the Tyne Regatta,
and by defeating the Tyne and Durham City crews made itself
master of the Grand Challenge Cup of the Tyne, while a second
Durham crew only just succumbed in the final of the Junior race.
These performances were welcome not only in themselves, but also
as being evidence that our withdrawal from the City Regatta was
not a confession of weakness cloaking itself under the plea of
privilege. However, in 1893 the split was mended, and the experiment of holding two regattas in Durham, by no means a successful
experiment, as has been already remarked, was discontinued.

The following year saw the 'Varsity put an exceptionally good
boat on the river, but owing to an unfortunate fouling of Elvet arch
by the cox in both the Wharton and the Grand, the crew failed to
win either race. The crew, however, stroked by Platt of Hatfield,
was in no way disheartened by the mishap at Durham. Later in
the season it entered for and won the Wirral Challenge Cup at the
Chester Regatta, and thus made a precedent for future crews. The
names of this crew are deserving of record. They were: J. Platt,
stroke; J. Gardiner, 3; J. Scott, 2; J. S Whitehead, bow; and
H S. S. Jackson (afterwards a most successful 'Varsity oarsman),
cox.

In the next year also—1895—the 'Varsity was represented by a
very strong crew, and a crew, too, which was more fortunate than

that of the preceding year, for both the Grand and the Wharton —the race open to Durham crews only—were won, the Wharton being just won on the post after one of the most exciting races ever seen on the Wear. The names of the 1895 crew were: G. C. Pollard, stroke; H. R. Hughes, 3; T. C. Tanner, 2, J. S. Whitehead, bow.

The next year in which the double event was won was 1898, only three years after the previous success—a fact which points to a distinct improvement in the standard of rowing at Durham. To have earned the distinction of being probably the best crew in the North twice within four years was one of which the University might well be proud. The 1898 crew was stroked by M. J. Buchanan, one of the best oars ever sent out from Durham school, and probably the best stroke the 'Varsity ever had. The other members of the crew were: L. Fallaw, 3; J. F, Palmer, 2; and J. W. Fell, bow. In 1902, when Buchanan was stroke again, the 'Varsity had a splendid crew, which had the misfortune to go the wrong side of the buoy in its first heat of the Grand. Though it won the ' row-off,' it could not do itself justice in the final, and was just beaten ; but some compensation was afforded by the winning of the Wharton. In addition to M. J Buchanan (stroke), this crew included H. L. Lloyd, 3 , W. Bettison, 2; and H. S S. Jackson, bow.

In 1904 a welcome step was made by the inaugurating of a race with the University of Edinburgh. The idea of a race with Dublin University had often been suggested before, but it had never been found possible, owing to the fact that Dublin found its trip to Henley as much as it could manage. Fortunately, however, it has been found possible to arrange a meeting with Edinburgh, and it is to be hoped that the race of this year, which Edinburgh succeeded in winning, will be the first of a long series. Nothing is more likely to stimulate 'Varsity rowing than inter-'Varsity competition. This date brings us up to the present time, and this account, therefore, may be fittingly concluded with a summary of the University records on the river. This is as follows . ten wins in the Grand Challenge Cup and six in the Wharton. No other club has won the Grand more times than the 'Varsity ; while, with respect to the Wharton, all six victories have been achieved since 1895—a record in both instances which will bear comparison with those of most other clubs in the North.

RUGBY FOOTBALL.

Next to rowing in order of precedence, if we take time as our standard, comes Rugby football. The date of its origin is in obscurity, but there are certain records of it as far back as 1876. In that year the team that represented the University had a most successful career, of ten matches eight being won and two drawn. But all this time the team appears to have been taken from the Durham side of the University, and it was not until 1884 that a University club was formed which combined the full strength of both Durham and Newcastle. The effect of this amalgamation was immediately apparent, the team of 1885 being an exceedingly good one, and containing several men who were thought worthy of a trial for the county. The reputation the Rugby team thus won for itself was well maintained, and in 1887 it had an unbroken record, most of the prominent teams in the district—namely, Westoe, West Hartlepool, North Durham (then one of the first-rate teams of the county)—all falling victims to its prowess. But Rugby football probably reached its high-water mark in 1889 and 1890. In both these years the University team was probably the best in the county, and it held a continuous record of victories. One match in particular is worthy of notice—viz., that against Westoe, this team, always pretty strong, being beaten by 6 goals 2 tries to nil. Three members of this University team were on the Durham County side —F A. Bulman, B Cox, C. T. B. Wilkinson, the latter of whom was also chosen reserve forward for the Rest of England v. Yorkshire, the champion county of 1890.

Unfortunately, this brilliance did not last, and the teams of the following years were much inferior, and matters were not improved by a lowering of the standard of fixtures. Weaker clubs were met, presumably to suit the altered conditions of football. This policy was not a wise one. Nothing was to be gained by playing clubs who made up for their minimum of skill by a maximum of energy, and a defeat at whose hands—a defeat, too, probably due not so much to inferior football as to utter inability to cope with the 'coarseness' (the word is used in the Scotch sense) of our opponents —did us infinitely more harm than a heavy defeat at the hands of stronger opponents could have done. Not that the team did badly during these years, but its results undoubtedly fell short of what we had a right to expect, considering that there were in the team representatives from the Midland Counties Football team and from Durham, Northumberland, and Cumberland counties. And one very good reason for this was the fact that too many clubs were met who did not play scientific so much as vigorous football.

In 1898, however, after two or three years of comparative weakness, a strong team was got together and better fixtures were insisted on. With the obtaining of these the standard of football greatly improved, and only two matches were lost during the season, while seven were won. So encouraging was this success that a Scottish tour was arranged. Glasgow University was met and defeated at Glasgow, while a very close match was played with the Watsonians, who were only victorious after a hard struggle. In this way was the policy of obtaining better fixtures justified. The team improved in every respect, several of its members playing for one county or another—F. J. Gowans for Durham, B S. Robson for Northumberland, and H. C. B. Cummins for Hampshire, etc. We had also a representative on the Rest of England v. England Team—W. Seymour, of the Medical College, who was also chosen as first reserve for England v. Ireland at three-quarters. This improvement has been maintained, and the team is now quite worthy to be ranked among the best in the district One thing to be regretted is that the fixtures with Edinburgh have been allowed to drop. Such matches are excellent in every way ; they foster keenness, and also teach useful lessons.

CRICKET.

Cricket at Durham has never been as good as it might reasonably be expected to have been from the position that the 'Varsity holds in the North. Several reasons account for this, the chief of them being the shortness of the season, which is practically over by the time a satisfactory team has been got together, and owing to the shortness of most men's stay at Durham it is more than probable that half of the team will have gone down by the time the next season comes round. In cricket, therefore, we are more dependent than in the other games on receiving from the public schools cricketers ready-made The time is really too short to try and train our own , hence, whenever the supply of cricketing Freshmen is limited, we can generally reckon on having only a moderate cricket team. In the football season the two winter terms do give us some time to knit together a good team, even if the prospects are unsatisfactory at the beginning But in cricket, unless we start with a good team ready to hand, there never is a chance of turning out a thoroughly representative one. And it is in cricket, too, that the amalgamation scheme has proved least effectual, excellent though it has been in other respects. To get off in the morning and afternoon means for most Newcastle men the dropping of a lecture or two, and this, though harmless enough on one or two occasions, is a serious matter if repeated too frequently. In addition, the constant travelling to and fro during a busy cricket season forms a by no means inconsiderable item in the cricket expenses; hence it is that it is very difficult to get together a team really representing the full cricketing strength of the University. With this preamble we may turn to some records.

It was not till 1888 that the University made for itself a cricketing reputation; but in that year an influx of good cricketers, coupled with great keenness in the University for sport in general, resulted in our attaining great prominence in the cricket as well as in the football of the North of England. One performance of 1888 is of such excellence as to merit a paragraph to itself.

Playing against Sunderland, the University team ran up the excellent score of 442 for eight wickets, a score which was believed at the time to be a record for North-country cricket. Of this score one member of the team, R. Bousfield, who has since that time done splendid service for Durham County, ran up 245 not out, while he also received great assistance from F. L. C. Hamilton, who, when at Haileybury, was one of the best public-school bats of his year

For two or three years this excellent form was maintained. The fixture-list was good, and included, besides our usual matches with the Yorkshire Gentlemen and the Borderers, a match with Northumberland County, who were defeated on two or three occasions. But we had no team equal to that of 1888 until 1898 and 1899, in both of which years the team was very strong, and in 1899 probably stronger than it had ever been before In both years the side was much the same, and stronger fixtures were arranged accordingly

In 1898 a visit to Lord's was arranged, and a match played against a strong team of Gentlemen of the M.C C. Though the match ended in a defeat, the experiment was nevertheless a distinct success, and the chief honours were carried off by a Durham man, Gillingham, the hero of many University matches, making 123

In the next year fixtures were arranged with Edinburgh and Dublin Universities, the latter being the first of its kind. The first match we won by an innings and 80, while the second resulted in a draw, though scarcely in our favour. Of the members of this team most have since played for second-class counties, and two of them for first-class counties, in one case—that of F. H. Gillingham for Essex —with distinguished success. The record for the season was a win

in every match except that against Dublin University, the highest
score for us throughout the season being 201 not out by Gillingham
against the Gentlemen of Durham—a score almost rivalling Bousfield's big score ten years earlier. But certainly the most gratifying
win was against Edinburgh University. Previously to that time we
had not done well against them, but our innings defeat of them in
this year somewhat atoned for earlier failures. The feature of the
game was an innings of 158 by the University captain, H. B. Fawcus,
who was a tower of strength all the time he was up. Altogether
this year was the high-water mark of Durham cricket, and it is not
to be wondered at that succeeding years have seen some decline.
Nevertheless, the mistake of adapting the fixture-list to altered
conditions has not been made. A wise step has been taken by the
arrangement of fixtures with Victoria University, and though the
balance is at present against us in these matches, it is nevertheless
only by such fixtures that the strength of former days can again be
approached.

Association Football.

Strange to say, Association football has always been somewhat
overshadowed by Rugby football in the 'Varsity. This is the case
at both Oxford and Cambridge, but why it should be so at Durham it
is difficult to say. Certainly the standard of Association football at
Durham has always been quite up to that of Rugby, the teams en-
countered have been of quite as good class, while the records of the
one certainly bear comparison with those of the other. It is, however, of somewhat later date than Rugby, there being no authorized
club in the University until 1886. For some years the team met,
and met successfully, most of the leading teams in the North—
Sunderland (at that time just beginning to show signs of future
greatness), Middlesboro' Ironopolis (the then champions of the
North), and Darlington; but, on the team showing signs of decline,
the unwise policy of lowering the standard of fixtures was adopted,
and the standard of play greatly deteriorated in consequence. In
later years, however, this retrogressive policy was checked, and the
team of 1899 proving exceptionally strong, a Southern tour was
arranged in that year. In the course of this, matches were to have
been played with Peterborough, the Casuals, and the Old Malvernians; unfortunately, only one of these matches could be brought
to a definite issue—viz., that against a strong team of the Old
Malvernians, containing several Blues. The result, a good victory
for Durham, only made the postponement of the two other matches

more regrettable. Quite recently inter-'Varsity matches have been arranged with Edinburgh and Victoria Universities; in the former we were successful, but unsuccessful in the latter.

Yet, win or lose, there can be no doubt that the policy of arranging such fixtures is the policy that pays in the long-run. From every point of view—from the prestige of the University, from the improvement in sport, from the increased enjoyment—it is a policy to be commended, and it is to be hoped that the Association team will arrange as many of such fixtures as possible. The class of football played for the most part by Association clubs round Durham is, to put it mildly, not educational, and the fewer we play of such rough-and-tumble matches the better for 'Varsity football.

ATHLETIC SPORTS

The Athletic Sports were discontinued in 1876, but were revived again in 1884 through the energy of Dr. Jevons, who showed his practical interest in sports by continuing as secretary until 1894. The sports have suffered from the fact that they are maintained for the most part by men who, having many other things to do, cannot find the time to specialize in running or jumping. In a larger place there would be room for men who could make athletic sports their one hobby, and could thus attain a high level of proficiency. But excellence in sports is impossible without specialization; hence it is that our sports have never reached a high standard, though there have always been some performances of the greatest merit, as will be seen from a list of the records .

Hundred yards: 10¼ seconds; C. T. B. Wilkinson.
Quarter-mile : 52⅔ seconds; F. G. B. Hastings.
Cricket ball : 107 yards; John Fowler.
Long jump : 19 feet 8 inches ; V. J. Jacka.
Mile : 4 minutes 39 seconds; F. L. C. Hamilton.
Weight : 33 feet 3 inches ; N. Raw.
Hurdles (120 yards) : 17 seconds; R. A. Morland.
Half-mile : 2 minutes 8 seconds ; W. D. Ross.
High jump : 5 feet 4½ inches ; A. L. Wilkinson.

So much for the separate branches of the sport. The general verdict on the whole must be that, considering the many disadvantages under which sport at Durham labours, the shortness of most men's study, and the separation of the University into two parts —a great disadvantage, despite the excellence of the amalgamation scheme—the University is and has been as prominent in sport of the North as could well be expected. In rowing the University is always prominent, while the cricket and football teams, on the average, are a match for most of the teams they meet, and there are at times teams so much above the average that an excursion into foreign parts to do battle with other Universities is fully justified by results. One thing is certain, that the keenness displayed and the results attained are more than proportionate to the size of the University.

APPENDIX X

LISTS OF PRINCIPAL OFFICERS

[Original Durham alumni are marked with an asterisk in these lists. The word ' in ' before a date means that the person named may have been in office for some little time before or after the date given.]

VISITORS.

William van Mildert, 1832 ;[1] died February 21, 1836

Edward Maltby, enthroned July 19, 1836; resigned October 1, 1856

Charles Thomas Longley, enthroned December 3, 1856; translated in June, 1860

Henry Montague Villiers, enthroned September 5, 1860; died August 9, 1861.

Charles Baring, enthroned November 20, 1861; resigned February 3, 1879.

Joseph Barber Lightfoot, enthroned May 15, 1879; died December 21, 1889

Brooke Foss Westcott, enthroned May 15, 1890; died July 27, 1901.

Handley Carr Glyn Moule, enthroned November 1, 1901.

WARDENS

Charles Thorp, appointed, provisionally, before December 9, 1831; appointment confirmed pursuant to Act of Chapter, dated April 4, 1834; he deceased October 10, 1862.

George Waddington, October 10, 1862 ;[2] died July 20, 1869.

William Charles Lake, installed as Dean October 2, 1869; resigned November 2, 1894

George William Kitchin, installed November 17, 1894.

---

[1] By Act of Parliament, 3 William IV., July 4, 1832

[2] As Dean, on the death of Archdeacon Thorp, by Order in Council issued June 4, 1841.

SUB-WARDENS.

Henry Jenkyns, December 12, 1839, to October 31, 1840.
Temple Chevallier, October 31, 1840, to October 26, 1841.
Henry Jenkyns, October 26, 1841, to June 22, 1842.
John Edwards, June 22, 1842, to June 21, 1843.
Temple Chevallier, June 21, 1843, to December 3, 1844.
Henry Jenkyns, December 3, 1844, to October 28, 1845.
John Edwards, October 28, 1845, to November 3, 1846.
Temple Chevallier, November 3, 1846, to December 15, 1847.
Henry Jenkyns, December 15, 1847, to 1848.
John Edwards, 1848 to June 19, 1849.
Temple Chevallier, June 19, 1849, to 1850.
Henry Jenkyns, 1850 to October 28, 1851.
John Edwards, October 28, 1851, to December 14, 1852.
Temple Chevallier, December 14, 1852, to November 1, 1853.
Henry Jenkyns, November 1, 1853, to January 30, 1855.
John Edwards, January 30, 1855, to June 17, 1856.
Henry Jenkyns, June 17, 1856, to June 16, 1857.
John Edwards, June 16, 1857, to June 15, 1858.
Temple Chevallier, June 15, 1858, to June 28, 1859.
Henry Jenkyns, June 28, 1859, to 1860.
John Edwards, 1860 to June 18, 1861.
Temple Chevallier, June 18, 1861, to 1871.
Thomas Saunders Evans, January 27 to June 25, 1872.
Adam Storey Farrar, June 25, 1872, to June 22, 1880.
Robert John Pearce, June 22, 1880, to December 10, 1895.
Alfred Plummer, December 10, 1895, to June, 1902.
Frank Byron Jevons, October 21, 1902.

PROCTORS.

(Nominated in June, and admitted to office in October.)

Senior.

Thomas Williamson Peile, 1836-1842.
Charles Thomas Whitley, 1842-1847.
David Melville, 1847-1848.
C. T. Whitley, 1848-1849.
D. Melville, 1849-1850.
C. T. Whitley, 1850-1851.
William George Henderson, 1851-1852.
C. T. Whitley, 1852-1853.

*John Pedder, 1853-1854.
C. T. Whitley, 1854-1855.
*J. Pedder, 1855-1857.
Robert Baldwin Hayward, 1857-1858.
*J. Pedder, 1858-1859.
James John Hornby, 1859-1860.
*Joseph Waite, 1860-1863.
James Barmby, 1863-1864.
*J. Waite, 1864-1865.
J. Barmby, 1865-1876.
*Joseph Thomas Fowler, 1876-1877.
Alfred Plummer, 1877-1893.
Archibald Robertson, 1893-1896.
Frank Byron Jevons, 1896-1899.
*J. T. Fowler, 1899-1901.
Percy John Heawood, 1901.
*Arthur Robinson, 1904.

Junior.

C. T. Whitley, 1836-1841.
John Thomas, 1841-1842.
Edward Massie, 1842-1845.
D. Melville, 1845-1847.
Steuart Adolphus Pears, 1847-1848.
W. G. Henderson, 1848-1849.
George Butler, 1849-1851.
Henry Harris, 1851-1852.
James Gylby Lonsdale, April, 1852-1853.
J. J. Hornby, 1853-1854.
*J. Waite, 1854-1855.
J. J. Hornby, 1855-1856.
R. B. Hayward, 1856-1857.
*J. Waite, 1857-1858.
J. J. Hornby, 1858-1859.
*J. Waite, 1859-1860.
J. Barmby, 1860-1863.
J. J. Hornby, 1863-1864.
J. Barmby, 1864-1865.
J. Waite, 1865-1873.
Frederick John Copeman, 1873-1875
A. Plummer, 1875-1877.
William Sanday, 1877-1882.

18

*J. T. Fowler, 1882-1886.
A. Robertson, 1886-1892.
Joseph Rushton Shortt, 1892-1896.
*Henry Ellershaw, 1896-1901.
*Arthur Robinson, 1901.
John Hall How, 1904.

PROFESSORS OF DIVINITY.

Hugh James Rose (acting), October, 1833, to March, 1834.
Henry John Rose (acting), April to June, 1834.
Henry Jenkyns (acting), October, 1834, to June, 1839-
Henry Jenkyns (actual), installed as Canon October 26, 1839; resigned professorship in 1864.
Adam Storey Farrar, appointed Professor December 18, 1864.

PROFESSORS OF GREEK AND CLASSICAL LITERATURE.

Henry Jenkyns, before July 20, 1833, to October, 1839.
John Edwards, installed June 25, 1841, died April 1, 1862.
Thomas Saunders Evans, installed June 11, 1862, died May 15, 1889.
Herbert Kynaston, installed August 8, 1889.

PROFESSORS OF MATHEMATICS.

John Carr, June to November, 1833.
Temple Chevallier,[1] July, 1835, to 1872.
Samuel Waymouth, March, 1872, to August, 1874.
Robert John Pearce, October, 1874, to June, 1895
Ralph Allen Sampson, October, 1895.

PROFESSOR OF HEBREW.

Henry William Watkins, July, 1880.

PROFESSORS OF MEDICINE.

Dennis Embleton, 1870, 1872.
Edward Charlton (acting), 1871-1872.
Edward Charlton, 1873, 1874.
Thomas Humble, 1874, 1876.
George Hare Philipson, June 13, 1876

---

[1] Professor of Mathematics and Astronomy, June 4, 1841, to November, 1871.

PROFESSORS OF SURGERY.

George Yeoman Heath, December 11, 1889, to March 4, 1892.
*William Christopher Arnison, May 7, 1892 to November 4, 1899.
Frederick Page, November 21, 1899.

PROFESSOR OF PHYSIOLOGY.

Thomas Oliver, December 11, 1889.

PROFESSOR OF ANATOMY.

Robert Howden, September 9, 1893.

HEATH PROFESSOR OF COMPARATIVE PATHOLOGY.

George Redmayne Murray, September 25, 1893.

PROFESSOR OF MUSIC.

Philip Armes, 1897.

READER IN LAW.

William Gray, before July 20, 1833, to 1872.

READERS IN MEDICINE.

William Cooke, before July 20, 1833, to March, 1842
Dennis Embleton, in 1854-1870.

READER IN HISTORY.

Thomas Greenwood, before July 20, 1833, to 1871.

READERS IN NATURAL PHILOSOPHY.

Charles Thomas Whitley, before July 20, 1833, to 1855.
Robert Baldwin Hayward, in 1856-1859.

READER IN MORAL PHILOSOPHY.

J. Miller, before July 20, 1833.

READER IN HEBREW.

Temple Chevallier,[1] November, 1835, to 1871.

---

[1] Mr. Chevallier lectured on Hebrew in Michaelmas term, 1834, and probably until he was appointed Reader.

READER IN CHEMISTRY.

Algernon Freire Marreco, in 1868-1871.

READER IN ENGLISH LITERATURE.

Herbert John Randall Marston, 1882-1889.

TUTORS.[1]

Thomas Williamson Peile, 1833 to 1841.
William Palmer, 1833.
Charles Thomas Whitley, c. 1834 to 1854.
John Thomas,[2] c. 1834 to 1842.
Edward Massie, 1842, 1843.
David Melville,[3] 1843 to 1845, 1847 to 1851
*Brereton Edward Dwarris, 1846.
William Hedley, 1846.
Steuart Adolphus Pears, 1846 to 1848.
William George Henderson,[4] 1849 to 1852.
George Butler,[5] 1849, 1851.
Henry Harris, 1852.
James Gylby Lonsdale, 1852, 1853.
Edward Henry Bradby, 1853.
*Joseph Waite, 1853 to 1873.
James John Hornby,[6] 1854 to 1864.
Edward Parry,[7] 1854 to 1856.
*John Pedder, 1855 to 1859.
Robert Baldwin Hayward, 1856, 1857.
James Barmby, October, 1860, to June, 1875.
Frederick John Copeman, c. 1865 to May 30, 1880.
Herbert Edward Booth, in 1873-1874.
Alfred Plummer, October, 1874, to June, 1902.
William Sanday,[8] October, 1876, to June, 1883.

---

[1] Entered in the calendars as of 'the University College' until 1850, in and after which year they are placed among the officers of the University.
[2] Late Canon of Canterbury.   [3] Late Canon of Worcester.
[4] Dean of Carlisle.   [5] Late Canon of Winchester.
[6] Provost of Eton.
[7] Late Bishop Suffragan of Dover.
[8] Dean Ireland's Professor and Canon of Christ Church, Oxford.

*James Atkinson, in 1881-1884.
William Edward Gabbett, October, 1880, to August 12, 1882.
Frank Byron Jevons, October, 1882.
Archibald Robertson,[1] October, 1883, to March, 1897.
Henry Alcock White, March, 1897, to July 30, 1898.
Dawson Walker, October, 1898.
Henry Gee, October, 1902.

LECTURERS.

HEBREW.

*Joseph Thomas Fowler, January, 1872.

CLASSICAL.

*Thomas Thornton, 1872 to 1876.
*James Atkinson, 1877 to 1880.
*Willmore Hooper, 1881 to 1886.
Joseph Rushton Shortt, 1887 to 1898.
*Henry Ellershaw, January, 1889.
Herbert Louis Wild, January, 1889, to 1893.
Dawson Walker, October, 1894, to October, 1898.
John Hall How, October, 1898.
*Arthur Robinson, April, 1899.

JUNIOR CLASSICAL.

*Willmore Hooper, 1879, 1880.

MATHEMATICAL.

*Joseph Morris, 1879 to 1886.
Percy John Heawood, 1887.

HISTORY.

George Harold Godwin, 1900.

MODERN LANGUAGES.

James Hamilton, before July 20, 1833, to 1844.

CHEMISTRY.

J. F. W. Johnston, before July 20, 1833, to 1855.
T. Richardson, 1856 to 1867.

---

[1] Bishop of Exeter.

TEACHERS OF MODERN LANGUAGES.

L. B. de Karp, 1862-1875.
Émile Wendling, 1877-1882.
William Clarke Robinson, 1883-1889.
James Grove White Tuckey, 1890-1895.
William Eddowes Urwick, 1896-1904.
Charles Frederick Herdener, 1904.

REGISTRARS.

Temple Chevallier, November, 1835, to December, 1865.
*Francis Frederick Walrond, December, 1865, to June, 1868.
*Thomas Thornton, October, 1868, to March, 1877.
Walter Kercheval Hilton, April, 1877.

UNIVERSITY LIBRARIANS.

Patrick George,[1] 1833 (died January 13, 1834).
Charles Thomas Whitley, July 21, 1834, to 1855.
*Robert Healey Blakey, 1857, 1858.
*Henry Frederick Long, 1859 to 1864.
*Francis Frederick Walrond, c. 1860 to 1868.
Thomas Forster Dodd, 1869 to 1873.
*Joseph Thomas Fowler, 1873 to June, 1901.
Edward Vazeille Stocks, October, 1901.

MALTBY LIBRARIANS.

*Henry Frederick Long (Routh and Maltby), in 1858-1868.
*John Dixon Hepple, in 1869-1871.
Frederick John Copeman, in 1872-1880.
Vacancy in 1880-1881.
*Joseph Thomas Fowler, 1881.

ASSISTANT-LIBRARIANS.

*John Cundill, 1838-1842.
*William Greenwell, 1843.
*Henry Frederick Long, 1857.
*Charles John Robinson, 1858.
*Francis Frederick Walrond, 1859-1864.

---

[1] Minor Canon, Chapter Librarian, Perpetual Curate of St. Margaret's.

Sub-Librarians.

*William Greenwell, 1844-1847.
*Joseph Stevenson, 1848, 1849.
*Godfrey Richard Ferris, 1850-1851.
*Stephen Poyntz Denning, 1852.
*Robert Healey Blakey, 1853-1856.
*Willmore Hooper, 1884-1886.

Observers.

Temple Chevallier, June 16, 1840, to 1841 (latter part).
John Stewart Browne, in 1841[1] (?).
*Arthur Beanlands, February 18, 1842, to February 3, 1846
- Robert Anchor Thompson, February 3, 1846, to June 25, 1849.
— Le Jeune, in June, 1849.
Robert Healey Blakey (acting), June, 1849, to October, 1849.
Richard Carrington, October, 1849, to March, 1852.
William Ellis, March, 1852, to May, 1853.
George Rümker, in 1854, 1855.
Albert Marth, in 1856 to January, 1863.
*Edward Gleadowe Marshall, in 1863-1864.
Mondeford Reginald Dolman, in February, 1865, to April, 1867.
John Isaac Plummer, in November, 1867, to February, 1874.
Gabriel Alphonsus Goldney, in June, 1874, to September, 1885.
Henry James Carpenter, in September, 1885, to September 24, 1900.
Frederick Charles Hampshire Carpenter, September 29, 1900.

Assistant-Observer.

John Stewart Browne, June 16, 1840.

Treasurers.

William Charles Chaytor, 1833-1858.
*John Pedder, 1859.
*Arthur Beanlands, 1860-1897.
R. A. Sampson (acting), 1897-1898.
F. B. Jevons (acting), 1898-1902.
Frederick William Ritson (acting), 1902.

---

[1] 'The Observer, Mr. Browne, attended' (Minutes of Curators, Dec., 1841). There is no record of his appointment as Observer. Professor Chevallier was recording observations in February, 1842.

SOLICITORS.

Messrs. Hargreaves and Joblin, 1888-1896.
Francis Edward Joblin, 1896.

AUDITORS.

William Lloyd Wharton, 1845-1848.
Nathaniel Ellison, 1849, 1850.
William Lloyd Wharton, 1851-1867.
John Fogg Elliot, 1868-1879.
John George Hargreaves, 1880-1893.
John Alexander Mackay Scobie, 1894-1897.
Harry Squance, 1898-1903.
Herbert Salisbury Squance, 1903.

MASTERS OF UNIVERSITY COLLEGE

Charles Thorp, c. 1839[1] to October 10, 1862.
*Joseph Waite, January, 1865, to June, 1873.
Herbert Edward Booth, July, 1873, to June, 1874.
Alfred Plummer, July, 1874, to June, 1902.
Henry Gee, 1902.

PRINCIPALS OF BISHOP HATFIELD'S HALL.

David Melville, October, 1846, to 1851.
William George Henderson, in 1851-1852.
Edward Henry Bradby, in 1852-1853.
James Gylby Lonsdale, in 1853-1854.
*John Pedder, in 1854 to June, 1859.
James Barmby, October, 1859, to June, 1876.
William Sanday, October, 1876, to June, 1883.
Archibald Robertson, October, 1883, to March, 1897.
Frank Byron Jevons, April, 1897.

PRINCIPALS OF BISHOP COSIN'S HALL.

*John Pedder, in 1851-1854.
James John Hornby, in 1854-1864.

PRINCIPALS OF NEVILLE HALL, NEWCASTLE-UPON-TYNE.

*William Greenwell, in 1852-1854.
*James Raine, in 1854-1856.

---

[1] Previously Head of ' the University College ' as Warden.

VICE-MASTERS OF UNIVERSITY COLLEGE.

Thomas Williamson Peile, in 1840-1841.
Charles Thomas Whitley, in 1842-1855.
Robert Baldwin Hayward, in 1857-1858.
James John Hornby, in 1859-1864.

CENSORS OF UNATTACHED STUDENTS.

Frank Byron Jevons, October, 1892, to March, 1897.
Percy John Heawood, April, 1897, to June, 1901.
Dawson Walker, October, 1901.

PRINCIPALS OF CODRINGTON COLLEGE.

William Thomas Webb, October, 1864, to June 18, 1884.
Alfred Caldecott, June, 1884, to June 18, 1886.
Frederick Meyrick (acting), October, 1886, to June 18, 1887.
Hubert Henry Hancock (acting), October, 1887, to June 18, 1888.
Richard Rawle (Bishop of Trinidad), October, 1888, to May 18,
    1889
Hubert Henry Hancock (acting), May, 1889, to June, 1890.
Thomas Herbert Bindley, June, 1890.

PRINCIPALS OF FOURAH BAY COLLEGE.

Metcalfe Sunter, 1870 to 1883.
Frank Nevill, 1884 to November 2, 1889.
William John Humphrey, September, 1890, to March 25, 1898.[1]
Edmund Henry Elwin, November 3, 1898, to December 20, 1901.
Thomas Rowan, February 6, 1902.

PRINCIPALS OF THE WOMEN'S HOSTEL.

Laura Roberts, April, 1899, to July, 1900.
Elizabeth Robinson, October, 1900.

PRESIDENTS OF THE COLLEGE OF MEDICINE.

Thomas Emerson Headlam, 1851-1864.
Charles Thomas Whitley, 1864-1872.
Edward Charlton, 1872-1894.
George Yeoman Heath, 1874-1892.
George Hare Philipson, 1892.

---

[1] Killed in the Hinterland of Sierra Leone by the natives,
March 25, 1898, while seeing to the safety of others.

PRESIDENT OF THE COLLEGE OF SCIENCE.

The Warden of the University, *ex officio.*

PRINCIPALS OF THE COLLEGE OF SCIENCE.

William Steadman Aldis (acting), 1871-1879.
William Steadman Aldis (actual), 1879-1884.
William Garnett, 1884-1893.
Vacancy, 1893-1894.
Henry Palin Gurney, 1894-1904.

REPRESENTATIVES IN THE MEDICAL COUNCIL OF THE UNITED KINGDOM.

Dennis Embleton, in 1868-1872.
*Thomas Thompson Pyle, in 1873-1888.
George Yeoman Heath, in 1889-1892.
George Hare Philipson, in 1893.

SECRETARIES OF EXAMINATIONS.

Joseph Rushton Shortt, in 1896 to April, 1898.
*Henry Ellershaw, April, 1898.

PRINTER TO THE UNIVERSITY.

Francis Humble, in 1837-1847.

CHAPLAINS OF UNIVERSITY COLLEGE.

*John Cundill, in 1839-1842.
*Thomas Garnett, in 1839-1841.
*Brereton Edward Dwarris, in 1842-1845.
Henry Wade Hodgson, in 1843-1846.
*William Greenwell, in 1846-1847.
*George Edward Green, in 1848-1849.
*Lewis Morgan, in 1847.
*Philip Rudd, in 1848-1852.
*Godfrey Richard Ferris, in 1850-1851.
*Joseph Waite, in 1852.
*Richard Chaffer, in 1853-1854.
*James Raine, in 1854.
*Robert Healey Blakey, in 1855.
Edward Parry, in 1855-1856.
*Alfred James, in 1856-1860.

*Charles John Robinson, in 1858.
*Henry Frederick Long, in 1862-1864.
*Francis Frederick Walrond, in 1865-1867.
 Chaplaincies vacant in 1868-1875.
*Thomas Thornton, in 1876-1878.
*James Atkinson, in 1875-1883.
 Alfred Plummer, in 1877-1896 [1]
 Hastings Rashdall, in 1885-1888
 Beresford James Kidd.[2]
*Henry Ellershaw, October, 1890, to 1893.
 James Grove White Tuckey, in 1894-1895.
 Dawson Walker, in 1896-1897.
 Henry Alcock White, in 1897-1898
 Vacancies in 1898-1899.
 George Harold Godwin, 1899.

CENSORS OF UNIVERSITY COLLEGE.

Thomas Williamson Peile, in 1837-1841.
John Thomas, in 1837-1842.
Edward Massie, in 1842-1845
David Melville, in 1843-1845.
Steuart Adolphus Pears, in 1848.
William George Henderson, in 1848-1850.
George Butler, in 1849-1851.
Henry Harris, in 1852.
James Gylby Lonsdale, in 1852-1853.
*Philip Rudd, in 1853.
 J. J. Hornby, in 1854.
*J. Waite, in 1854-1864.
 Edward Parry, in 1855-1856.
*H. F. Long, in 1862-1864.
*F. F. Walrond, in 1865-1868.
 Frederick John Copeman, in 1865-1878.
*Thomas Thornton, in 1869-1877.
*James Atkinson, in 1878-1883.
 Walter Kercheval Hilton, 1884.

[1] With one or two intermissions of a single term.
[2] Appointed towards the end of 1888, but never came to Durham

BURSARS OF UNIVERSITY COLLEGE.

Luke Ripley, in 1837-1840.
John Thomas, in 1841-1842.
*John Cundill, in 1843
*William Greenwell, in 1844-1847.
William George Henderson, in 1848 .
*John Pedder, in 1848-1851.
*Philip Rudd, in 1852-1853.
*Robert Healey Blakey, in 1854-1858
*Alfred James, in 1859-1860.
*Henry Frederick Long, in 1862-1864.
*Francis Frederick Walrond, in 1865-1868.
*John Dixon Hepple, in 1869-1870.
*Thomas Forster Dodd, in 1871-1873.
*Thomas Thornton, in 1874-1877.
Walter Kercheval Hilton, 1878.

CHAPLAINS OF BISHOP HATFIELD'S HALL.

*Robert Taylor, in 1847-1850.
*Hon. Arthur Gascoigne Douglas, in 1851.
*Robert Healey Blakey, in 1852.
*Henry Frederick Long, in 1853-1860.
*Francis Frederick Walrond, in 1861-1865.
*Thomas Forster Dodd, in 1865-1870.
*Joseph Thomas Fowler, January, 1871.

ASSISTANT-CHAPLAIN.

*Henry Ellershaw, 1899.

CENSORS OF BISHOP HATFIELD'S HALL.

*Robert Taylor, in 1847-1849.
*Stephen Poyntz Denning, in 1850-1852.
*Henry Frederick Long, in 1853-1862.
*Francis Frederick Walrond, in 1853-1864.
*Thomas Forster Dodd, in 1865-1870.
*Joseph Thomas Fowler, January, 1871, to 1890.
Joseph Rushton Shortt, 1889-1891.
*Henry Ellershaw, 1891-1898.
John Hall How, 1899.

Junior Censors.

*Willmore Hooper, in 1884-1887.
Joseph Rushton Shortt, 1887-1889.
Edward Vazeille Stocks, 1901-1902.

Bursars of Bishop Hatfield's Hall.

*Francis Frederick Walrond, in 1860-1864.
*Thomas Forster Dodd, in 1865-1870.
*Joseph Thomas Fowler, January, 1871, to December, 1888.
Joseph Rushton Shortt, January, 1889, to June, 1898.
*Bertram Henry Algernon Hanbury-Tracy, October, 1898, to
    March, 1899.
*Arthur Robinson, April, 1899.

Chaplains of Bishop Cosin's Hall.

*James Frederick Turner, in 1853-1854.
*William Greenwell, in 1855-1863.

Censors of Bishop Cosin's Hall.

*James Frederick Turner, in 1853-1854.
*William Greenwell, in 1855-1863.

Resident Medical Tutors of Neville Hall.

Arthur Umphelby, in 1853-1854.
James Champion Penny, in 1855-1856.

APPENDIX XI

MR. BRADLEY'S SKETCHES OF 'Yᴱ FRESHMONNE'
AT UNIVERSITY COLLEGE, DURHAM

THE following memorandum occurs in connection with the original sketches:

'The sketches originated "Verdant Green." I showed them to Mark Lemon, Editor of *Punch*, to which I was then a contributor with pen and pencil, and he asked me to adapt the sketches to Cambridge, and said that he would publish them in *Punch*, with letterpress by Professor Tom Taylor (of Trinity College, Cambridge, afterwards Editor of *Punch*). I declined this offer, but said that I would adapt the sketches to Oxford, which I did, and Mark Lemon accepted them for publication in *Punch*. Some of those on the opposite page [Part II.] were utilized for "Verdant Green." About fifty were drawn and engraved for *Punch*, where they were to appear, a page at a time, when Mr. Herbert Ingram, of the *Illustrated London News*, started a series of special supplements to his paper, chiefly contributed by "*Punch* men"—Douglas Jerrold, Mark Lemon, Tom Taylor, Shirley Brooks, G. A. A'Beckett, John Leech, John Tenniel, etc.—and Mark Lemon proposed to me to exchange the series of sketches to the *Illustrated News* supplements, where twice the number of sketches could appear at once, on their large page. I consented, and two large pages had appeared, when Mr. Ingram changed his mind, and decided to have musical supplements by Charles Mackay and Bishop. So the "Verdant Green" sketches, with their few lines of letterpress, were summarily stopped. Subsequently I wrote letterpress to the sketches, and they were published as a railway book.—CUTHBERT BEDE.'

'Yᴇ FRESHMONNE,' AFTERWARDS 'VERDANT GREEN,' PHOTOGRAPHED
BY EDIS, FROM THE ORIGINAL SKETCHES

'YE FRESHMONNE,' AFTERWARDS 'VERDANT GREEN,' PHOTOGRAPHED
BY EDIS, FROM THE ORIGINAL SKETCHES

APPENDIX XII

NOTICE OF THE AUTHOR

As the Publishers of this work feel that it would be far from complete without some reference to the Author, with the consent of Canon Fowler and by permission of Messrs. A. and C. Black, they include this notice from ' Who's Who ?' for 1904, as complementary to Chapter V :

FOWLER, REV JOSEPH THOMAS, M A , Hon. D.C.L. Dunelm , F.S A., M.R.C.S., L S.A.; Vice-Principal of Bishop Hatfield's Hall, Durham, since 1870; University Hebrew Lecturer, 1872; Librarian, 1874-1901; Keeper of Bishop Cosin's Library, 1889; Hon. Canon of Durham, 1897; *b.* Winterton, Co. Lincoln, 9 June, 1833, *e s.* of Joseph, *e. s.* of William Fowler, the Antiquary and Engraver, of Winterton, and Elizabeth, *e. d* of Thomas Fowler, Owmby, near Spital, Co. Lincoln; unmarried. *Educ.:* at home (by his father); West Riding Proprietary School, Wakefield , St. Thomas's Hosp., London , Bishop Hatfield's Hall, Durham Hospital appointments at St. Thomas's; Hebrew Prizes; Theological, Entrance, and Barry Scholarships at Durham. House Surgeon St. Thomas's Hosp , 1856-57 , Bradford Infirmary, 1857-58 ; Curate of Houghton-le-Spring, Co. Durham, 1861-63, Chaplain and Precentor at St. John's College, Hurstpierpoint, 1864-69; Curate of North Kelsey, 1870; a Local Sec for Durham of Society of Antiquaries ; a Vice-President of Surtees Society. *Publications:* Editor of Ripon Chapter Acts; Newminster Cartulary; Memorials of Ripon, 3 vols. ; Metrical Life of St. Cuthbert (Surtees Society); The Coucher Book of Selby, 2 vols. (Yorkshire Record Society); Cistercian Statutes (Yorkshire Archæol. Society); Adamnani Vita S. Columbæ, and Translation; Durham Account Rolls, 3 vols

(Surtees Society); Rites of Durham (Surtees Society); Durham
Cathedral; Life and Letters of Dr Dykes; St. Cuthbert, a sermon
preached in York Minster; Rites of Durham. *Recreations:* formerly part-singing and bell-ringing; now indexing and cycling,
particularly touring. *Addresses:* Bishop Hatfield's Hall, Durham;
Winterton, Doncaster.

INDEX

BILLING AND SONS, LTD., PRINTERS GUILDFORD

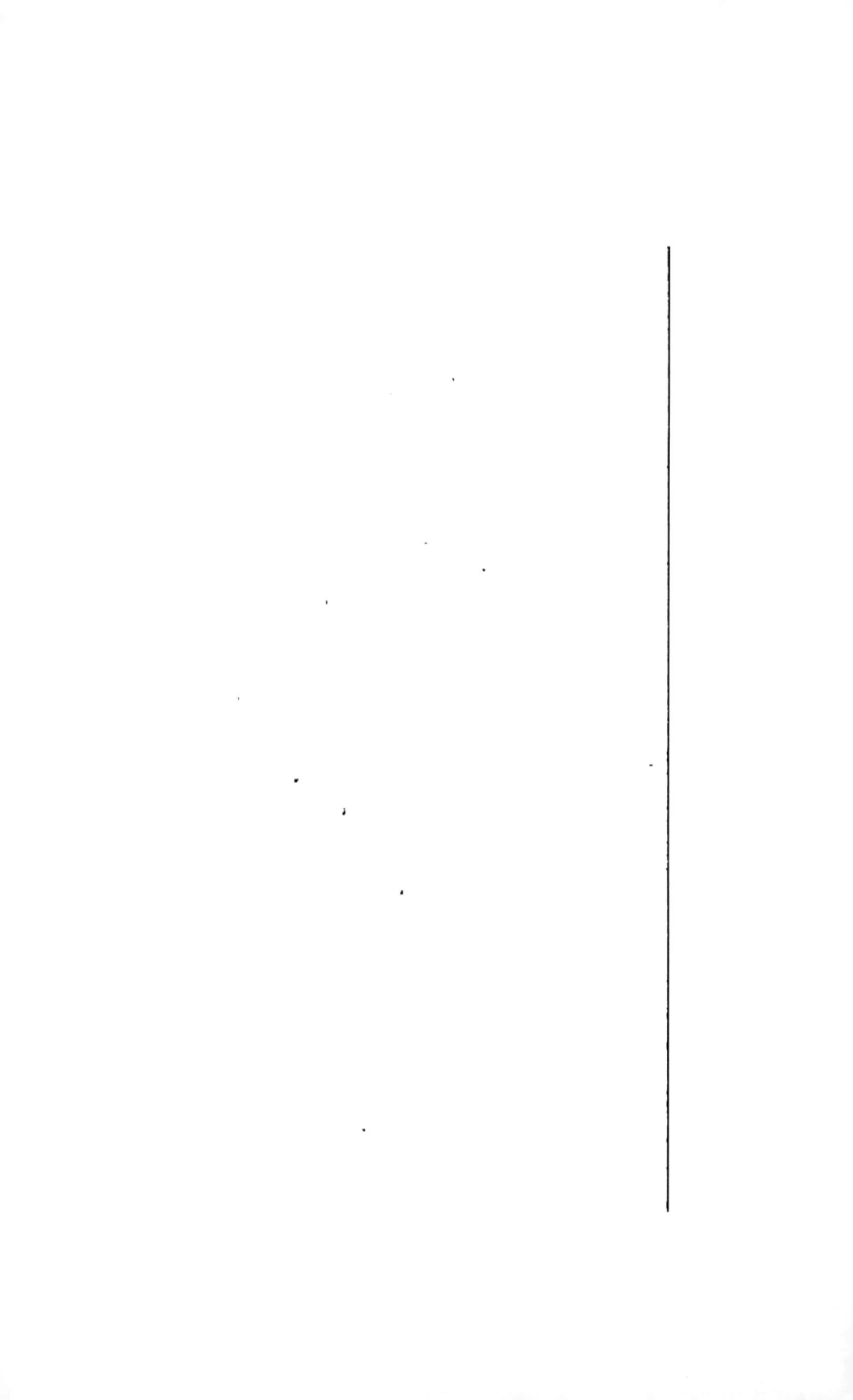

Ingram Content Group UK Ltd.
Milton Keynes UK
UKHW020838190423
420422UK00006B/408

9 781019 217443